Earth Politics

Narrating Native Histories

Narrating Native Histories aims to foster a rethinking of the ethical, methodological, and conceptual frameworks within which we locate our work on native histories and cultures. We seek to create a space for effective and ongoing conversations between north and south, natives and nonnatives, academics and activists throughout the Americas and the Pacific region. We are committed to complicating and transgressing the disciplinary and epistemological boundaries of established academic discourses on native peoples.

This series encourages symmetrical, horizontal, collaborative, and auto-ethnographies; work that recognizes native intellectuals, cultural interpreters, and alternative knowledge producers within broader academic and intellectual worlds; projects that decolonize the relationship between orality and textuality; narratives that productively work the tensions between the norms of native cultures and the requirements for evidence in academic circles; and analyses that contribute to an understanding of native peoples' relationships with nation-states, including histories of expropriation and exclusion as well as projects for autonomy and sovereignty.

Combining, as he himself explains, ethnography, biography, and history, Waskar Ari traces the deep roots of Bolivia's current decolonization agenda and debates in the multiple forms of indigenous political creativity and conflictual politics of twentieth-century Bolivia. *Earth politics* emerges as a creative umbrella concept under which different Aymara, Quechua, and Uru activist intellectuals developed notions of Indian law that articulated indigenous beliefs and practices with the colonial notion of the Indian republic in innovative and unique ways. Ari provides us with fresh perspectives on the Bolivian National Revolution of 1952, the Indianista and Katarista movements, and Evo Morales's complex and contested project for decolonized and radical democracy.

Earth Politics

Religion,
Decolonization,
and Bolivia's
Indigenous
Intellectuals

WASKAR ARI

Duke University Press   Durham and London   2014

Printed in the United States of America on acid-free paper ∞
Typeset in Quadraat by Tseng Information Systems, Inc.

Library of Congress Cataloging-in-Publication Data
Ari Chachaki, Waskar.
Earth politics : religion, decolonization, and Bolivia's indigenous
intellectuals / Waskar Ari.
pages cm — (Narrating native histories)
Includes bibliographical references and index.
ISBN 978-0-8223-5613-4 (cloth : alk. paper)
ISBN 978-0-8223-5617-2 (pbk. : alk. paper)
1. Alcaldes Mayores Particulares (Bolivia)
2. Indians of South America—Bolivia—Politics and government.
3. Nationalism—Bolivia—History—20th century.
4. Bolivia—Race relations—History—20th century.
I. Title. II. Series: Narrating native histories.
F3320.C43 2014
984.05′1—dc23 2013026428

Mamitaxataki, Eduarda Chachaki, jupaw awkitraki
taykatraki nayatak akapachan sayt'awayi

To my mother, Eduarda Chachaki, who has played
the role of both father and mother in my life

Contents

Acknowledgments

Acknowledgments perform the essential intellectual task of situating the production of an individual work in a long chain of influence, collaboration, and encouragement. I've worked over this section several times, more than any other part of the book, so I'll just stop here, apologize to anyone I may have missed, and start at the beginning.

Originally from Bolivia and having spent most of my life in La Paz, I had the good fortune to have first been taught the connection between politics and history by Silvia Rivera Cusicanqui, Ivonne Farah, Julio Mantilla, Hugo Bedregal Romero, and Danilo Paz Ballivian while at the University of San Andrés. Aymara scholars and activists such as Julian Ugarte, Clemente Pimentel, Anacleta Ventura, Prudencio Peña, and Ricarda Torricos first introduced me to the complicated history of Andean indigenous activists. I also benefited from extensive academic discussions on the topic with Tomas Huanca, Carlos Mamani of the Taller de Historia Oral Andina (THOA), and Roberto Choque.

In 1998 I began my journey toward earning my PhD at Carnegie Mellon University, where I had the privilege to work with outstanding scholars such as Tera Hunter, who first taught me about the history of race. Soon thereafter, however, I received an offer to continue my studies at Georgetown University. Having only recently left Bolivia, I felt unsure about making the move, but friends like Forrest Hylton convinced me that Georgetown and Washington, DC, would offer me a rich intellectual and personal experience. Indeed, I used the opportunity to take several classes at Howard University with Professor Emory Tolbert to expand my knowledge of the history of race. Beyond thanking them for their contributions, I want to take this opportunity to appreciate the friendship of Erick Langer, Joanne Rappaport, Thomas Klubock, John Voll, and Jo Ann Moran-Cruz. They helped me to understand this work in relation to larger issues of government and power in Bolivia and Latin America.

I owe my greatest intellectual debt to Erick Langer, Thomas Klubock, and Joanne Rappaport. Every good thing about this work is a result of their observations, criticism, and support. Erick Langer read early versions of this work not only repeatedly but meticulously, and Joanne Rappaport inspired me with her incredible knowledge of indigenous activists in Latin America and the world, pushing me to reach beyond clichés, facile observations, and easy critiques of past work. It has been an honor and a privilege to work with such impressive and generous scholars. But, more than this, Erick, Tom, and Joanne formed a network of creative support and encouragement.

Regarding my research, I have accumulated many debts over thirty years of researching the Alcaldes Mayores Particulares (AMP). A number of people in Sucre, Bolivia, made research and writing possible. Above all are indigenous teachers and friends in the Yachaywasi literacy program, religious groups such as the Hermanos Espirituales, and the Central Agraria de Marawa, Cantar Gallo, Jatum Mayu, Pampawasi, and Marapampa. In particular, I'd like to thank Nabil Saavedra, Ezequiel Orieta, Juan Carlos Saavedra, Agapito Ponce Mamani, Julia Rivera (the best *papawaykus* and dinner in all of Chuquisaca), Elena Limachi, and Petrona Luque. These friends made returning to Tarwita, Cantar Gallo, and Tarabuco feel like coming home, no matter how long I had been away.

In Oruro and northern Potosí I especially want to mention Matilde Qulqi, Blas Pacheco, Julio Mamani, Valerio Trigori, Agustin Quispe, and Valentin Quispe, who were constant companions throughout this work, sharing *chismes*, *tristezas*, *alegrías*, and *esperanzas* in addition to helping to make life in the *ayllus* and communities of Oruro and northern Potosí a great experience, at least when Lucas Marka bothered to get enough blankets and corn to eat in Wayllamarka (alta puna), since digestion can often be difficult at sixteen thousand feet. In search of indigenous archives, Lucas and I took so many *vueltas* around the villages of Tallixa, Pasto Grande, Muxlli, and Warwi Tutura that this is as much his project as it is mine. I also cannot thank enough the leaders of the ayllus of Qariphuyu, Arampampa, Acasio, Arumani, Saqaqa, Chiarjaqi, and Tarukamarka for allowing me access to their valuable archives, known as "viejos documentos que nadie debe ver" (old documents that no one should see).

In southern Cochabamba and the Tapacari Province, I want to mention Genara Rocha, Luciano Negrete, and the leadership of the indigenous communities of Raqaipampa, Molinero, Pasto Grande, Muxlli, and Tallija, who not only facilitated my work at the indigenous archives of the region but also made it enjoyable with warm and thick corn soup. The great *tata* Fermin Vallejos's interest in this study provided me with a powerful incentive to get it right. I hope that in some small way my interpretation of their history helps them in their work; however, the recent transformations in Bolivia have gone so far that my efforts seem small in comparison with the doors, and challenges behind them, now open in Bolivia. I am also grateful to Dorotea Vallejos, Santusa Terrezas, and Franz Quispe for graciously sharing their memories and photographs. Special appreciation goes to Walter Callizaya for sharing Gregorio Titiriku's stories and for reminding me that his history did not end in 1953.

In La Paz and other places around Bolivia, I have to thank the many people who helped me with images, especially Victor Alanoca and Reina Juanaquina. In La Paz I also want to mention Nicolas Anawaya, Ramon Arwitru, Daniel Sallacuchu, Pedro Ilaqita, Vicente Ojira, and the leaders of the centrales campesinas de Sisani, Qaxiata, Ancoraimes, Chuxnnapata, Ambana, and Timusi who helped me discover the connections between their communities and the AMP network in the first half of the twentieth century. Special thanks go to my wonderful friend Ramón Arwitru, who traveled extensively with me. I will never be able to adequately express my appreciation to Marina Murillo for her help and support as my research assistant over all of these years.

I am also grateful to the many people in the public archives of Sucre, Oruro, and La Paz who were so very generous in helping me find and access materials.

A book needs more than ideas and research. Linda Farthing, Elizabeth Shesko, and Anitra Grisales were so wonderful in helping me develop and edit my writing. Linda Farthing helped me in the initial stages of editing. Liz Shesko had the patience to correct my prose whenever it did not make sense—I am a nonnative English speaker—and, as a historian and a Bolivianist, she became so familiar with the text that she was able to make many superb suggestions. I do not have enough words to articulate my appreciation for Liz Shesko's meticulous proofreading and suggestions. Anitra Grisales helped me polish the prose in the later stages of revision. With all of their help, this book is now totally understandable to an English-speaking audience.

Many others read and commented on this work as it progressed. I greatly appreciate the interest that Sinclair Thompson, Brooke Larson, John Wunder, and Margaret Jacobs showed in this work. Brooke Larson brought insightful ideas to this project that have been crucial to its development. Sinclair Thompson offered a wealth of practical suggestions, especially in regards to facts and historiography. John Wunder and Margaret Jacobs have been wonderful friends in supporting this work and providing me with interpretations from comparative indigenous history.

I would also like to recognize the funding institutions that made this work possible: the Rockefeller Postdoctoral Fellowship at the University of Texas, Austin (Race and Resources in Latin America) and the Arts and Humanities Enhancement Fund Award at the University of Nebraska, Lincoln.

I owe particular thanks to a group of institutions and friends who made it possible for me to return to American academia and publish this book. In the aftermath of September 11, 2001, I was prevented from assuming my post at the University of Nebraska, Lincoln from 2005 to 2007. I have never received an official explanation as to why. After the U.S. Customs and Immigration Services failed to take action for two years on my visa application, there was much speculation that this stemmed from ideological issues due to my indigenous background, my association with indigenous movements, and the political situation emerging in Bolivia on the eve of the current transformations that have reshaped Bolivian society. The American Historical Association, especially presidents Linda Kerber and Barbara Weinstein, stood up and protested on my behalf. The Latin American Studies Association (LASA) and American Civil Liberties Union (ACLU) were also crucial in this struggle. I also cannot forget the wonderful contributions of Michael Maggio, a prestigious immigration lawyer who took my case pro bono and pressed for it to be resolved. Only after his efforts made my case public did it begin to move. Of all those who worked to bring me back, I especially want to mention Diana Negroponte of Georgetown University, who fought like a *cruzada* for justice to be done. Her work was crucial, and I will never have the words to express my appreciation! Jo Ann Moran Cruz, Erick Langer, Maurice Jackson, and Xenia Willkinson, all from my alma mater Georgetown, and Patrick Jones, Kenneth Winkle, and Marcela Rafaeli, from the University of Nebraska, Lincoln, devoted their time and support to help with my situation. Patrick Jones, in particular, worked so intensely that it is hard to find words to thank him. When I finally got the green light to enter the country again, I had already started a new life in Bolivia, but I chose to return because I was so impressed with and touched by the willingness of so many to work on my behalf. After my plight ended, and I took my post as assistant professor of history and ethnic studies and Latin American studies at the University of Nebraska, Lincoln, I was relieved to find everything to be so collegial and to feel as though I could teach and speak freely; indeed, now I am even a permanent resident.

Finally, this work is dedicated to my mother because, in her own way, she was the first one to teach me to be persistent and stay strong in life's difficult moments. It is thanks to her that I am now publishing this book.

Chapter One

Building the Indian Law and a Decolonization Project in Bolivia

The evening of May 17, 1936, eighty *jilaqatas* and *apoderados* from indigenous *ayllus* and haciendas gathered in La Paz to discuss their place in the world evolving around them. Gregorio Titiriku, one of the apoderados, told them that "land and territories are only given and blessed by Pachamama [the Mother Earth] and the Achachilas [the hilltops, protectors of humankind] and not by Spaniards [whites] and their law."[1] Titiriku insisted that the then-popular tactic of searching for colonial titles in the struggle for land and communal rights was no longer necessary. The hacienda expansion that began in Bolivia in the late-nineteenth century had pushed community leaders and activists to search for ways to prevent further appropriation of indigenous lands, and they had successfully used colonial documents in that effort. Their success had led indigenous workers on many haciendas to believe they could also use this process to confront haciendas owners, and many of them started searching—often to no avail—for colonial titles to back their claims.

Gregorio Titiriku, however, claimed that written records such as property titles were irrelevant to indigenous people and their beliefs. Titiriku argued that continuing to pay rent to the *hacendados* and levies to the state harmed the foundations of the indigenous religion that the Quechuas, Urus, and Aymaras shared.[2] Instead, he advocated for the legitimacy of what he and the three other indigenous activists profiled in this book called the Indian law, which was a reinterpretation and re-elaboration of parts of the seventeenth-century colonial Law of the Indies (Leyes de Indias). The Indian law was a specific ideology framed with resources and tools available at the time that considered segregation itself as a response to racism and articulated a project of decolonization. This "law" basically elaborates a discourse of indigenous rights and cultural affirmations, and though it was not recognized by any Bolivian government officials, indigenous activists and their followers used handwritten and printed copies of it to defend their rights and way of life.[3] The indigenous activists whom I profile in this book synthesized Aymara religious and political ideas to ultimately articulate a project of decolonization. A major ideological component of this decolonization project, as articulated in the Indian law, advocated for two separate republics: one Indian and the other white (or Spanish).[4] Titiriku legitimized the Indian republic through an Aymara religious and cultural worldview that reflected the beliefs of a new ethnic movement I am calling earth politics.

Titiriku was responding to the efforts of indigenous leaders such as Mariano Qhispe from the hacienda Sumala (Chuquisaca) and Feliciano Inka Marasa from the ayllus of Quntu (Oruro), who had traveled by foot, train, and truck to the historical archives of Peru in an unsuccessful search for documentation of indigenous colonial ownership in the great Qaranqa ayllu network.[5] Insisting that these titles were meaningless, at the meeting that night Titiriku asked the mallkus and apoderados if Pachamama and the Achachillas "are not suffering themselves by seeing their own children in pain and suffering for not doing the right thing."[6] This invocation of the Aymara gods to delegitimize the tactic of searching for colonial land titles was a critical element that set Titiriku and his network apart from their contemporaries. This novel combination of colonial law and religion won Titiriku an audience in the pre-1952 indigenous world, which was eager for new strategies in their fight to obtain rights and emancipation.

Like most of his colleagues at the meeting, Gregorio Titiriku only had a very tenuous grasp of written language. However, these Aymara chiefs and activists called on the assistance of lawyers and volunteer secretaries (called escribanos in Spanish) linked to projects of Indian education to help them search for documents in the Archivo Nacional de Bolivia (Bolivian National Archives) in Sucre. While there in the early 1920s, Titiriku came across the Law of the Indies, which would later become key to his career as an activist. Based on that document, Titiriku developed a new discourse that emphasized the potential of certain aspects of early colonial legislation to be repurposed as a tool in the Indians' struggle. He explained: "Our law [Indian law] is the best one for us; no law made by whites for Indians is good. The only [exception] was the Law of the Indies that the king of Spain made for us and that now the whites have taken away. We need a law again that is just for us."[7] However, Titiriku's discourse also called on elements from his own local tradition, Janqulaime oral history. He told the assembled representatives that "before the Spanish came, our jilaqatas ruled everywhere. They ensured justice and that everybody had enough to eat and that there was no hunger."[8]

Titiriku drew on oral histories passed down by generations of Indians that told of a distant past free from injustices and colonial domination.[9] This version of the past became crucial to the creation of the indigenous activist network he helped to found, the Alcaldes Mayores Particulares (AMP), and was influential in the debate about whether they should use colonial land titles or resume traditional mallku practices to confront the power of Bolivia's white minority and the usurpation of indigenous lands by the haciendas.[10] Titiriku's use of Indian history and spirituality to challenge the apoderados' legal strategies brought the Aymara gods, such as the Pachamama and the Achachilas, back into the discussion in order to reach a broader audience.

Gregorio Titiriku, Toribio Miranda, Melitón Gallardo, and Andrés Jach'aqullu all lived on haciendas or as members of ayllus and were defined as Indians in the racial categories of the mid-twentieth century. These four indigenous activists together formed the AMP, a political network that included at least 489 cells in five regions or departments of Bolivia.[11] The AMP existed during a time of upheaval in Bolivian history and rose to prominence by creating a discourse that addressed the specific context of the prerevolutionary era of 1921–1951. In response to major changes following the Bolivian National Revolution from 1952 to 1971, the AMP reinvented their movement to address new forms of coloniality. Active during the same period as the indigenistas, an elite group who argued in favor of retaining traditional indigenous cultural practices and opposed modernization or change for indigenous peoples, these indigenous intellectuals epitomized an alternative vision of liberation. By framing issues, gathering audiences, and creating networks and social movements from inside the Indian world, these actors provided alternative understandings of nation making in modern Latin America.

This book narrates the history of AMP indigenous activists and the dissemination of their message on local, regional, and national levels. Their story does not follow a linear narrative; instead, it is multisited, moving between social locations in political hierarchies, geographical regions, and temporal periods. Through the Indian law, the AMP presented a new interpretive frame and a new language for articulating collective interests, identities, and claims across Bolivia's indigenous communities. They created ideological consensus, forging a discourse and a way to interpret society by interacting with their specific audiences: local constituencies, local allies and politicians, and national supporters. In its fifty years of existence, the AMP used this discourse to challenge first the landlords and then the peasants unions, state institutions, and the Catholic Church. The second generation communicated its message to a broader international audience in the U.S. embassy, the International Labour Organization, the United Nations, and other diplomatic delegations. These international connections also gave them a certain legitimacy with their indigenous audience.[12] The AMP's influence reached into the 1980s and 1990s via the Indianista and Katarista civil rights movements, and its legacy is still seen in contemporary Bolivia in the political and cultural transformation taking place under the country's first indigenous president Evo Morales.

Melitón Gallardo referred to indigenous peoples as *jallp'a sangres* (the "blood of the earth") and summarized the AMP's platform in the following way: "nuestra política es la tierra, nuestra política es la Pachamama" (our politics is the earth, our politics is the Mother Earth).[13] When they spoke about the earth, the AMP referred to land, territory, nation, faith, religion, rights, and Indianness.[14] Based on this holistic interpretation, I refer to the AMP practices and discourse as *earth politics*. In recounting the history of the AMP's earth politics over the course of fifty years, I hope to show how they developed and implemented a unique project of decolonization based on the reinterpretation and re-elaboration of colonial law. They affirmed Aymara religious, cultural, and gender practices and took direct action against oppressive social and labor policies. My analysis focuses on connections between the making of an Indian peasantry, the emerging labor movement, and the modern nation-state, as well as AMP leaders' relationships with national and regional public intellectuals. I examine how these activists produced mobilizing ideas, strategies, and organizations based on their own experiences of both segregation and assimilation policies in Bolivia.

MAP 1. Republic of Bolivia.

A Brief History of the AMP

In 1874 agrarian reform was passed in Bolivia, officially eliminating ayllus, dissolving Indian representation, and openly appropriating Indian land in the name of civilization and modernity. The War of the Pacific that was fought between Bolivia, Peru, and Chile from 1879 to 1883 delayed the full implementation of the reform, but once the war ended it was put into practice with the goal of promoting individual private property and rural capitalism in the countryside. At the same time, the liberal ruling government worked to move the national economy from dependency on Indian tributes to exporting raw materials, particularly silver from the 1880s to 1890s, rubber in the 1900s to 1910s, and tin from the 1910s to 1920s.[15] Between the growth of the mining sector and the expansion of the haciendas, the market economy in Bolivia peaked in the 1920s. Using little technology and mostly Indian labor, the haciendas sold their products to mines eager for food supplies. At the birth of the AMP, Bolivia's economy was undergoing a radical change as the haciendas expanded, and even the ayllus attempted to take advantage of the high price of food in the years prior to the Great Depression. Through their control of the state, the ruling elite attempted to spread the market economy throughout the country, regardless of groups that were abused in the process.

It was in this context that the AMP emerged from the network of apoderados and caciques led by Santos Mark'a T'ula in the 1920s. At first the AMP was only one of many factions in the network; only in 1936 did it become a completely different group and take the name Alcaldes Mayores Particulares. Between 1920 and 1960, the AMP nurtured two different generations of activists; the four cases I study in this book represent important leaders of the movement, but they were certainly not the only ones. Toribio Miranda and Gregorio Titiriku are the two founders that all adherents recognize, and they, along with Melitón Gallardo, formed part of the earlier generation and offered strong national leadership from 1921 to 1951. Andrés Jach'aqullu emerged as a leader of the second generation in the AMP following the national revolution in 1952, during a time when the original network was gradually dissolving. Over the course of fifty years, these AMP leaders petitioned the republican-era state and provided activist training to grassroots leaders on the haciendas in the post–Chaco War era (1936–1952) and in the sindicatos (unions) and commandos (revolutionary committees) during the long cycle of the national revolution (1952–1971). The four cases I examine here are part of a long trajectory of Bolivian indigenous activists who have based their authority on different types of available representations of Indians: caciques, mallkus, jilaqatas, apoderados, and alcaldes. Although most of the AMP's leadership came from the Aymara world, their audience was predominately from the Uru and Quechua groups.

While the Aymara ayllus in the highlands were mostly concerned with fighting hacienda expansion and white power, the Quechua peoples were largely confined to haciendas and were involved in numerous labor conflicts between 1920 and 1940.[16] In southern Bolivia *latifundios* (large landed estates) had a long history of oppressing the peons who labored on them. For these Quechua peons, Santos Marka T'ula's strategy of defending indigenous rights with colonial titles would not be effective because such titles had never existed for their lands. The AMP, by contrast, proposed claiming rights based mostly on reapplications of early colonial legislation. Certain concepts in the Law of the Indies made more sense for regions such as Chuquisaca, south of Cochabamba, and even the valleys of northern Potosí. After the national revolution in 1952, most Aymara communities quickly appropriated newly formed peasant unions to meet their goals, while in southern Bolivia Quechua indigenous communities did not join the unions until the late 1960s. For this reason, Quechuas south of Cochabamba, Chuquisca, and northern Potosí formed the AMP's main audience.

Origins and Breaks

A central figure in the indigenous movement of the first half of the twentieth century was Santos Marka T'ula, who built a leading network of apoderados in the ayllus and communities of Bolivia to denounce government practices and institutions. He and his associates, like Feliciano Inka Marasa, worked diligently to find colonial titles that supported indigenous land claims. Based on the confederation of Carangas ayllus that had enclaves in Chuquisaca, Inka Marasa built a network that spanned the Chuquisaca and Oruro regions. Toribio Miranda and Melitón Gallardo emerged from this early connection between the regions. Santos Marka T'ula's generation also developed a new form of activism through the publication of documents that protested oppressive treatment and claimed certain rights for Indians. These took the form of newsletters called *garantías*. The garantías had a long genealogy that went back mainly to late or early colonial property titles and the Law of the Indies, which had established special protections for Indians. Marka T'ula thought that these official documents might be useful in helping to protect Indians from abuse two centuries later. Garantías were produced in print shops in La Paz and Oruro and were often addressed to local, regional, and national authorities. Some indigenous activists, like Gregorio Titiriku, began copying these garantías by hand and distributing them throughout the countryside in the early 1920s.

Toribio Miranda and Gregorio Titiriku eventually split from Santos Marka T'ula's movement because of his emphasis on enforcing colonial land rights granted to *caciques de sangre* (descendants of mallkus, the main indigenous chiefs in the eighteenth century). Over time, Miranda and Titiriku became seriously disillusioned with this strategy because it failed to provide hacienda peasants with sufficient means to advocate for their land rights in the latifundio system, and it also did not target the internal colonial institutions of the postcolonial state. The other reason behind the split was that the early leaders of the AMP—Feliciano Inka Marasa, Toribio Miranda, and Gregorito Titiriku—had strong religious beliefs. Their faith in Pachamama led them to be known as *pachamámicos* and to develop a politics based on the earth that emphasized native religion and gods. Miranda and Titiriku began circulating their own garantías that deemphasized colonial property titles and focused instead on reviving certain ideas about indigenous rights that they found in the Law of the Indies, as well as incorporating new issues such as education. These new garantías articulated what would eventually become known as the Indian law.

Conceptualizing an Indian Law and Gaining Followers

One of the main concepts that Titiriku and his followers would adapt from the Law of the Indies was the idea of two republics, which they used to provide historical and political justification for founding a republic of Qullasuyu, a nation of Aymara ancestry. Titiriku and Miranda empowered their Indian network to establish a peasant and Indian nation in response to the subjugation of Indians within the early twentieth-century Bolivian nation-state, a situation known as internal colonialism.[17] They advocated for *particular* schools (reflected in the name Alcaldes Mayores Particulares) that would serve autonomous educational interests and be controlled by Indians. The AMP was not alone in this endeavor; other indigenous movements of the 1930s and 1940s also sought to establish elementary schools run by Indians that had different emphases and purposes than state-run schools. With the support of indigenous activists such as Melitón Gallardo, the new AMP network took a much greater hold in some Quechua-speaking valleys. During this period the AMP represented the Indian sharecroppers of the south, and Miranda and Titiriku's political ideas accompanied many rebellions, revolts, and instances of peasant resistance, especially in Chuquisaca and Cochabamba during the turbulent year of 1947. The AMP, especially Miranda and Titiriku, called for a return to worshipping the

Aymara gods; in the Bolivian political sphere, they also demanded an end to segregation in public plazas and streetcars, worked for autonomous education for Indians, and created alternative institutions of citizenship.

New Generations

The gradual decline of the AMP occurred between 1952 and 1971 after the Movimiento Nacionalista Revolucionario (MNR, Revolutionary Nationalist Movement) came to power during the national revolution. When Miranda could not travel anymore after 1953, a second generation, led by Andrés Jach'aqullu, took over the leadership of the AMP just as a new modernizing paradigm of de-indigenization and assimilation was emerging in the wake of the national revolution. In response the second generation of the AMP shaped their discourse more in terms of rights, re-elaborating the Indian law to oppose forced participation in peasant unions and other MNR policies enacted after the agrarian reform in 1953. In this period the AMP was less influential in the Aymara-speaking highlands than in the Quechua-speaking southern Andes, where mestizos controlled local institutions and prevented indigenous peoples from assuming positions of power.

Earth Politics Intellectuals versus Indigenistas

In discussing the AMP, I do not use the term "intellectuals" to mean scholars but rather activists. Antonio Gramsci referred to such intellectuals as "organic." Gramsci places strong emphasis on the conditions required for the emergence of the activist intellectual, one of whose functions is to produce a specific discourse, which is a "complex of signs and practices" that "organizes social existence and social reproduction."[18] As such, I consider Miranda, Titiriku, Gallardo, and Jach'aqullu to be activist intellectuals because they constructed an ideology to contest the political system in which they lived. The AMP produced a discourse to speak out against the challenges indigenous people in Bolivia were facing in the mid-twentieth century, particularly at the hands of the colonial institutions of the postcolonial republic.

My conception of the AMP's leaders, beyond their elaborating and spreading a particular ideology, follows Edward Said's notion that intellectuals also take on a role of actually "representing, embodying, and articulating a message, a view, and an attitude."[19] He emphasizes that the task of intellectual activists is to speak truth to power and utilize the art of representing an agenda.[20] The AMP embodied this idea in its use of representations of indigenous religion and culture to develop and legitimize its agenda. The AMP activists emphasized a return to worshipping Pachamama (Mother Earth), *uma jalsus* (water), *qixuqixu* (lightning), and the Achachilas (the spirit of the mountains). They also began conducting their own indigenous ceremonial weddings, baptisms, and funerals, challenging the Catholic Church's authority while still incorporating certain aspects of Christianity in a more syncretic way. Their audience was mostly made up of indigenous peoples, mainly *jaqis* (Aymara) or *runas* (Quechuas), but they also spoke to indigenistas and international organizations interested in indigenous issues.[21]

It is important to distinguish between the AMP and the indigenistas, who were articulating an ideology of *indigenismo* during the same era. They can be seen as a sort of counterpoint to the AMP. Associated with political groups on both the Right and the Left, indigenistas throughout Latin America shared a cultural agenda that glorified and defended Indian culture while simultaneously infantilizing indigenous peoples. Although most indigenistas belonged to the margins of the ruling elite and were from mestizo backgrounds, they were not interested in doing away with the dominant order. Latin American historiography has long focused on the role of indigenismo (or its indigenista proponents) in the construction of the nation-state. In Mexico, for example, indigenismo glorified *mestizaje*, the racial mixing of whites and indigenous people, in the national imagination but also rejected native languages and excluded minorities.[22] The writings of José Vasconcelos exemplify the promotion of this discourse.[23] In the struggle against the whitening project of Lima's elite in Peru, Luis E. Valcarcel opposed education and unions for Peruvian peasants as part of the indigenistas' efforts to keep the Indian race "pure."[24] In Bolivia Franz Tamayo defended indigenous people but wanted to shield them from modern life and education, which would essentially keep them in a subaltern condition.[25] Though they had different interpretations of history and visions for the future, the indigenistas and the AMP did interact and influence each other in Bolivia, as I will show through Fernando Diez de Medina's connections with Gregorio Titiriku and Andrés Jach'aqullu. These types of connections between indigenistas and indigenous activists were frequent in Bolivian history and continued beyond the

AMP's active years, passing from one generation to another, even though the content of these messages were heavily negotiated. For example, the Bolivian public sphere learned about the AMP's ideas of Indian revolution through Fausto Reinaga, an indigenista working in the 1970s. In this way both movements ended up influencing more contemporary indigenous politics and contributing to the construction (or reconstruction) of Indianista and Katarista movements in Bolivia from 1970 to 1990. An Indianista, in this context, is an Aymara or *originario* who seeks an Indian revolution. Katarismo, by contrast, is an ethnic movement that emerged in the late twentieth century that, inspired by the eighteenth-century Aymara hero Túpac Katari, argues in favor of indigenous rights. These movements, in turn, shaped the rise of Evo Morales and indigenous empowerment in Bolivia today. In sum, by examining the AMP movement as a distinct yet concurrent indigenous movement in Latin America, I hope to provide a new perspective and a more complex understanding of the history and current state of indigenous activism in Bolivia and of other ethnic movements in Latin America today.

Critical Frames for Understanding the AMP's Earth Politics

Coloniality and Decolonization

In this study *internal colonialism* refers to a broader narrative that applies the colonial legacy, or the repercussions of the conquest from centuries ago, to modern inequality and the reproduction or continuation of a rigid social hierarchy. Internal colonialism is the bedrock on which all economic, cultural, and power relations have been built throughout Bolivian history, despite change and restructuring.[26] It is internal colonialism that has kept indigenous peoples and their descendants in a subordinate condition in relation to the other social groups in Bolivia, particularly those of Spanish and mestizo descent. The AMP developed within this particular national and international context, shaped by the legacy of colonialism, liberal ideologies, new institutions, and Bolivia's place in the global economy.

Since the nineteenth century, the Liberals' mission of domestication had constructed paths of citizenship and individualism that formed the social context in which the AMP worked. New institutions such as military service, public schools, voting rights, and pro-state unions influenced popular discourse and reinforced the cultural discipline of the era. Finally, the Bolivian nation-state's mission to produce raw materials for the global economy profoundly shaped its economic development and political stability, in turn shaping the lives of all Bolivians, including AMP activists. Extremely low social mobility helped to re-create discourses of ethnic and racial differences and perpetuated inequality between the descendants of Indians and Spaniards, those living in the country and the city, and speakers of native languages and Spanish. In this context of internal colonialism, mestizos (the children of whites and Indians) identified with and chose to side with the whites in order to gain power. In Bolivia's case mestizos perpetuated the inequalities that originated in the colonial period and subjected indigenous people to a coloniality that the AMP directly resisted.

My work on AMP activist intellectuals is in conversation with recent work on indigenous peoples and nation making in the Americas and especially the ongoing revisionist Bolivian historiography of the mid-twentieth century. Some of the crucial contributions on the Bolivian Andes during this era have come from the members of the Taller de Historia Oral Andina (THOA), which is a think tank of mostly Aymara scholars whose purpose in the 1980s was to reconceptualize the agency of indigenous peoples and the meaning of citizenship. Published by the THOA in 1984, a short biography of Santos Marka T'ula opened up a new understanding of indigenous agency regarding the modern institutions of the Bolivian state in the twentieth century.[27] Whereas mainstream historiography at the time had attributed all agency to pro-state peasant unions, this work showed that ayllus and independent communities prior to the national revolution had developed strong political organizations and a complex ideology that challenged the modern state's discourses of ethnic domestication.[28]

Based on the insights of the THOA's work, Silvia Rivera Cusicanqui elaborated a new social theory that redefined the meaning of internal colonialism in twentieth-century Bolivia. Rivera Cusicanqui argued that internal colonialism was not only a legacy of colonial times but also that it was reinvented in liberal and populist Bolivian ideologies. Coloniality, she argues, is habitus;[29] in other words, it is ingrained in the habits and experiences of everyday life and in Bolivian nation making, which has reproduced a hierarchical organization of society.[30] Other scholars, such as Javier Sanjinés, have defined internal colonialism as coloniality because both concepts address the problem of ethnicity, race, and inequality in nation making. Consequently, coloniality re-creates and re-elaborates a controversial modernity and becomes associated with the trajectory of "postcolonial states."[31]

Race versus Ethnicity

In this study I explore how the historical process of restructuring power relationships and racial discourses between the 1920s and the 1960s shaped and reshaped the emergence of the AMP's decolonization project. I consider how the elite's racial discourse was restructured and how assimilation policies emerged, often alongside segregationist policies, throughout the making of the modern Bolivian nation. My study thus examines how hegemonic nationalism was articulated through a discourse of mestizaje by national intellectuals. Before delving into that history, however, I will clarify how I understand and use the concepts of *racialization* and *coloniality* in this work. Racialization signifies the extension of dehumanizing and racial meanings to a relationship, social practice, or group that was previously unclassified racially. In the Bolivian experience, this racialization happened as a result of colonization and has forged Bolivia's social hierarchy. In other words, racialization is the form and colonialism is the content.

In terms of the notion of *race*, I understand it to be a discourse that categorizes people related to their exterior appearance and constructs social hierarchies, while *ethnicity* is more related to discourses that emphasize cultural difference.[32] Indeed, Jeffrey Gould has argued that Latin American countries such as Nicaragua used mestizaje as a racial discourse of homogenization in the making of nation-states during the twentieth century.[33] Mestizaje as a discourse, he argues, "refers both to the outcome of an individual or collective shift away from strong self-identification with indigenous culture, and to the myth of cultural homogeneity which elites imposed from above as a standard part of their repertoire of nation-building."[34] In Nicaragua the national elite used the state to promote the idea that indigenous peoples were no longer a living part of society and that the country was becoming increasingly mestizo. This perspective often worked as a justification for ignoring the rights of indigenous peoples, which occurred in Nicaragua, where indigenous people lost their land between 1870 and 1930 at the hands of supporters of this new discourse. Other authors, such as Diane Nelson, have argued that hegemonic racial discourse works "as a racial regulatory schema" in the process of the making of the nation-state.[35] As a result, elites are able to keep indigenous peoples in a subaltern position. Nelson argues that the schema of mestizaje discourse works to domesticate the Maya in Guatemala and to make them "the worst destroyers of their culture" by converting them into mestizos—which is to say, nonindigenous people.[36] Similarly, in considering Aymara regions of contemporary Bolivia, Aurolyn Luykx argues that education is used to consolidate and propagate mestizaje as a national identity and to push Aymaras to reject—or at least assume a passive attitude toward—their own identity.[37]

Throughout the history of the Bolivian state, intellectuals and politicians frequently discussed issues of ethnicity and race, referring to them as the "Indian problem." However, their policies and ideas about solving this problem, either through segregation or assimilation, fluctuated from 1920 to 1960. Embedded in colonial legislation, segregation was based on the idea that Indians and the descendants of Spaniards should have separate places in society. In the 1920s proponents of segregation such as Alcides Arguedas believed that neither education nor citizenship was necessary for Indians. In practical terms Indians were defined by how they dressed, what language they spoke, their illiteracy, and their lack of formal education. Individuals displaying these markers were thus racialized and targeted for exclusion. Beginning in the 1920s, a process of mass migration to La Paz and other cities gradually encouraged indigenous people to reject their racial markers and ethnic origins. According to census records, La Paz rose from a population of 40,000 in 1900, to 350,000 in 1950. Oruro—the third largest city in the country—increased from 15,000 to 75,000 in the same time period. Indeed, when many Indians in Bolivian cities faced strong discrimination because of their Indianness, they began adopting some elements of Western dress, gradually becoming full-fledged cholos—meaning they no longer self-identified as Indian—and joining the urban working class and sometimes the tiny middle class.[38]

Institutionalizing Indian dress as an emblem of race and ethnicity, municipal orders forbade Indians from entering certain urban spaces. During the 1920s, men were forced to abandon their ponchos and Andean pants for Western suits whenever they went to the city. Likewise, women were allowed to wear a mixture of Indian and Western dress, but they had to use manufactured fabrics rather than traditional handwoven textiles. Urban chola women in the main cities of Bolivia refined this fashion. In La Paz the term ch'ukutas was invented to reflect these changes.[39]

In discussions about the so-called Indian problem, assimilation was a marginal idea prior to the Chaco War between Bolivia and Paraguay from 1932 to 1935. However, the war and the collateral effects of the Great Depression initiated a long phasing out of segregationist policies, and assimilation slowly became central to the construction of the Bolivian state. Gradually, most elites began to support this option both rhetorically and through policies, encouraging Indians to abandon markers of indigeneity to reinforce their modernization project.[40] This position was strongly promoted by mainstream intellectuals after the national revolution of 1952 and by the government through policies of national integration. The Bolivian intellectual Astenio Averanga wrote that "Bolivia had effectively repopulated itself" by "modernizing . . . indigenous peoples."[41] Given elites' widespread belief that the country's failure to achieve modernity was due to the large Indian population, Averanga argued that by discouraging Indianness, the country could indeed become "modern." Averanga, like other intellectuals such as Manuel Rigoberto Paredes, explained that Bolivia could "whiten" and achieve modernity by means other than miscegenation and white immigration. Paredes saw Indianness as basically a dress code, arguing that when people gave up indigenous dress, they would be "de-Indianized," and the country would essentially become whiter. Thus, despite the shift from segregationist to assimilationist policies, attitudes toward race and ethnicity changed very little, as illustrated by the fact that ethnic dress was an emblem of racial and ethnic subordination both before and after 1952.[42] When the Bolivian National Revolution was finally consolidated in the 1960s, indigenous dress was increasingly seen as old-fashioned or primitive, and popular literature associated Indianness with prerevolutionary times.[43] Until the mid-1960s, people who did not change their style of dress continued to face restrictions when entering urban businesses such as movie theaters and restaurants.[44]

In the countryside the "modern style of dress" continued to be enforced after 1952, when mestizos controlled peasant unions and revolutionary dictates prohibited indigenous people from having long hair or wearing traditional textiles. As I will describe in chapters 2 and 5, the AMP's encouragement of new gender paradigms also became a tool for opposing the hegemonic conception of modernization, which resulted in the greater success of the modernizing process with men than with women. Women's dress changed very slowly in the countryside over the subsequent decades, and chola dress became a symbol of Indianness in Bolivian cities in the early 1960s.

From the 1920s to the 1960s, the de-Indianization process divided cholos and Indians along racial lines; the Chaco War and the national revolution were both watersheds in this process. Jach'aqullu and Titiriku focused their main struggle on resisting the whitening that cholo identity usually signified. Urbanization and modernity in Bolivia converted cholos, who were one generation away from being ch'utas or Indians, into the "mestizo or white" category (or dominant group). In other words, the children of Indians in the 1920s would become the cholos or ch'utas of the 1940s. There were, of course, some exceptions among cholos in the labor movement, such as Luis Cusicanqui, who defined himself as Indian Aymara.[45] For the most part, however, the racial system in Bolivia did not allow Indians to retain an Indian identity upon entering the working and middle classes.[46] In response the AMP elaborated new notions of Indian fashion as an external representation of indigenous culture and religion that exemplified their radical opposition to the de-Indianization that ch'utas and cholos represented. They created their own dress code as a signifier of the republic of Indians.

On Language and Race

Since one of the goals of this study is to lay bare the symbolic and tangible violence of racism and colonialism in modern Bolivia, I use the racial conventions and terminology of the time throughout this book. I understand race to be a social construct, and I attempt to discuss all levels of the racialized hierarchy in an individualized and humanizing way. However, I also show how racialized words, hierarchies, and images were deployed at the time. I do this in order to analyze and expose rather than to reinforce the very racial categories interrogated in this study. Thus, words like peon, cholo, chuta, Indian, and mestizo appear throughout the book and are critical to giving voice to the AMP's development and discourse. I have also included a glossary that provides definitions for these and many other Aymara and Spanish terms used throughout the book.

Religion and Politics

Unlike other indigenous activists, the AMP activists drew on religion not only as a critical part of their ideology but also as a way to present and legitimize their discourse to a wider group of people. From the 1920s to the 1960s, the AMP's earth politics was grounded in Aymara religiosity, the spirituality of the Bolivian Andes. In fact, I argue that combining indigenous religion and politics was fundamental to the AMP's ethnic social movement.[47] The dominant Bolivian culture of the mid-twentieth century assumed that Aymara spirituality was based on "superstition." In fact, Aymara religious practices were so derided that they were mostly practiced clandestinely. As the AMP consolidated its discourse, both the cult of Pachamama and the worship of wak'as on the mountain tops became central to its followers. For example, Melitón Gallardo sought to practice a spirituality based on the Saxama mountain in Oruro, one of the great spiritual centers of the Aymara world, and Andres Jach'aqullu enlarged the role of religious rituals by creating new ones, such as weddings and death rites. This discourse at first challenged the church and the landlords, but later it was also useful in organizing against the peasants unions and state institutions.

Indigenous spirituality proved fertile ground for the production of Indian law because it provided the AMP with a foundation of oral tradition with which to combine religion and politics.[48] The AMP's primary goal was the expansion of Indian law, which they promoted as a decolonizing text that contained their version of pre-Incan religion and heritage.[49] Their social movement, infused with religious content, spread from core regions, such as Jach'aqhachi and Saxama, to valley regions, such as Misk'i and Icla. The AMP's rituals included the burning of symbolic "packages of sweet and other aromatic essences" called *mesas* and offerings to Pachamama. During these rituals, several followers, including Francisco Rivera and Atiliano Peñaranda, burned currency, birth certificates, and other documents as a rite of passage to mark their passing from "white society" into the "republic of Indians" and as a symbol of separation from "whites."[50] These AMP rituals also symbolized the rejection of Christianity. One site of worship was Cantar Gallo, where white roosters were frequently sacrificed to Pachamama and the spirits of the Saxama and Sawaya mountains. By the early 1950s, such sacrifices had become Melitón Gallardo's favorite mode of worship, which he promoted as a way to mark the republic of Indians.[51]

The idea of a pluri-ethnic Qullasuyu (an imagined community that referred to the land primarily populated by Aymara) was central to the thinking of Toribio Miranda and subsequent AMP activists. With the name Qullasuyu, Miranda initiated a discourse that encompassed the complexities of a multiethnic region. Also crucial to Miranda's religious vocabulary of Qullasuyu is the Aymara word *puchu* (vestige), which refers to the origins of different ethnic groups, or a historical construction of *first peoples*. In his terminology reconstructed from oral sources, the monte-puchus (Uru), quchapuchus (Aymara), and chullpapuchus (Quechua) are the "remnants" of the "white invasion" and four centuries of colonialism. I will discuss these religious and political concepts at greater length in chapter 3, devoted to Miranda's activist intellectual production.

Studies of activist intellectuals among indigenous peoples mostly focus on urban, middle-class indigenous movements. Diane Nelson focused on a professional group of indigenous activists, and Kay Warren addressed a mixture of indigenous activists in an urban context.[52] This linking of urban and professional indigenous activists with ethnic nationalism has been reinforced in Latin American studies. Greg Grandin's work on the history of the indigenous elite in Quetzaltenango (Guatemala) epitomizes such a perspective.[53] Grandin argues that the Maya elite was "no less elitist than its Ladino counterpart" and shows that this group made decisions based on their own interests, uniting with the Ladino elite to emphatically oppose the struggles of Maya peasants for land.[54] In contrast, by focusing on indigenous activists in both rural and urban areas, I explore the cultural contexts in which Aymara religiosity produced a different type of ethnic social movement.

Patriarchalism and Gender Relations

The THOA has already shown the many ways that indigenous women participated in the Indian struggle during this time, but their work has not addressed the issues surrounding the structure of Andean patriarchy. This form of patriarchy was characterized by ideas about parity and comple-mentarities among men and women; however, these ideas existed within a patriarchal structure in which the father and older men were the primary or official actors in Andean societies.[55] In recounting the life stories of Melitón Gallardo, Toribio Miranda, Gregorio Titiriku, and Andres Jach'aqullu, I also focus on how their relationships with their wives, mothers, and female relatives affected their activism, as well as how gendered discourses shaped the way they interacted with audiences both on haciendas and in ayllus.

The AMP's history reveals the existence of two different stages of patri-archy in Bolivia. The Western form of patriarchy predominated in the urban sphere and with the rural elite from the 1920s to the 1940s and then had a greater impact on the rural sphere from the 1950s to the 1960s. The first generation of the AMP used patriarchal strategies from indigenous traditions to exercise their power and influence in different ecological regions of the Andes. Kinship and patriarchal ideas about the roles of husbands and fathers were essential to the early construction of the AMP network. Rosa and Santusa, Titiriku's first and second wives, were part of networks of Indian power that he used to help the AMP expand. Toribio Miranda's mother, Juana Flores, was a powerful influence in his life, pushing him to recuperate ancestral land by returning to his father's community. Miranda knew that marrying a local woman would open considerable connections and resources for him, given the fact that in the 1920s land often passed from women to women. He organized his network based on alliances that he built through marrying women in the regions where he worked. He was married three times in the course of his life, to women from Cochabamba, Chuquisaca, and Oruro, which allowed him to operate as an indigenous activist in different regions from the 1920s to the 1950s.

The second generation put more emphasis on Andean ideas about marriage and reinvented some ideas about women's participation. In the 1940s Gallardo lived between the ambivalences of the indigenous patriarchal system and internal colonialism, while, as an activist, he also promoted an indigenous form of marriage. Gendered ideas were also present in other dimensions of AMP indigenous activists' work, and helped to spread the AMP's ideas. As women tended to have closer ties to indigenous spirituality than men during this time, they helped to nourish that aspect of the movement.[56] Matilde Qulqi and Manuela Quevedo used their influence on Jach'aqullu and Miranda, their respective husbands, to include ancient rites in AMP discourse. Finally, Andrés Jach'aqullu promoted the values of reciprocity and complementarity between men and women in the years after the revolution of 1952, when dominant patriarchal ideas were spreading throughout Bolivia.

Although the national revolution gave women the right to vote, the Bolivian National ID Office started to issue identification cards to women that included their husbands' last name.[57] The peasant unions established that households must be represented by males, since in "modern times" only men represented the community. They frequently rejected documents from communities that included the names of women. This move kept representation out of women's hands, fundamentally changing the role of wives in rural society and women's status in the community. Indigenous women were no longer welcome to participate in local community issues

FIGURE 1.1. A group of Aymara women in the main plaza
of Uncía (Potosí), circa 1926. Indigenous women liked to
be photographed in the urban context of plazas, and in this
picture Matilde Qulqi (wife of Andrés Jachaqullu in the 1940s)
is at the right. In 1929 the City Council of Uncía led by the
mestizo elite banned Indians from entering the main plazas.
Courtesy of Eusebio Quyu, Qala Qala, Potosí.

since they were seen as more Indian because of their clothing; in this sense
urban and rural women had different experiences. Although the AMP's
leadership was dominated by men, the organization promoted Aymara
gender relations as way to confront Western patriarchy's attempt to erase
women's roles in rituals and in the signing of official documents. The
AMP indigenous activists strongly encouraged participants to bring their
wives to meetings and to include their names when signing documents.
Women from remote indigenous communities throughout the Bolivian
Andes came to La Paz with their husbands to fight for their rights in government offices. In this way, as we will see, the AMP emphasized elements

of Aymara tradition that empowered women and advocated for equal participation in public affairs.

The experience of the AMP sheds light on the specific ways in which earth politics and gender dovetailed in Andean societies and how these, in turn, linked with indigenous politics. Marisol de la Cadena has argued that in Peruvian markets people from the cities considered peasant women to be Indians.[58] Indeed, Indian women were more visible than men because their dress was seen as part of the Indian heritage in the Andean World. After the national revolution, the association between female Indianness and Andean textiles became more prevalent, encouraging more and more Indian men to stop including Andean textiles in their dress. This solidified the perception that women were more Indian because they retained Indian dress. Indeed, the idea that men should wear hats and suits had become so widespread that the masculinity of Indian males who chose other forms of dress would be questioned.

The indigenous activists of the AMP not only understood this racialized urban perception of Indian women but also saw the potential for Indian women to nourish the movement. In other words, the AMP challenged the national revolution's conceptions of male-oriented modernization. Although Aymara and Andean gender practices became part of the AMP's counter-hegemonic actions, the AMP had their own forms of patriarchalism too. While the AMP attempted to keep spaces open for women to participate, it was always in a subordinate position, and there seemed to be no room for single women or women who disagreed with their husbands. Even so, and although the role of women was still primarily symbolic, the AMP insisted that women remain part of the public sphere. This stood in stark contrast to the new ideas of the revolution that insisted, at least through the peasant unions, that "modern" women should retreat to the private sphere.

The four stories I present in this book show how the restructuring of patriarchalism and gender in Bolivia overlapped with internal colonialism, race, class, and the relationship between urban and rural areas. In some cases AMP indigenous activists established connections with different regions and ethnic groups through marriage and kinship. Their responsibilities to parents, children, and some state-sponsored institutions, such as military service, crucially shaped these four lives in the context of the constant imagining and reimagining of the Bolivian nation. Along with modernization in the 1940s and revolution in the 1950s, modern patriarchal ideas shaped the institutions of the new nation-state, especially in marriage practices, surnames, dress code, women's union participation, ethnicity, public schools, citizenship, the spread of Spanish, and the corresponding eradication of native languages. In contrast to the dominant contemporary ideas about women's role in the public sphere, AMP activists emphasized the participation of women in their social and political movements, while they still embodied a native patriarchal system fundamentally tied to coloniality.

Telling Stories: Sources, Archives, and Methods

I review the production, consumption, and circulation of these ideas of decolonization in the context of the AMP based on personal and public archives located in Oruro, La Paz, Chuquisaca, and Cochabamba. The archives that are in the hands of indigenous families include sources such as the memoirs of their ancestors and family members and collections of letters addressed to intellectuals and to government, diplomatic, local, and church officials, including corregidors, subprefects, prefects, the U.S. embassy, the United Nations, the Bahá'í Council, and the Methodist Church. The most important source in archives held by indigenous families and other rural archives in southern Cochabamba are notarized testimonies of life stories. These documents were created when AMP activists, especially those living in ex-hacienda regions, visited public notaries between the 1950s and 1970s in order to give testimony regarding some episodes from their lives. The AMP's members were concerned about recording their perspective and preserving their land rights, especially while the agrarian reform and its legal procedures were in force, given that the AMP had mixed feelings about it.

The records also include transcriptions of the titles of colonial agrarian properties and newspapers with records of some of the denunciations of AMP activists made to the Bolivian national government. These private archives aid in comprehending the internal organization, life histories, and other issues related to these intellectuals' political ideas. Despite having the same ethnic background, indigenous language, and friendly relationships with the AMP leaders' descendants and relatives, I did not easily gain access to these archives. In the process of researching and collecting materials for over thirty years, my knowledge of indigenous activists and their struggle has grown, and I became increasingly able to distinguish exaggeration from useful material.

The texts that I draw from in this book were produced in different circumstances, which necessarily affects my interpretation of them as sources. An important example is a set of memoirs produced in the 1970s when Radio Mendez (La Paz), Instituto de Investigación y Cultura para la Educación Popular-Oruro (INDECIP), Centro de Investigación y Promoción del Campesinado-La Paz (CIPCA), and other nonprofit organizations focused on literacy and organized a local campaign to collect indigenous memoirs, some of which featured AMP leaders.[59] These memoirs were subsequently kept in local archives. Similar memoirs were produced when, in the early 1980s, Bahá'ís and Methodists also organized a campaign to promote literacy. These and other life stories ended up in NGO and indigenous archives.

These memoirs circulated in a very limited way at the local level in some indigenous communities in the Bolivian countryside. Although these resources offer an indigenous perspective, in some cases they create silences about activists' political and religious connections. Sometimes they overemphasize their subjects' activism, but they also provide insights into the era and the types of concerns that these activists had. In some cases I found that accounts were created one generation later and use concepts and ideas a posteriori to the facts. For example, Maria Titiriku refers to indigenous people as Aymaras, while, in her father's generation, they would have been referred to as jaqis. Historians should be aware of the differences in these terms and of their implications. In some cases there is no language discrepancy, but the emphasis on some events or actors is excessive and needs to be correlated with other accounts. So while they provide a unique source, historians need to carefully analyze the factual and discursive nature of these accounts. In general the indigenous archives are a slippery terrain, just like many other sources.

In addition I also conducted oral history interviews with some indigenous intellectuals and their descendants and family members in the 1980s. I especially focused on the families and communities of Melitón and Lucia Gallardo (Sucre), Andrés and Matilde Jach'aqullu (Oruro), Gregorio and Rosa Titiriku (El Alto, La Paz), Fermín Vallejos (Raqaypampa, Cochabamba), Luciano Negrete (Aiquile, Cochabamba), and Felix Paqusillu (Wayllamarka, La Paz). As Alessandro Portelli argues, oral history is historically produced and represents a fixed identity and thus should be read, like any other document, with care.[60] At the same time, oral history can facilitate an understanding of social realities that are frequently omitted in documentary sources; for instance, the experiences of indigenous intellectuals who lived between the countryside and the city, the relationship between this group of *cabecillas* and their associates in different parts of the countryside, the internal workings of their organization, women's role in the organization, and the family life of these intellectuals. Oral histories have provided me with a better understanding of the "structures of feeling" and emotions at play within the AMP movement.[61]

With regard to my methodology, I started to collect data about indigenous movements more than thirty years ago after I met several AMPs in the early 1980s, when many were (or recently had been) Bahá'ís, a religion that had arrived in Bolivia in the 1940s and started to gain indigenous members in the late 1950s.[62] Despite the religion's Muslim origins, it had thousands of believers in the Bolivian highlands in the 1960s, many of whom converted to Bahá'ísm because of the legal support this religion could offer them in the era after the national revolution. Bahá'ís have suffered persecution in Iran since the nineteenth century and thus were especially sensitive to the fact these indigenous activists and their networks were also under a "kind of persecution" in Bolivia. At some level these Bahá'í leaders wanted to believe that these indigenous leaders were being persecuted because of their conversion to Bahá'í. Whether or not this was an exaggeration, the Bahá'ís did provide AMP leaders with lawyers in the 1960s. As an Aymara teenager belonging to the community of Marka Hilata, Carabuco, La Paz, I also converted to this religion for an important period of my life, although I left it in the 1980s. During my years in the Bahá'í faith, I participated in several congresses organized by the Bahá'ís in order to bring AMP indigenous activists back to the religion since so many had left the faith in the 1970s. As a teenager and during my later years in the Bahá'í faith, I got interested in hearing about these activists' lives, struggles, and failures. At that point, I was only curious about whether they had really been persecuted because they were Bahá'í. Over the last thirty years, I have discovered that another, deeper story lay behind the apparent persecution of Bahá'ís in Bolivia.

In the 1980s people like Andres Jach'aqullu, Melitón Gallardo, Fermín Vallejos, Luciano Negrete, and Dorotea Vallejos embraced me and told me some of the secrets hidden behind their official lives as Bahá'ís. They likely trusted me because my first language is Aymara and because, like them, I also come from an ayllu, or indigenous community. Through these contacts, I also met AMP members' descendants and families in hacienda regions that did not have the ayllu tradition. These connections later brought me to other AMP indigenous activists who had rejected the Bahá'í faith even earlier than me, had become Methodists, or had built up native religions in the 1960s. In the process I also learned how to create new connections and find new indigenous archives in different regions of Bolivia. This work also taught me that I had a responsibility to work in the areas of development and human rights, which I did by building up NGOs for about twenty years. This work in the 1980s and 1990s taught me about the diversity and richness of the Bolivian indigenous heritage. Even now that I live in the United States for most of the year, I maintain strong connections with the indigenous world, and when I do go back to South America I mostly live in rural Bolivia. I am dedicated to communicating what I have learned and am still learning from indigenous archives and oral sources to many different academic audiences, the indigenous audience, the Bolivian national audience, and the U.S. audience, all of which have different priorities and interests.

Tracing a Movement: Four Case Studies

Chapter 2 reviews this history and illustrates the local, regional, national, and global factors that contributed to the persistence of internal colonialism, which helped shape the AMP's discourse. Through the cases of Toribio Miranda and Gregorio Titiriku, chapters 3 and 4 recount the development of the Indian law, the AMP's response to racial segregation, and explain gender relations in the era prior to the national revolution in 1952. Chapter 3 details how Miranda's earth politics emerged in the Aymara and Uru highlands and draws out the connections of these areas with large estates in the Quechua-dominated southern Andes. This case reveals rich connections with previous indigenous movements, the complex elaboration of discourses of race and decolonization, and the role of the indigenous women and men who traveled among the AMP in the 1920s. Gregorio Titiriku, the focus of chapter 4, was a contemporary of Miranda's, and he took a leadership role in elaborating the Indian law during the era of segregation. Titiriku covered a lot of ground, moving between the cities of La Paz, Oruro, and Cochabamba, actively confronting segregationist

FIGURE 1.2. Gregorio Titiriku, during one of his meetings with an officer of the International Labour Organization in La Paz, circa 1950s. The whole delegation that went with him to the meeting is in the background, including both men and women. Archivo Privado de Pedro Mamani, Qariphuyu, Potosí, Bolivia.

policies and factionalism between cholos and Indians from the 1920s to the 1960s. Like apoderados, jilaqatas, and other indigenous activists did at that time, from 1920 to 1935 Titiriku used garantías—written declarations of rights—to empower Indians, but he also used them to spread the notion of Indian law and the republic of Indians much more widely.

By the mid-twentieth century, assimilationist discourse began to dominate national politics. The cases of Melitón Gallardo and Andrés Jach'aqullu, in chapters 5 and 6, narrate how earth politics emerged, transformed, and spread in that context. When Melitón Gallardo entered Indian politics in the 1940s, the ideology of de-Indianization was so powerful that most urban Indians had become cholos or ch'utas. His history shows the intricate ways that ethnic social movements overlapped with religion.[63] It also shows the workings of the caste system in society prior to 1952 and the era's hegemonies of race, dress, and language. Through Jach'aqullu's case, I analyze Indian law in action during the national revolution, when the dominant revolutionary party, the MNR, went from supporting segregation to emphasizing assimilation in Bolivian society. Like Titiriku, Jach'aqullu experienced class conflict between Indians and cholos, who had Indian heritage but followed so-called whitening practices. Like Miranda, Titiriku, and Gallardo, Jach'aqullu advocated a project of decolonization that included autonomy for a nation of Indians and relied heavily on Aymara religious practices. In Jach'aqullu's case we also see another example of the importance of women in the AMP's activism. Finally, I conclude by reviewing the role of religion, politics, and memory in the AMP movement and then evaluate some of its impact in Bolivia after the election of Evo Morales.

The AMP in Comparative Perspective with Other Ethnic Movements in the Andes and Mesoamerica

Indigenous activists like the four profiled in this book, who worked throughout the Andes and Mesoamerica in the mid-twentieth century, demonstrate the construction of indigenous identities. However, the modern evolution of ethnic politics in these regions goes back at least as far as the mid-nineteenth century and includes indigenous intellectuals such as Manuel Quintín Lame in Colombia;[64] Teodomiro Gutierrez Cuevas in Puno, Peru;[65] Pablo Zárate Willka in Bolivia (who figures into this story as well);[66] and Ismael Coyoc in Quetaztelnango, Guatemala.[67] Their petitions and letters denouncing abuse, as well as their organizational experience, represent the postcolonial indigenous voice in the Andes and Mesoamerica, and their work and audience are mostly known in the field of Latin American studies as ethnic political movements.

Among these ethnic movements there were some important differences in terms of strategies in the construction of indigenous identity, but they all sought and defended indigenous rights in an unequal battle with the nation-state, which was firmly within the grasp of white and mestizo elites. Three cases from Chile, Ecuador, and Guatemala stand out when viewed in a comparative perspective with Bolivia's AMP.[68] According to Thomas Klubock, the Mapuche Indians wanted to create an Araucana republic in 1934 in Ranquil and Cautil that would have involved the return of land and the restoration of indigenous language in 1934.[69] These Mapuche activists operated in conjunction with the Communist Party and the labor movement in Chile. The peasant intellectuals of Ecuador studied by Marc Becker were also linked to the Communist Party in Cayambe. In both of these cases, the link to external leftist ideologies in Ecuador and Chile was a strong factor. The Communist Party represented a strong voice in favor of labor and peasant rights in the first half of twentieth century, and, consequently, indigenous peoples in Ecuador and Chile adopted the political strategy of working with the Left and the labor movement in forming their movements. Those involved in the Guatemalan case treated by Greg Grandin also had ties, if more partial and tenuous, to the Communist Party. During Guatemala's Ten Years of Spring (1944–1954) under Juan José Arévalo and Jacobo Árbenz, Grandin argues that the pro-Maya educational association called the Sociedad El Adelanto, which sought land and education for Maya Indians, was divided by pro- and anticommunists in the time of the Cold War. In all of these cases the construction of indigenous identity in the first half of the twentieth century remained linked to metropolitan ideologies.

In contrast, while the AMP also had connections to the Communist Party and other leftist and indigenista movements, they followed a different pattern because they strategically expressed indigenous identity in relation to colonial law, specifically the seventeenth-century Law of the Indies. By basing their work on a historical concept rather than a contemporary political party, the AMP could create their own worldview, discourse, and ideology and could reject the overtures of the Left. Since the Indian law also included ideas about autonomy and land claims, they could use it to emphasize a worldview that combined politics, land, and religion. The AMP built their struggle on a long tradition of indigenous activism based on networks of caciques, alcaldes, mallkus, and apoderados that had existed since the nineteenth century and were organized to fight land usurpation and the state's liberal policies. In the first half of twentieth century, indigenous Bolivians had their own intellectuals and sources of discourse, in which Pachamama and other Aymara deities played important roles and acted as mobilizing factors.

The fact that the AMP based its discourse on colonial legislation did not make it unique among ethnic movements in the Andes. Indeed, indigenous peoples were already defending their rights based on legislation from before the foundation of Bolivia to the end of the nineteenth century. In Ancash, Peru, leaders such as Pedro Pablo Atusparia based their struggle and uprising on certain aspects of the Law of the Indies.[70] Similarly, in the Colombian case indigenous peoples used colonial ideas about caste to defend their land and rights.[71] What is new about the incorporation of colonial legislation in Bolivia's case is that the AMP created a discourse that combined it with ideas drawn from Andean religion. The four AMP activists studied in this book not only moved from their interpretation of the Law of Indies to an Indian law discourse but also built up an ideological corps in the process, constructing an organization with the goal of defending their rights.

The second-generation AMP re-created the Indian law discourse and even deployed it against the goals of the Bolivian National Revolution of 1952. The AMP's audience during this revolutionary era had some similarities with the Maya indigenous peoples in a different revolutionary era of the 1930s in Chiapas, Mexico. Indeed, Stephen Lewis argues that the Ministry of Public Education of Mexico had poor results in promoting the goals of the revolution, including labor laws and agrarian reforms. This was particularly difficult in the Maya highlands given the fact that the teachers did not show an interest in native languages. Followers of the second generation of the AMP in the countryside of Chuquisaca and southern Cochabamba also rejected the goals of the Bolivian National Revolution, including the agrarian reform and state-run education promoted by peasant unions. Instead, they wanted cultural autonomy, education in native languages, and indigenous forms of land tenure that were not based on individual ownership.

Bolivia's AMP movement is part of a long evolution of ethnic politics in the twentieth century, particularly noteworthy because it was able to re-create its discourse and ethnic movement over two generations, both before and after the national revolution. Bolivia's AMP epitomizes the complex construction of indigenous identity in the long and unresolved struggle for heterogeneity, civil rights, citizenship, and autonomy in the twentieth century.[72] The AMP's ideas continue to resonate in the political transformations that Bolivia is undergoing in the early twentieth-first century.

Chapter Two

Nation Making and the
Genealogy of the AMP
Indigenous Activists

The Alcaldes Mayores Particulares (AMP), also known as the *kollasuyus* group and *phawajrunas* (the flying men), came from a long genealogy of indigenous activists and a Bolivian civil rights movement that goes back at least to the passing of the agrarian reform in 1874. The first generation of indigenous activists, led by Luciano Willka and Pablo Zárate Willka, were called apoderados or caciques. These activists were mostly mallkus, alcaldes, or jilaqatas of indigenous communities, and they created extensive networks to resist the new polices of the liberal state, especially the agrarian reform of 1874, and its actions during the civil war that took place from 1898 until 1899. Some of the future generations of AMP members were descendents of those early activists, whose stories of the conflict were fundamental to the founding of the AMP.

In the early twentieth century, a new network of indigenous activists emerged under the leadership of Santos Marka T'ula and Feliciano Inka Maraza, among them Toribio Miranda and Gregorio Titiriku. Santos Marka T'ula's network and strategies emphasized literacy and the validity of colonial titles and was rooted in the historical conditions of the period.[1] But by the 1930s Marka T'ula's apoderado and cacique movement was collapsing after decades of work. The Chaco War between Paraguay and Bolivia from 1932 to 1935 brought about political changes that gave indigenous peoples the opportunity to create new political strategies, such as establishing clandestine schools and demanding civil rights. The con-

fluence of these factors sparked the formation of a new group of indigenous activists in 1936, the AMP, led by Miranda and Titiriku. Emerging
from the structures of racial domination, the AMP embodied a new face
that drew on the legacy of the early colonial period and faith in wak'as
and Achachilas.

The Agrarian Reform of 1874: Sowing the Seeds of the AMP

The impact of liberal nationalism and the first Bolivian agrarian reform in
1874 was fundamental to the emergence of the AMP. During the second
half of the nineteenth century, liberalism, which was associated with both
military and civilian regimes, spread throughout Latin America. Agustín
Aspiazu, Félix Reyes Ortiz, Vicente Ochoa, and Julio Méndez, the founders
of Bolivian liberalism, emerged in the early 1860s from an elite La Paz lit-
erary club. During the following three decades, they formed the first Liberal Party under the leadership of Eliodoro Camacho.[2] Like other liberal
groups in late nineteenth-century Latin America, Bolivian Liberals came
from the elite and, consequently, were all white or mestizo. Not unlike
other liberals of the time, they believed that individual freedom was the
only path to equality and progress. Promoting individualism in Bolivian
society, they rejected all forms of collective Indian existence, including
the Indian ethnic organization of ayllus.[3] They promoted a liberal agrarian
reform called the Ley de Exvinculación (Disentailment Law), which originated in the mid-1860s, when Donato Muñoz convinced Mariano Melgarejo's government to introduce a law that mandated the sale of community land at public auction unless communities obtained new property
titles from the government within three months. When the Bolivian state
started to sell Indian land to white and mestizo purchasers in 1869, it led
to a general Indian uprising in the Altiplano and to the overthrow of the
Melgarejo regime. In 1871 Aymara jilaqatas and alcaldes mayores led by
Luciano Willka installed a new caudillo, Agustín Morales, to rule Bolivia.[4]
This marked the first direct participation of Indians in Bolivian politics.
However, Liberals quickly reorganized to end Agustín Morales's regime
and install Tomás Frias. Agustín Aspiazu, a leader of the Liberal Party and
the president of Congress at the time, passed a long-planned agrarian
reform in 1874, asserting that it was the Liberals' highest achievement.
However, given the emergency provoked by the War of the Pacific, which

broke out in 1879 between Bolivia, Peru, and Chile, implementation of the law was delayed until the mid-1890s.[5]

The law forbade indigenous corporate or group landowning, which meant the official abolition of ayllu and marka systems in which Indians were represented by alcaldes mayores (who were also known as mallkus and jilaqatas).[6] The Disentailment Law stated that ethnic representations were "no longer accepted" and required that indigenous people act as individuals and appoint apoderados whenever they wanted to address problems with land tenure. This law substituted liberal ideas of individual titles for the Aymara "corporate" paradigms that had previously governed land tenure. This facilitated the "dissociation of the communities" and the appointment of agrarian bureaucrats to visit indigenous communities in order to impose "individual private property."[7] However, a complementary law passed on November 23, 1883, stated that ayllus and communities did not have to be divided into individual tracts of private property if they presented colonial property titles.[8] The application of these laws over the next three decades revived the relevance of the colonial titles that many Aymara mallkus had purchased in the sixteenth century with gold or services. Although it was extremely difficult for communities to find titles that dated back three centuries, the ayllus and markas began searching in order to stave off the division of their communities. This legal provision became critical for indigenous activists, including the AMP.[9]

The entire creation and application of the agrarian reform of 1874 was based on racist assumptions. To promote "progress," Liberals quickly concluded that land must be taken away from Indians. As one prominent Liberal asserted, land should be taken out of "unproductive Indian hands" and be given to the "creative white race."[10] Although the Bolivian constitution did not explicitly mention race during the 1860s and 1870s, the government defined citizenship in terms of literacy, urban property, and Christian education, which essentially limited it to the white population because very few Indians knew how to read or write.[11] Liberals' ideas of equality and freedom simply did not include Indians and women; their actions showed that progress and modernity only applied to white men, and appropriating Indian resources to achieve these goals was acceptable.

The Liberals' racialized view of civilization and progress did not include the problems and needs of the country's vast Indian majority. In fact the focus of this first generation of Liberals on the destruction of the ayllus and markas demonstrated that they did not understand the connections between indigenous networks and the market economy. Tristan Platt has argued that groups of ayllus were well integrated into the market economy in the mid-nineteenth century and that the existence of ayllus did not hinder the country's modernization.[12] For instance, the Aymaras of northern Potosí produced great quantities of wheat for the mines of Potosí, and the ayllus of Paqajaqi dominated the transport of mining production and imported goods between La Paz and Arica during the second half of the nineteenth century. The Liberals' viewpoint essentialized the collective dimension of ayllus and ignored the role of the individual within the ayllu. In her study of the links between liberal ideology, Bolivian whites, and the role of skin color, Danielle Démelas called the history of Liberals in the late nineteenth century "darwinismo a la criolla" (Creole-style Darwinism).[13] Liberals were influenced by European social Darwinism, an ideology based in pseudoscience that posited the existence of superior and inferior races and considered nonwhites to be intrinsically incapable of achieving modernity or progress. The historian Charles A. Hale has argued that Latin American liberals during this era turned away from liberal universalism and toward positivism's strong proclivity for practical, disciplinary, and authoritarian reform.[14] Therefore, despite their rhetoric of equality and freedom, Liberals only succeeded in restricting indigenous communities and transferring control of indigenous lands to the country's white minority.

Aymara Nationalism and Hybrid Religiosity in the Civil War Era

Since the 1880s the Bolivian and global economies had been linked mostly through the mining sector. In the early twentieth century, Liberals constructed railroads between the country's mining centers and the Chilean ports of Antofagasta and Arica as well as between the principal cities in the western highlands. This occurred in the context of growing urbanization due to the agrarian reform of 1874, which had led to the enlargement of haciendas and to the expulsion of Aymara peasants from the ayllus and markas.[15] As commercial agriculture expanded in the valleys of Cochabamba, Chuquisaca, and La Paz, the city of La Paz increased from 40,000 people in 1900 to 350,000 in 1950, and Oruro—the country's third largest city and an important mining center—grew from 15,000 to 75,000 in the same period.[16]

As the silver economy slowly collapsed, the power of the southern elite from Sucre and Potosí, who were mainly part of the Conservative Party, diminished. This elite wanted to maintain Bolivia as a unitary state with its capital in Sucre in order to enhance its power. However, as the northern tin-mining economy rose in importance, the northern elite from La Paz and Oruro, who were mainly members of the Liberal Party, advocated a federal system and moving the capital to La Paz. This confrontation initially played out in the Bolivian Congress, but President Severo Fernández Alonzo rejected the idea of moving the capital, despite the fact that presidents had tended to reside in the more dynamic city of La Paz since 1825. The northern elite subsequently rejected President Fernández Alonzo's constitutional regime and organized a federal government in La Paz in the name of the Liberal Party. Since both party politics and regional elite interests were embodied in La Paz's rebellion, Fernández Alonzo decided to lead the army into the highlands to quell the insurrection. The subsequent civil war lasted from December 1898 to April 1899.[17] José Manuel Pando, the Liberal leader of the mestizo and white elite, emerged as a northern federalist leader, basing his power on relationships with important mallkus and indigenous activists that he had cultivated before the civil war. He obtained part of this power through his wife Adela Warachi, who, as a descendant of a rich and important member of the eighteenth-century Aymara elite, still enjoyed prestige among indigenous communities. Warachi owned large tracts of land around Sik'a Sik'a and Luriway (La Paz), where Aymaras rose up en masse during the civil war. Pando had also been corresponding informally since 1896 with Pablo Zárate Willka, one of the mallkus or apoderados from Sik'a Sik'a who demanded Aymara separatism during the civil war. The informality and frequency of visits between Zárate Willka and Pando show that they forged a strong collaboration when both leaders were emerging as caudillos in the 1890s.[18]

Since the 1880s Zárate Willka had belonged to a large network of Aymara alcaldes mayores and jilaqatas that included Melchor Marka (Qaranqas), Lorenzo Ramirez (Moxsa), Marcelino Mamani (Janqulaimes), Isidro Qanqi (Qallapa), Juan Lero (Puxpu), and a hundred others from disparate parts of the country.[19] Trying various strategies to defend ethnic territories from the agrarian reform of 1874 quickly turned these apoderados into indigenous community activists. They attempted to assist their people by learning to read legal dispositions, writing letters of complaint, dealing with lawyers, and attending meetings with judges and other authorities, all while crafting a "politics of memory" for their communities.[20] In other words, they constructed a system of ideas and strategies that used history and memory to influence the present. Although they were not formally educated, these apoderados were frequently trained by the long-standing traditional networks of alcaldes mayores and jilaqatas. For the actual work with documents, they relied on the assistance of escribanos.[21]

The first generation of apoderados started their careers as part of Luciano Willka's network of indigenous activists in the early 1860s. Willka was a well-known Aymara activist from the region of Waichu (La Paz) who developed strong ties to General Agustín Morales in the 1860s. When Morales became president in 1872, he resurrected the abolished community status for Indian lands. Thus, through uprisings against Melgarejo and supporting Morales's rise to the presidency, the first "postcolonial" Indian network led by Luciano Willka achieved an important victory. This helped them gain power for future activists who would defend the autonomy of ayllus and markas.[22] Pablo Zárate Willka, who became the best-known Aymara activist of the end the nineteenth century, emerged in this context. In his early years as an indigenous activist, Willka met his wife Aida Aguilar, who belonged to a family of mallkus from Qhupaqawana (Copacabana) on the border with Peru, and her kinship ties gave him wide access to ayllu and marka networks in the Lake Titikaka basin.[23] Apoderados like Luciano Willka and Zárate Willka were in frequent contact with national and regional caudillos such as Agustín Morales and José Manuel Pando, constructing an identity as leaders and as indigenous intellectual activists. Within the ayllus and markas, indigenous activists with reliable information and knowledge of Bolivian politics could garner a wide audience. But white caudillos like Morales ignored the political strategies of the alcaldes mayors and jilaqatas and probably never understood the complexity of indigenous demands for lands, territory, and civil rights, instead believing that the indigenous leaders would not cause trouble and would provide unconditional support. Epitomizing this misunderstanding, José Quintín Mendoza, a member of the Liberal elite and a local caudillo who presided over the federal government in La Paz, announced that he thought that the Aymara peasantry and their indigenous activists "were committed to liberal ideas and the 1898 federal revolution."[24]

In the years prior to the civil war, Zárate Willka visited ayllus and markas and communicated the mostly oral but occasionally written message that

"Indians must have their own government as was the custom before the Spaniards arrived."[25] As shown by his frequent references to the fifteenth-century (before Inka and Spanish domination) Aymara ethnic groups of Umasuyus, Paqajaqis, and Qarangas, Zárate Willka imagined a nation that would include a strong ethnic dimension of the Aymara world. This pre-Inka perspective used ethnic signifiers from the Aymara heritage to represent its nationalism. During the 1890s Zárate Willka used the names of the ten Aymara nations to refer to Bolivian regions that had different legal names. For example, he used the older name of the Paqajaqi nation to refer to the region of Taraqu (Ingavi Province) and rejected the republican denomination of Manco Capac Province, instead speaking of Qhupaqawana as a part of Umasuyos.[26] Zárate Willka's discourse also embodied the construction of an Indian identity that included many Catholic and Aymara religious practices. Studies like Thomas Abercrombie's help us to understand that religious identities included European forms of historical consciousness and Andean ways of understanding the past.[27] Zárate Willka even visited the famous Qulla and Catholic sanctuary of Qhupaqawana in April 1896; from there he wrote to his future ally Pando that "he prayed for him," which shows the role of Catholic rituals in the process of legitimizing Indian activism. While José Manuel Pando probably thought that Zárate Willka prayed to the Virgin Mary, he was probably praying to Pachamama through the figure of Mary. The Catholic Church's role as a legitimating factor is reflected in other statements, such as when Zárate Willka insisted that even "Catholic priests should be Indians."[28] In this case he was probably referring to an extremely hybrid Aymara-Catholic version of religiosity. In addition Aymara religion strongly emphasizes Pachamama as the main religious character, which made for an easier assimilation of the Marian cult since both focused on female figures. In his messages to Indian communities during the civil war, Zárate Willka argued that his struggle was based on the idea of "equality that comes [from the] Pope and the Vatican."[29] References to the Catholic Church became a necessary element in a hybrid society, in which the dominant groups made Catholicism the official religion and indigenous peoples embraced a hybrid religiosity.[30]

When the Liberals realized that indigenous activists sought autonomy, they became extremely worried. Indigenous participants in the civil war referred to Zárate Willka as the "president" of the republic and to his army staff (headed by Manuel Mita Willka, Feliciano Willka, and José Willka) as his cabinet.[31] The civil war slowly evolved from a struggle between Liberals and Conservatives into a confrontation between Indians and whites, becoming very violent in some regions. This change was provoked by soldiers' mistreatment of the Aymara civilian population in Muxsa; the communities responded by killing 110 soldiers. As the civil war became a racial war, a discourse of Aymara nationalism emerged that promoted the Aymaras' goals.[32] During the civil war, the leaders of the ayllus and markas learned how to operate in the white-dominated society. This group included Santos Marka T'ula and Isidoro Kanki from Qallapa (La Paz), Cirilo Flores from Paria (Oruro), Federico Peralta from Peñas (La Paz), Feliciano Miranda from Quntu (Oruro), and Feliciano T'ula from Wayllamarka (La Paz). This group of activists played a key role in the development of an indigenous politics that helped the AMP gain prominence in the 1930s.[33]

At the end of the civil war, the Aymara communities declared Zárate Willka the "president" of the indigenous Aymaras in Saqaqa, Moxsa, Qulqichaca, and Qaraqollo. However, even more radical was the installation in Phiñas (Oruro) of an independent and sovereign government. Juan Lero, mallku of the region, acted as "president" of the Republic of Phiñas and appointed a full staff of government officials that included Manuel Flores as secretary (also called minister of state), Ascencio Fuero as judge (also called supreme judge), Feliciano Mamani as intendant, and Evaristo Wariqallu as colonel and chief of the new army. To emphasize his indigenous nationalist claims, Lero announced that anyone who wanted to enter the new republic had to present passports. He recognized Zárate Willka as supreme leader of the new Aymara revolution and decided that the citizens of the new Indian republic should dress as "Indians" to display their ethnic pride and nationalism.[34] The Republic of Phiñas enjoyed almost a full month of autonomy before the Bolivian government sent the army to destroy it. For the first time since Bolivia's independence, Aymaras ruled themselves, and for the first time since Inka domination, Aymaras were in full (if only temporary) control of a vast region.[35] The Republic of Phiñas had at least three grassroots signifiers that informed its nationalism and would later influence the concept of the republic of Indians:[36] a shared Aymara language; a politics of memory grounded in a hybrid religiosity and consciousness that Zárate Willka and his followers developed over the course of the rebellion and Republic of Phiñas; and a dress code that required the cholos of Phiñas to wear regional Indian clothes, which were typically grey or white.[37]

During the civil war the Liberals sought to end the indigenous movement for autonomy by exacerbating already existing fissures in that community. For example, Umala's indigenous communities in La Paz had an ongoing land dispute with Sik'a Sik'a (where Zárate Willka originated). The people of Umala, who had enjoyed exemption from cattle taxes since 1872 due to their alliance with President Morales, were also jealous of the widespread support and influence that the jilaqatas and alcaldes mayores of Sik'a Sik'a had gained in the region. Pando, aware of this strife, proposed that a railroad pass through Umala, with a train stop in the village. In exchange Pando requested that the Indians of Umala place a large indigenous army under his command, which gave him an Indian army independent of Zárate Willka and allowed him to argue that not all Indians depended on Zárate Willka's leadership.[38] Meanwhile, Pando's forces, including the Umala Indians, concentrated in Panduro, Qharaqullu, and Phiñas. This type of strategy undermined indigenous cohesion and ensured that separatist movements like Phiñas did not extend to the rest of the Aymara world. Over the next few years, Zárate Willka was gradually marginalized and criminalized. While the autonomous Phiñas government under Juan Lero's leadership was an early version of subaltern Aymara nationalism, it was regionally restricted to Phiñas and did not involve most qullas (Aymaras and Quechuas). Despite its regional specificity, the concept of the Republic of Phiñas would later impact Toribio Miranda, as evidenced by his frequent references to it, and influenced how the AMP constructed a politics of memory.

Aymara nationalism in 1898–1899 was shaped by internal colonialism and its own segregationist policies. It emerged as a response to the appropriation of community lands through the agrarian reform of 1874 and the application of liberal ideas that further disenfranchised indigenous peoples. In the individualizing, anti-communitarian agrarian reform, the liberal government of 1874 ignored the importance of community and ethnic ties to the national economy. Liberal policies led to the ruin of indigenous enterprise and trade, which increased this sector's marginalization. This context profoundly influenced the desire of these communities to create their own country after the civil war. Although the movement was guided by activists with some education, the vast majority of the participants were peasants with no schooling. Without international connections, the collaboration of other indigenous peoples, or even that of other Aymara regions, their attempt at autonomy for the Qullasuyu could not be sustained. However, these efforts would eventually be key to the evolution of Qulla and AMP nationalism. Some of the activists of this period, such as Isidro Kanki (Qallapa) and Feliciano Inka Marasa (Quntu), would later help to reconstitute the new generation of indigenous activists that shaped both the AMP and the network led by Santos Marka T'ula.[39]

Literacy and Legality in the Indian Struggle of the 1920s

The dominance of La Paz's Liberal elites after the conclusion of the civil war in 1899 shaped the counter-hegemonic efforts of a new group of indigenous activists. Liberals' desire to continue implementing the agrarian reform of 1874 meant that agrarian commissions, called *revisitas*, operated at an accelerated pace in communities, measuring and dividing land into individual plots. Although community members in some regions, such as northern Potosí, opposed these actions with armed resistance, land tenure in the La Paz region, which had strong links to the mining and commercial economies, changed significantly as a consequence of these revisitas.[40] Although the white elite claimed to have purchased indigenous lands, their methods of land transfer and appropriation were often illicit, fraudulent, and illegitimate.[41] For instance, Juan Mamani from Ch'aquma (La Paz) borrowed twenty-five bolivianos to pay for his wife's burial from Jorge Monrroy, a hacienda owner in the region. Despite the fact that Mamani was illiterate, Monrroy made him sign a document in which he agreed to repay the debt by a specific date or lose half of his property. Since Mamani did not know how to sign, the names of other peons were put on the document to prove that he had agreed. When Mamani could not pay, he lost part of his property and had to work as a peon on the very land he had lost.[42] Similarly, the local lawyer Inocencio Vargas claimed to have bought half of the Ispaya community's lands as payment for his services and produced paperwork signed by community representatives.[43] The elite "purchased" these lands without the full knowledge of the indigenous peoples, who often did not understand liberal paradigms such as private property. Apoderados contested the legality of those purchases, rejecting the elite's tactics as illegitimate.

During this time community members had to serve both the local priest and state officials such as *corregidores* (magistrates) and subprefects. Some, in fact, turned to the haciendas to escape this servitude. Juan Fábrica from the community of Condor Ikiña (Oruro), for example, negotiated to become a peon on the Qunquriri hacienda because he was tired of serving for free. He explained: "As servitude [I] had to work for the priest and also for the corregidor. . . . I was tired of doing that job and not getting any compensation. The hacienda's peons worked for their *patrones* and they got coca and drinks as treats."[44] Many community members were tired of working without the reciprocity that used to exist between hacienda owners and peons in the early twentieth century. Julián Quispe from Condor Ikiña (Oruro), for example, chose to run away from his region and work in the city to avoid performing free services for state authorities.[45]

New hacienda owners maneuvered their way onto ayllu lands through the semi-legitimate acquisition of many of the plots close to the hacienda and then used either force or the judicial system to enlarge their holdings.[46] These pressures consolidated hacienda expansion and led to the partial collapse of the ayllus and communities. Paqajaqis lost 44,687 hectares between 1900 and 1920 through such sales, a figure that exceeds the 33,401 hectares lost in a similar manner from 1880 to 1899.[47] Often the new owners were important members of the new ruling elite: Jose Manuel Pando extended his property in Imilla Imilla (La Paz), Ismael Montes acquired a huge hacienda in Taraqu (La Paz), and Benedicto Goitia and Julio Sanjinés became the owners of new haciendas.[48] This usurpation of lands by the elite brought about several indigenous rebellions, such as Taraqu in 1920, Jesús de Machaqa in 1921, and Chayanta in 1927.

In response to this new assault, a second generation of indigenous activists regrouped, calling themselves apoderados. The indigenous activists Martín Vásquez and Santos Marka T'ula were originally from a region heavily affected by hacienda expansion, land expropriation by mining companies, and the construction of a railroad between Arica and La Paz in 1904. For example, the mining company Guillermita started operating in 1910 in Santos Marka T'ula's community of Imilla Imilla.[49] Worried about this situation, Martín Vásquez went to Lima with his lawyers and returned with his community's titles, which he later presented before more than one hundred apoderados. Vásquez successfully defended his community's rights by partially stopping the expansion of haciendas within his ayllu. He then appointed Santos Barco, a descendant of an eighteenth-century cacique de sangre, as apoderado; together they initiated a comprehensive new strategy to defend ayllu lands. Caciques de sangre were descendants of early colonial mallkus, who had paid cash and gold for legal land titles. Vásquez and Barco (who changed his name informally to Marka T'ula) thought that descendants of indigenous colonial leaders might be able to request land rights because the titles were under their ancestors' names. Vásquez's success in partially stopping the expansion of a hacienda onto his ayllu lands encouraged other indigenous people to use his strategy to benefit their communities.[50]

Although Marka T'ula did not play a leading role in the apoderado network of the 1890s, he agreed to take up the banner and to consult with the Aymara gods in order to faithfully represent the community and the ayllus' interests in the mid 1910s. He joined the large network of apoderados that included Felix Pantipati, Feliciano Inka Marasa, and Francisco Tancara. From 1900 to 1920 this movement restored the mallkus as apoderados of the ayllus and markas and became the cornerstone of efforts to defend community lands from becoming individualized private property.[51] Marka T'ula and Vásquez's strategy of using colonial documents became very popular. For instance, Julián Siñani, the apoderado of Jach'aqhachi, had such high hopes for it that he asked the local parish priest to search for the descendants of the caciques de sangre in the baptismal records because he believed that they were key to protecting the rights of the ayllus and markas of the Qullasuyu.[52]

Santos Marka T'ula focused on the strategy of colonial titles and converted it into a political tool by extending his alliances with other indigenous networks, such as the movement called República del Qullasuyu (Republic of Qullasuyu), which was headed by Eduardo Nina Quispe, a well-known educator of the 1920s.[53] For strategic reasons, Marka T'ula and his network were especially interested in working with the Federación Obrera Local (FOL, Local Worker's Federation) in La Paz and Oruro, which drew its members from a largely cholo and indigenous working-class population. Although the FOL had an anarchist approach, it was also open to indigenous nationalism. Indigenous activists and anarchists shared a counter-hegemonic role since both targeted the elites, who mostly self-identified as "white." In groups like the FOL, activists such as Marka T'ula could find people who understood indigenous concerns, which was a rarity in urban settings. The Federación Obrera de Oruro (Oruro Worker's Federation) appointed Santos Marka T'ula as secretary of peasant issues in 1926, which meant that some Aymara networks subsequently appeared as peasant sindicatos (syndicates) in FOL paperwork even though they remained autonomous and had their own ayllu structure.[54]

Marka T'ula developed close connections with the activist Luis Cusicanqui, who was one of the leaders of La Paz's anarchist movement in the late 1920s, and Jorge Amado, a Trotskyite socialist leader in Oruro during the 1930s.[55] In many documents Marka T'ula defended the rights of the working class and artisans, particularly La Paz slaughterhouse workers' rights to racial inclusion, arguing that they all came from the "same [Aymara] race."[56] Marka T'ula also developed strong connections with new actors such as the Adventist missionaries who had arrived in the early 1920s. Marka T'ula was especially sympathetic to them because they created the first network of Aymara schools in the countryside, which were linked to mallkus and other ethnic leaders. Through his visits to many indigenous communities, Marka T'ula became one of the best-known ayllu apoderados of the era. Many mallkus, mostly from the La Paz region, organized to write petitions for Marka T'ula to present to the central government in La Paz. By 1930 he had been made apoderado general of all the indigenous communities of the republic by the apoderados of more than one hundred large ayllus. However, the liberal governments of the era strictly monitored indigenous activists, frequently calling Marka T'ula's meetings in La Paz "conspiratorial." He was twice (in 1917 and 1923) forced into exile in Río Cajón, which is located in the Alto Beni region of the Bolivian jungle.[57] Marka T'ula then created the Sociedad Indígena (Indigenous Society), a powerful civil organization that for several years represented indigenous peoples on land issues and denounced the abuse of hacienda peons. Since the Sociedad Indígena had bylaws and a legal status, it provided Marka T'ula with some protection from government accusations of subversion. During the 1930s the Catholic Church supported Santos Marka T'ula in founding the Centro Bartolomé de Las Casas, a pro-indigenous rights organization, in La Paz. Marka T'ula served as its president while simultaneously expanding his reach to include lowland communities; eventually he became an apoderado of the Guaraní communities. The chief of the Izozog Guaranís, Captain Barrientos, was a Marka T'ula ally.[58]

Marka T'ula's leadership relied on the support of his wife and family. When Marka T'ula was jailed, his wife Manuela Barco took over his position and presented a memorandum to La Paz's archive on February 9, 1931, introducing herself as an "apoderado's wife" and requesting that they "give her back some documents that her jailed husband left."[59] However, during Marka T'ula's time as an apoderado, his family fell victim to the hostility of a local hacienda. Marka T'ula's daughter Santusa recalled in her oral history how the Antaqi hacienda made fun of her and of her father's struggle. Local hacienda admistration use to call her racist nicknames that broke her heart as a child.[60] Her mother Manuela had to take care of six children, tend the fields, and support Santos while he was jailed and in exile, sending him food, medicine, and supplies. Her ascension to the position of apoderada reveals the Aymara ideology of gender, which rests on the idea of complementarity between women and men.[61] This support along gender lines was more evident and necessary during the Chaco War (1932–1935), when the government restricted protests. To counteract these restrictions, Marka T'ula mobilized Aymara women from the communities, arriving in La Paz in November 1934 with almost two hundred women requesting both the return of their sons from the Chaco and respect for community landholdings.[62] These types of protests slowly increased opposition to the war.[63]

Literacy and written documents played an important role in constructing Santos Marka T'ula's indigenous activist network, as evidenced by the legal documents and papers produced by his movement and as a result of its relationship with the labor movement. As a political strategy, Marka T'ula focused on the potential benefits of the application of the agrarian reform of 1874, which permitted corporative ownership of land if colonial titles could be proven to have existed. Although Marka T'ula did not know how to read and almost everybody else in the network was illiterate, they enlisted the help of escribanos and lawyers in order to understand the archives' contents. They memorized the most important laws and kept extensive records of their demands and struggles. In their meetings these mostly Aymara-speaking chiefs and indigenous activists discussed documents written in Spanish, such as the Disentailment Law of 1874, and strategized about legal issues and how to confront state policies in the 1920s.[64]

A garantía that was published in 1926 starts by demanding official recognition of selected documents "that are in the National Archives of Bolivia" after being deposited there by Marka T'ula. It then discusses a request made by seventy-five mallkus and apoderados from different communities to the Bolivian Congress for the "verification of the limits of their ayllus with the adjoining haciendas." In the document Santos Marka T'ula represents himself both as apoderado general and as a representative of the ayllus of Paqajaqis. The names of regional activists Feliciano Inka Maraza (apoderado de los ayllus Quntu y Qhuphawillki), Daniel Tanqara (ayllus de Ancoraimes), Ismael Turrini (ayllus Laimes), and Ignacio

Aduviri (ayllus Muru Muru) are also there. The garantía includes the response of the Bolivian Congress to the mallkus' and apoderados' request, which argued that they "could not verify the limits between haciendas and ayllus" because there was "no such thing as [ayllus] in the current legislation."[65] In another garantía published in the late 1930s, the apoderados and mallkus presented the International Catholic Congress with a special request to address the abuses suffered by indigenous peoples in Bolivia. They told the meeting that "Spaniards should leave the country and abandon occupied land."[66] Along with this request they included copies of letters sent to the Ministry of Indigenous Affairs that repeatedly requested the establishment of rural elementary schools.[67] Although this type of discourse was dominant among indigenous activists at the time, Santos Marka T'ula distinguished himself by insisting on using legal measures to gain indigenous rights that would be officially recorded in writing.

The apoderados, including Santos Marka T'ula, referred to themselves in the garantía as the "first Bolivians" and as being "more Bolivian than anyone else."[68] During the early twentieth century there was no concept of aboriginal or first peoples that could have legitimized the role of Indians in the history of the country. The word *Indian* had a racialized meaning in a highly hierarchical society. By calling themselves the first Bolivians, the activists used the idea of aboriginal or first peoples in a way that only became widespread at the end of the twentieth century. Considering that almost all of the congressional representatives at this time self-identified as white, the idea of first Bolivians and the notion of aboriginal or indigenous peoples was very novel indeed. The garantías transmitted the idea that because indigenous activists had been unsuccessful in their petitions to "democratic" institutions such as the Congress, they were justified in demanding the separation of indigenous peoples from whites. This strategy was meant to create an imagined community of an Indian nation that was reinforced by the circulation of garantías and other printed documents.

Martín Mamani from Jach'a Qhaxiata, one of the first communities to harbor indigenous activists, remembered when the first garantías showed up in his community in the 1930s. These documents arrived with petty traders selling sugar, who told them: "While sugar is to make people's lives sweet, this other long paper [the garantía] is to show the whites that they [the peons] are not alone. Their brothers [from the ayllus] might be ready to come to the [haciendas], and these Indian allies [from the ayllus] would come quickly to support [the peons] when their belongings are taken away."[69] This type of document not only introduced the issues and the purposes of the apoderados but also presented a mythic vision of what the garantías could achieve. The spread of the garantías also demonstrates how Indians participated in the market economy as a way to seek empowerment in an unequal world. In this way printed documents helped shape the idea of a subaltern nation separate from "whites," a category that included hacendados and the dominant elite. Therefore, the oral and written transmission of garantías not only achieved modest results within its limited goals but also played an important role in shaping ethnic and racial consciousness in the region. These documents spread as the circuits of economy expanded in Bolivia from the cities to the countryside and vice versa. Seasonal workers, such as miners and *pongos*, also helped diffuse them in hopes that the documents might protect them and their villages from mestizos' and whites' abuses of power. These peons, *tatalas* (Aymara elders who traded in interethnic zones), and miners used a combination of oral and written communication to learn about their civil rights.[70]

Linking the idea of first Bolivians to the notion of garantías and publicizing discussions between the National Congress and apoderados to an audience in the indigenous communities revealed the internal contradictions of the Bolivian system and presented Indian intellectuals' perspective on so-called equality and freedom. Garantías were widely used by the AMP years later, circulating them among a wide audience of more than four hundred networks of ayllus or markas, from southern Potosí to northern La Paz and from Qarangas (on the border with Chile) to the valleys of Cochabamba and Chuquisaca.[71] This network played a key role in organizing the petitions submitted by ayllus and communities during the 1920s. Petitions were requests to the institutions of the state and usually asked for the state's attention to the areas of justice, land, and conflicts with haciendas and labor. Garantías often resulted from these petitions and contained ideas about protection and the rights of Indians. Laura Gotkowitz, who also writes about the role of the law in the construction of the Indian movement prior 1952, argues that this strategy eventually led to a situation in which Indians became the bearers of their own law.[72]

This focus on documents follows a pattern of mediated literacy that dates back to the colonial period and was made possible by a relatively small number of lettered escribanos. By the 1920s there were enough literate Indians that they could become scribes, writing letters and transcribing other legal documents for the apoderados. This change formed a new relationship between indigenous activists, as both the apoderados and the escribanos engaged in Aymara activism, communicated in Aymara, and shared common concerns. It also allowed indigenous activists to use writing as a new political tool. Leandro Condori, one of these escribanos, managed indigenous activists' correspondence, which was a task that previously had been fulfilled by whites. Condori's own writing vividly narrates the escribanos' work and responsibilities during 1920s: "there were men who used to work with [the indigenous activists]. They . . . supported the apoderados. However, they were lawyers, . . . [leftists and anarchists], politicians . . . and they were Spaniards; indeed, they were not Indian. These men used to defend Indians and the poor. [On the other hand], Aymara escribanos believed in the law that says Indians should not pay taxes. The Spaniards used to talk about salary and labor . . . nothing about Indians. They did not understand [the Indians' problems] because they were . . . [not Indians]."[73]

Garantías help us to understand the literacy- and legality-based indigenous social movement produced by Santos Marka T'ula's network in the 1920s. The widespread interest in these documents shows that while most members of indigenous communities were illiterate at this time, they actively penetrated the literate world by constructing counter-narratives based on the written word. This type of social movement differed from earlier forms such as the Peruvian peasant nationalism of Atusparia in the late nineteenth century.[74] While the peasants of Atusparia sought to ally and collaborate with Peruvian mestizos, Marka T'ula's network developed a politics of legality and literacy, drawing on the earlier indigenous networks that operated during the civil war between 1898 and 1899, the experience of the independent Republic of Phiñas, and previous indigenous movements such that of Zárate Willka.[75] However, the role of literacy in building a politics of memory extended throughout the Andean region. In 1920s Colombia, for example, José Gonzalo Sanchez established an organization called the Supreme Council of the Indies that included Manuel Quintin Lame and a network of indigenous cells called cabildos. Like Marka T'ula, Sánchez constructed a politics of memory based on literacy and oral tradition, referring to colonial institutions in building his activist network.[76]

The Birth of the AMP and the Radicalization
of Indian Struggle

Gregorio Titiriku and other AMP members would eventually resist the strategies of legality and literacy, preferring leadership under an apoderado since they felt that the actions available to caciques de sangre were not inclusive of all indigenous people. Titiriku's focus on the Indian law rejected the idea that the Indian struggle should be built around the validity of colonial land titles and the official culture of Spanish literacy. As such, he also rejected the ideological implications of these strategies, which had led to the acceptance of the agrarian reform of 1874 as valid. Indeed, Titiriku opposed the very concept of property titles as a legitimization of land tenure because he did not want the Indian struggle to be restricted to a fight for lands and property within the framework of the dominant sectors' laws. Although he published garantías and employed the tools of literate culture, Titiriku argued in many meetings from the early 1930s to the 1950s that "colonial land titles are evil pathways written with the blood of our grandparents."[77] His work also appealed to many communities and ayllus that were not only interested in preserving their lands but also in more complex political ideas as well.

By the 1930s the apoderados of Chuquisaca, southern Cochabamba, and parts of northern Potosí became frustrated with the strategy that Martín Vásquez began and Santos Marka T'ula continued. Additionally, some hacienda peons started to move away from a politics of legality and literacy because it did not address their problems. For example, the peons of the Wisk'anchis hacienda (Chuquisaca) were eager to liberate themselves from harsh labor obligations and had hoped that the decades of research into colonial titles conducted by Mariano Qhispe and members of nearby Puxpu hacienda would allow them to claim ownership rights over the land and demonstrate that the current owners of the hacienda were actually usurpers. Because he had found colonial titles from several haciendas in Paqajaqis region, Qhispe thought that he could do the same for his own community. However, he discovered that the land had never been officially granted to the indigenous community and had been a hacienda for centuries. Antonio Garcia, an apoderado from Sumala (Chuquisaca), had even searched the baptismal records of Icla and Tarabuco in a desperate effort to find out if the mallkus of Sumala had at some point bought the hacienda from the colonial rulers. Since both Garcia's and Qhispe's efforts failed, the peons of Wisk'anchis grew frustrated with attempts to legally support their claims.[78]

Many hacienda peons who had limited connections to the twentieth-century ayllu system of land tenure experienced similar marginalization. Few hacienda peons or even ayllu members could benefit from colonial titles because it was so difficult and expensive to find them. Trips to Lima, Sucre, or Buenos Aires were expensive for communities and indigenous groups, and they frequently had to hire lawyers to conduct research in national archives and state notary records. For example, the peons of Sunimuru hacienda (La Paz) sent two people between 1925 and 1936 to the archives of Buenos Aires to search for their colonial titles, and they also spent 1,500 bolivianos commissioning research at the archives in Sucre and La Paz.[79] The experience of the apoderados of Tomata Palqa (Charcas Province, northern Potosí) demonstrates the limits of relying on locating colonial titles. After extensive research, the apoderado Guillermo Córdoba discovered that his family had belonged to the nineteenth-century category of *forastero*. Forasteros had fewer land tenure rights than other categories such as the originarios who could trace their tenure to the seventeenth century.[80] A third category of *agregados*, on the other hand, had ancestors in the ayllu since the eighteenth century who had received land from the originarios and therefore could trace their land rights back to the colonial period. Forasteros came from other communities, while agregados might be a new generation from the same ayllu or from another region. Most forasteros had become part of the ayllu in the nineteenth century in order to benefit from the ayllus' practice of redistributing land among its members once every generation. Although the majority of the community in Tomata Palqa were agregados and forasteros, and therefore did not have large tracts of land like originarios, they were all united in their struggle against the appropriation of plots by the local hacendados. After discovering the forastero status of the current occupants of his community, Guillermo Córdoba understood that they had little chance of reclaiming hacienda land through colonial titles. He also realized that the full restitution of ayllu land would not solve the ayllu's problems because it would not help those categorized as agregados and forasteros.[81] Other apoderados, such as the influential Feliciano Inka Marasa, also had poor results in regaining the lands of the ayllu of Qarangas in the region of Poroma, Chuquisaca. This prompted him to join the emerging opposition group that would later take the name Alcaldes Mayores Particulares in the mid-1930s.[82] So few ayllus in Oruro and Chuquisaca won legal battles against the haciendas in court that, over time, Marka T'ula began to lose the support of the very apoderado networks that had brought him to prominence in the first place.

By the mid-1930s the strategy of Santos Marka T'ula and his network suddenly seemed very limited because it did little to satisfy the needs of other groups of indigenous people, such as hacienda peons and marginalized people within the ayllu structure. Discontent within his network grew, particularly in Chuquisaca, southern Cochabamba, and some of the valleys of northern Potosí, where many haciendas were of colonial rather than more recent origin.[83] Because Santos Marka T'ula's strategy did not work everywhere, some indigenous activists carefully considered Gregorio Titiriku and Toribio Miranda's project. According to the testimonies of Julian Ugarte, the first AMP groups emerged between 1935 and 1936 in La Paz, with Poroma Indians. Feliciano Inka Marasa was among them and other forasteros in the ayllu. Other AMP groups then formed in the haciendas of Laqaya and Sunimoro in La Paz. The next year peons from the haciendas of Wisk'anchis and about seven other groups of hacienda peons from Inqawasi (North Cinti, Chuquisaca) also decided to support the new group of indigenous activists. These new supporters were people who had smaller plots of very poor quality land; they were the disenfranchised among the disenfranchised. This does not mean that the Marka T'ula movement lost all of its adherents, but the fracturing did lead to the breakdown of his indigenous activist network.

While Santos Marka T'ula continued to focus on colonial land titles, Toribio Miranda and Gregorio Titiriku spoke of returning to the worship of Aymara gods and restoring the Qullasuyu to its sixteenth-century state.[84] In terms of political discourse, this was a radical step for their time and circumstances. The purpose was to re-create the indigenous movement of apoderados, which by then was already in decline. In the face of a deeply colonial nation-state, many of the AMP's goals were difficult to achieve on a wide scale. However, in terms of twentieth-century indigenous movements, the AMP epitomized a new activism that eventually grew into the twenty-first-century indigenous struggle for civil rights. But even at its inception, this discourse found a receptive audience of hacienda peons who were frustrated with Marka T'ula and felt that he was "poor in initiatives and ambitions."[85] Apoderados like Mariano Qhispe and Eusebio Qhoyu felt that Marka T'ula's relationship with the labor movement in La Paz, the Left in Oruro, and the Catholic and Adventist churches did not enhance the ideology of the ayllus and markas but rather promoted integration into mainstream white society. They even argued that Marka T'ula "was selling . . . out" to "Adventists and the government."[86] Despite the fact that Marka T'ula asked the Catholic Church to promote the idea of a separate Indian nation from the "Spaniards" during 1925 Eucharistic Catholic Congress of 1925, the discontent among some apoderados continued to grow.[87]

With almost thirty years of experience working with Marka T'ula, Miranda and Titiriku set out to promote new local, regional, and national leadership. Gregorio Titiriku, Feliciano Inka Marasa, and Toribio Miranda, among others, took on national leadership roles, while people like Melitón Gallardo from Chuquisaca became a regional leader. Years later, Titiriku and Miranda would also organize the leadership of the next generation of AMP, including activists like Jach'aqullu. All of these steps certainly helped to spread the AMP's message and foster indigenous activists.

Toribio Miranda, whom I profile in chapter 3, gained prominence in the mid-1930s. He was an Aymara-Uru from Quntu (Oruro) who had long participated in Santos Marka T'ula's activist network. Miranda had the advantage of having lived under the Aymara Republic of Phiñas in 1899 and later worked with both highland ayllus and the peons of the valleys of Chuquisaca. His social origins were not distinct from those of the caciques apoderados, and he belonged to ayllus and communities of Oruro. By 1935 he had developed ideological disagreements with Marka T'ula's strategy, particularly because it did not promote education in the Aymara language.[88] When Bolivian intellectuals debated what language indigenous education should be conducted in, some indigenous activists, such as Santos Marka T'ula, did not take a public position. On the other hand, along with many leftists, some Indian activists considered learning Spanish to be a priority. For example, Elizardo Perez and Avelino Siñani, the founders of the Warisata School, the first Indian school in South America, thought that education should be in Spanish.[89] Siñani, who was a school instructor at the beginning of the twentieth century, said: "we know Aymara and there is nothing more to learn about it."[90]

Titiriku, apoderado of the region of Janqulaimes (Umasuyus), agreed with Miranda and thought that the expansion of Spanish in the communities would mean that the Spaniards had invaded and permeated the Indian world.[91] Like Miranda's, Titiriku's social origins were similar to those of the caciques apoderados. He belonged to ayllus and communities of the city of La Paz and was familiar with urban culture. Titiriku also disliked the literacy program developed by Eduardo Nina Quispe, an urban Aymara from La Paz, because it promoted the Spanish language. Eduardo Nina Quispe's and Santos Marka T'ula's projects did work in favor of Indians: with the first more focused on indigenous education and the latter more focused on rights for Indians; compared to the AMP's project, however, both were too receptive to Westernization and assimilation.

Although the people of the communities wanted to learn to read and write, it was not clear why they needed to do so in Spanish. Memories of Felipe Beltran's efforts to promote literacy in Aymara in the 1870s indicated that teaching in native languages was feasible. As a child, Miranda met Beltran and was convinced that the use of Aymara in educational programs was both possible and beneficial.[92] For similar reasons, Titiriku eventually became another critic of Marka T'ula even though he had supported him for many years. Titiriku was the secretary for Juan Mamani, the principal apoderado of Omasuyus. One of the few literate apoderados, Mamani argued that "reading in Spanish [would] make Indians 'blind.' They [would] not be able to read the words of Pachamama and other good spirits. Spanish readers do not understand the Indian Law, and our people will follow the same path . . . the path of the whites and cholos."[93]

This argument was also frequently used by critics who believed that instead of searching for colonial property titles, the ayllus and markas should lobby for the Bolivian Congress to accept and implement Indian law. Titiriku and the AMP's decision to draw on Indian law resulted from several generations of historical analysis and ideological thought. The AMP's promotion of Indian law in the name of Pachamama and Achachilas advocated for traditional Aymara ways of living based in ethnic organizations and spirituality, which I will detail in the chapters to come.[94] Under these circumstances, a subaltern Indian movement that used religious perspectives to express their earth-based politics emerged. In light of the changes in Bolivian politics in the 1930s, Miranda and Titiriku felt that communities and hacienda peons needed an alternative to Santos Marka T'ula's strategy. Initially, Titiriku's perspective was not popular among the ayllus and markas, but he slowly gained a larger audience due to Marka T'ula's failure to focus on the long-term ideological implications of the expansion of the Bolivian state into the countryside during the

1930s. Even though Santos Marka T'ula was also deeply concerned with any law that benefitted Indians, regardless of whether it was colonial or republican, the movements' political discourses differed sharply, which gradually separated them in the 1930s. As part of this widening breach, Titiriku accused former ally Marka T'ula of worshipping colonial property titles and legal documentation as if they were connected to Pachamama and other Aymara gods.[95] Titiriku argued that this was a distortion of the native religion, which he strongly defended and always put at the core of his discourse. He focused on the potential of the Aymara religion to make people rise up and generate an opposition movement. He wanted to re-Indianize the country, which the AMP argued could be achieved through the application of Indian law.

Titiriku and Miranda chose the name Alcaldes Mayores Particulares to show their rejection of the apoderados who had been promoting the communities' acquisition of land titles since 1874. The phrase *alcaldes mayores* came from the late colonial and nineteenth-century terminology for town authorities and Indian leadership in some regions.[96] By the 1930s the term was also used to refer to indigenous activists interested in founding schools in the countryside.[97] In 1936 Titiriku and Miranda added the word *particulares* to express that the movement did not support state-sponsored schools, which they critiqued for reinforcing the internal colonialism of the Bolivian state. Instead, the name Alcaldes Mayores Particulares was associated with the time of two separate and parallel republics in colonial Andean societies.[98] The AMP constructed an oppositional discourse grounded in various political strategies, which they eventually articulated in the Indian law (examined in chapter 3). Their new brand of subaltern nationalism was based on a reconstructed memory of an ideal community from before both the Inka and Spanish conquests. These activist intellectuals proposed a new politics grounded in an Aymara worldview in conjunction with legal efforts to demand and defend Indian rights from state institutions.

A New Leader

From 1921 until his death in La Paz in 1959, Don Toribio Miranda elaborated and promoted the Indian law. Like that of his colleagues, Miranda's goal was to resist the postcolonial state's anti-Indian stance by denouncing the oppression of indigenous peasants in the haciendas of the Bolivian

Andes. He advocated for an end to segregation in public plazas and street-cars, worked to secure autonomous education for Indians, and created alternative institutions of citizenship. Miranda also fought for women's participation in politics and for the redistribution of land to Indian communities. Rejecting symbols of white and mestizo hegemony, he advocated for the use of indigenous last names and traditional *bayeta de la tierra* clothing. Like him, his adherents eventually opposed agrarian reform in 1953, rejected state-issued identification cards and the civil registration of weddings and births, resisted public and Spanish-speaking elementary schools, and rejected the practice of females changing their surnames after marriage. In so doing Miranda and his network of activists marked a new age of indigenous struggle in the relationship between national modernity and internal colonialism in mid-twentieth-century Bolivia.

Chapter Three | # The Beginning of the Decolonization Project

Toribio Miranda's Framing and Dissemination of the Indian Law

On the night of April 13, 1943, the chilly Oruro jail became a meeting place for the Alcades Mayores Particulares (AMP) when policeman Andrés Cerrogrande (who had rejected his Indian identity like many other urban indigenous people) met Toribio Miranda, one of the founders of the AMP. Cerrogrande was conducting his nightly rounds in the cell block before turning off the lights when he began a conversation with the seventy-year-old Miranda, telling him that an older man should not get involved in fomenting revolts. But Miranda's ideas about the rights of Indian people and his insistence that his participation was needed struck a chord with Cerrogrande, as did Miranda's penetrating eyes, which closely followed Cerrogrande's reactions to his words. While Cerrogrande's police training had taught him to oppose Miranda's promotion of rebellion in the countryside, the discussions he had with the old man transformed his worldview, eventually causing him to leave his position with the police in order to fight alongside other indigenous activists and become a key indigenous intellectual during the 1950s.[1]

After Miranda had spent eight months in the Oruro jail, the Peñaranda government (1940–1943) was unable to prove that he had been involved in a conspiracy and was forced to release him. During those months of incarceration, Miranda told Cerrogrande that he thought the apoderados working with Santos Marka T'ula could not stop "white-mestizo Bolivians" from increasing their power over indigenous peoples. He argued that the literacy programs promoted by Marka T'ula and run by Protestant churches fostered "anti-indio teaching in their discourse."[2]

During the 1940s Miranda was not the only apoderado or AMP in jail during President Peñaranda's regime. Many indigenous activists filled the jails of La Paz, Oruro, and Cochabamba, accused of spreading subversive ideas among hacienda peons and inciting rebellions, which occurred more frequently during the 1940s.[3] More than two hundred indigenous activists and militants in leftist and anarchist movements were forced into exile in the Bolivian jungle, where some of them, including AMPs Mariano Qhispe and Antonio García, died.[4] Others, such as Antonio Alvarez Mamani, one of the organizers of the National Indigenous Congress of 1945, and the anarchist indigenous activist Luis Ramos, returned to struggle for indigenous rights after the Bolivian National Revolution of 1952.

The Great Depression created a tumultuous political situation that was aggravated by Bolivia's defeat in the Chaco War (1932–1935). President Gualberto Villarroel (1943–1946) had tried to reform the political system by insisting on abolishing servitude (pongueaje). The traditional elite responded by showing some support for newly instituted civil rights, like the eight-hour workday and protections against servitude, but only in order to prevent the collapse of the segregationist racial structure through limited change.[5] Frequent military coups and short-term civilian regimes made for great instability, and despite their efforts, the administrations of Peñaranda, Hertzog, and Urriolagoitia (1947–1951) failed to successfully reestablish the traditional power structure. However, the traditional elite did not finally collapse until the national revolution.[6]

Toribio Miranda framed the Indian law discourse as a way to combat the Bolivian state's politics of exclusion against Indians, and thus he initiated a long struggle to build a decolonization project. He spent his early years in both Uru and Aymara communities, where he made connections with earlier indigenous activist networks and then eventually launched his own brand of activism. He concentrated his work on framing a new path for indigenous traditions by combining Uru oral traditions and Aymara ideas about the Qullasuyu to produce a multicultural vision for an audience that included Quechua speakers. Miranda started building the AMP network during commercial trips to the indigenous villages, where he was able to begin spreading his ideas about the Indian law; later he would focus exclusively on traveling to promote the AMP agenda. His three wives played important roles as he gained a wide audience among the peons of

Chuquisaca and Cochabamba and the members of the ayllus of northern Potosí, where liberal state policies had little effect due to the abusive power of the haciendas. These areas were characterized by a system of local bossism, in which the rural elite, who were mostly owners or administrators of the haciendas, concentrated political power and legitimized it by cultivating good relations with the Catholic Church there.[7]

Miranda traveled widely to hundreds of indigenous villages, haciendas, ayllus, and communities in most of the Bolivian Andes. The purpose of his trips was to cultivate and monitor the development of the AMP indigenous movement, an umbrella organization of various local and regional activists in the Bolivian indigenous world. In contrast to other movements of his time (such as those of Santos Marka T'ula, Tomas Ramos Quevedo, and Eduardo Nina Quispe), Miranda particularly emphasized that the Indian struggle must be based on indigenous religion and the Indian law. He strongly believed in the power of faith in the Aymara gods, especially Pachamama (or mother earth) and the Achachillas, the power of the mountains. In contrast, other movements believed there was a role for republican law, emerging socialist ideas, or even the support of the Catholic Church in securing indigenous rights. Miranda mainly disseminated this new discourse in the 1940s, when Bolivia experienced a significant change in its political system.

Decades later, in 1979, Agapito Ponce Mamani remembered that in Miranda's time, people who did not understand the Indian law used to tell him that there is a "new" law and that it was not necessary to rely on colonial legal structures.

> Miranda would reply that the "ancient law" is better because it contemplates real rights for Indians while the law of current times gives only "superficial rights" to Indians. Once Bautista Saavedra told him that Bolivia was a republic and it had its own laws.[8] Miranda replied that those laws are probably good for *mistis* [whites and mestizos] but not for Indians. Colonial law, he said, goes to the roots of Indian rights, tells us who we [Indians] are, and is a path for us. Bautista Saavedra did not like such opinions.[9]

Miranda disagreed with the fact that even the most progressive law focused on individual rights to the exclusion of collective rights. Indigenous notions of property, culture, and religious practices were all centered on the ideas of community and collectivity, which the new law did not validate. These ideas also provided a frame for elaborating more on the idea of the Indian nation and identity. In addition to emphasizing the importance of the collective in the Indian law, Miranda argued that Indians needed to enhance their relationship with Pachamama. He argued that if indigenous peoples—whether they were peons, belonged to ayllus, or lived as urban Indians—worked to re-create a strong faith in the Aymara gods, the energies and ideas that stem from that faith would help them fight social exclusion. During a time when women were not considered full citizens and could not vote, Miranda also decried gender discrimination and promoted parity between the sexes as in his discourse. This was an important part of his understanding of the AMP's version of the Indian law, which attempted to unite all Indians in order to overcome ethnic oppression. Based on an indigenous version of the importance of the earth, indigenous religions, recent history, and the politics of memory, he created an earth politics that would go on to have a strong impact on social movements in the 1940s.

Roots and Early Influences

When Toribio Miranda was a teenager during the civil war of 1898–1899, he saw a world where Indians and whites not only dressed, ate, and interpreted their dreams differently but also lived in a strictly hierarchical system. It was a time of consolidation for the modern segregationist Bolivian state, in which citizenship was granted on the basis of the following requirements: literacy, the ability to speak Spanish, urban property ownership and a regular cash income or salary, and being a good Christian. Indians, however, spoke mainly Aymara or Quechua, were mostly illiterate, did not have urban property or a regular income, and practiced a hybrid religion that incorporated into Christianity elements of Aymara beliefs and rituals. This situation began to change in the first half of the twentieth century, when Indians slowly gained citizenship through learning to read and write in Spanish (thus becoming more "civilized" and assimilated), obligatory military service, debt peonage, and "campesinoization," which abrogated the ayllu or Indian community and gave out small individual plots of land.

Miranda, who was born into an Uru-Aymara family, saw the liberal regime take over power in La Paz, and he witnessed the failed attempt to create an Aymara republic in Phiñas. His father, Francisco Miranda, from the Uru community of Phuñaca, died when Toribio Miranda was just a year old, leaving his mother, Juana Flores, little choice but to move back to her Aymara community, where she had a better chance of survival than in the more precarious Uru communities. In the late nineteenth century the Urus suffered long periods of famine during which their economy, which was based on fishing as well as the high *puna* (arid plateau) crops of quinua and qañawa, failed. Sadly, Juana saw that this led to a high rate of infant mortality in many large Uru families.[10]

Miranda was raised in the middle of the Aymara ayllus and markas of Quntu and Paria in the Department of Oruro (known as Phuxpu in Aymara). In Quntu his young mother married Pablo Choque, an older man who held significant local power. Choque and his extended family had supported Juan Lero, the apoderado who initiated the "short summer" of Aymara autonomy in the nearby town of Phiñas in 1899. As a teenager, Miranda saw his stepfather and relatives leave to participate in the Phiñas rebellion, and the experience was etched indelibly into his memory.[11]

The Catholic Church also had an early influence on Miranda, which sets him apart from the other AMP indigenous activists profiled in this book. As we will see later, other AMP indigenous activists, especially in the second generation, were frequently in conflict with the Catholic Church. Miranda on the other hand, had a somewhat fluid relationship with the Catholic Church. It developed during his childhood, when he met the priest Felipe Beltran, who ran a pioneering Aymara literacy program between 1872 and 1890 at several churches in Paria, Phiñas, and Killakas (Oruro). Beltran later founded a similar program in the city of Oruro and began teaching Quechua as well. Beltran sought to improve the teaching of Catholic religious doctrine through literacy. Although he was of Aymara origin, in the racial categories of the mid-nineteenth century Beltran was considered a mestizo because he was educated and dressed in a Western style.[12] Aware of his heritage, he became interested in Indian history, using the church to promote both his native language and Quechua. He was strongly concerned with the situation of indigenous people, which led him to publicly support the populist president Agustín Morales in 1874.[13] Despite Beltran's support for indigenous people and culture, there is no evidence that any other AMP leaders interacted with him. In later years, when Miranda had become an activist, he drew on his teenage experiences in Beltran's program to argue that education in Aymara was possible. Although he only infrequently attended Beltran's parish schools, he often talked about them. He learned to sign his name and to read Catholic prayers in Aymara, which did not render him fully literate but gave him a "taste" of reading and writing.[14] In the 1910s Miranda married Candelaria Mamani, a member of his Quntu ayllu, and showed interest in reconnecting with his Uru Indian heritage, possibly for the practical reason of increasing his access to land.[15] While Miranda was partially raised by his stepfather, his mother, Juana Flores, also had a strong influence on him. In fact she may have influenced him to retain his father's rights within the Uru community in Puñaca.

Concentrated in the department of Oruro, Uru communities had an ayllu system similar to that of the Aymaras.[16] According to documentation of the Tinta María community, the Uru ayllus in the late 1880s controlled large pastures and agricultural lands in a region called Markawi, where they grew quinua and qañawa. As they did not depend on agriculture or have llama herds, they mostly used these lands for hunting ducks in winter.[17] Indigenous people in Bolivia during the 1920s had various types of economies and lifestyles, even in the highlands. While the Aymaras and Quechuas primarily lived from farming on haciendas and in independent communities and ayllus, some ethnic minorities in the highlands, such as the Urus and Chipayas, lived mostly from hunting and had little involvement with agriculture.[18] The habitats of the Urus and Chipayas were located at more than twelve thousand feet above sea level, which limited agricultural possibilities.[19]

In the seventeenth century the Markawi region controlled by the Uru ayllus had been part of the Aymara Urinuqa ayllu and the Qaranqas nation. Seeking a return of this land, they instituted violent attacks on Puñaca and other Uru communities between 1915 and 1923. They planned to cultivate potatoes and barley to sell at markets serving the expanding mining towns of Llallagua and Wanuni, which had been increasing their demand for agricultural produce since 1910. Presenting colonial titles to support their claims, the Urinuqas argued that the Markawi lands belonged to them and had only ended up in Uru hands because of interethnic marriages between Aymara Urinuqas and Phuñaqa Urus in the eighteenth century.

When Miranda found out that Uru communities were immersed in problems with the Urinuqa ayllu, he got involved, hoping that his experiences with the Aymara apoderados of the Quntu ayllu might prove useful. When the Aymaras of Urinuqa forcibly took some of the territory back in 1915, the Uru communities appointed Miranda to defend their rights as the apoderado of Tinta María and Phuñaqa.[20] Miranda took the opportunity to serve the community, as he not only had land in Phuñaqa from his first marriage but also possessed the necessary legal skills, thanks to his partial literacy and his close relationship with apoderados in Quntu.[21] The Uru communities knew that Miranda could assist with their legal needs because of his experience and the training he received from his stepfather, a well-known apoderado, in presenting petitions to the government and working with lawyers in Oruro and La Paz.[22] By the 1920s Miranda had established a base in his father's native community of Phuñaqa, but his wife and children lived in the Aymara community of Quntu.[23] As apoderado from 1920 to 1923, Miranda presented several demands to Oruro's prefecture opposing the Urinuqas ayllus' incursions onto Uru lands. He obtained a court order from the sub-prefecture of Phuxpu (Oruro) in favor of the Uru communities, and the departmental government of Oruro finally came to the defense of the Urus' rights in 1921 and 1925.[24]

In the early twentieth century identification along ethnic lines was mostly limited to Oruro, which meant that neither Aymaras nor Urus elsewhere acted as separate ethnic blocks. For instance, the Urus of Tinta María and Phuñaqa had a close relationship with the Aymara Quntu, where they sold goods such as qañawa. Despite this relationship with Quntu, these two Uru communities had problems with the Aymaras of Urinuqas. Uru communities, such as the Phuñaqa and Qutsuña, differed over how to respond to the violent confrontations during the 1910s.[25] Their antagonistic relationship with the Urinuqas allowed the emergence of a leader of Miranda's importance to rise out of a minority ethnic community like the Urus in the 1920s. This context of multiethnic identities, conflicts, and solidarity between ayllus, and the memory of the autonomist experience of Phiñas, profoundly shaped Miranda's discourse and goals.[26] Living in both Uru and Aymara communities helped Miranda to focus on needs beyond those of his own ethnic group. The Oruro region's localized Indian identities would soon play an important role in the construction of a counter-hegemonic discourse through networks of apoderados.

Miranda later joined the network of apoderados headed by Santos Marka T'ula, eventually coming to identify strongly with the apoderados' struggle. He adopted Santos Marka T'ula's style of dress, which consisted of a gray poncho and pants made from sheep and llama wool that apoderados had traditionally worn since the nineteenth century.[27] These gray ponchos were part of the ceremonial dress of Aymara chiefs in many ayllus, such as Jach'a Irpa (La Paz), and were similar to the ones used by the Uru in the 1920s.[28] This clothing was highly valued by indigenous activists; Miranda used to say that "it allows your body to communicate better with the mother earth."[29] Although Miranda would develop strong differences with Marka T'ula in later years, he retained this style of dress for the rest of his life and emphasized the importance of maintaining sartorial traditions in his own movement, the AMP.[30]

Feliciano Inka Marasa also shaped Miranda's views. As a young activist, Marasa was active in the Phiñas rebellion and was a supporter of Pablo Zárate Willka's ideas in the 1890s. After the civil war ended in 1899, Marasa organized various Aymara ayllus, including Quntu and Killakas, to defend their lands on the eastern side of the Andes in the valleys of Chuquisaca.[31] Under Feliciano Inka Marasa's leadership, these ayllus challenged the expansion of haciendas in the 1920s. Marasa believed that the ayllus' legal battle based on colonial titles could be extended through the use of other colonial legislation, including the seventeenth-century Law of the Indies. In the early 1910s he was one of the first apoderados to base his perspectives on this early colonial legislation. Although these laws lost their validity with the arrival of the republic, Marasa used them along with republican legislation to promote his political agenda for over fifty years, until his death in the 1940s.[32] However, Marasa did not organize a wide network in order to frame and disseminate his belief in the Law of the Indies throughout the Andes, like Miranda did with the AMP.[33] Thus, Miranda continued along the path Marasa had pioneered in terms of using colonial law (not republican law) to frame indigenous demands. This was a necessary step because, according to Marasa and then Miranda, colonial law offered protections to Indian rights that republican law did not.

Framing a Multiethnic Jaqi Nationalism
with Uru Oral History

When Toribio Miranda settled in Phuñaqa in 1910s, he was introduced to Uru understandings of history. Uru communities elaborated a politics of memory based partially on oral history. Since the region was predominately Aymara, the Urus represented themselves as embodied in an imagined community called Qullasuyu, which by this time had become a generic name for Aymara lands (mainly the highlands of modern-day

Bolivia).[34] Since late colonial times the Urus of Paria mostly spoke Aymara and had created their own hybrid blend of Aymara religiosity and Catholicism.[35] However, their perspectives differed significantly from Aymara ones, at least in Quntu where Miranda grew up.[36] While the surrounding ayllus represented themselves through their Achachilas and illas (wak'as and other deities), the Uru ayllus represented themselves as a vestige of their own ancient civilization. In this sense Miranda developed a new and unique political discourse from the interethnic frontier where he lived that incorporated both Aymara and Uru notions of history.

The fact that the communities of Phuñaqa, Tinta Maria, and Llapallapani appointed Miranda as an apoderado in 1919 was central to the construction of his discourse.[37] An early document produced by Miranda portrays the Uru nation as "the people who are residuals of the original flood. [The Uru] are qhuchapuchus [the vestige of the flood]. We are the vestige of the [Puxpu] lake and we have been on the lake for thousands of years. The [Puxpu] lake is our home and all of those pampas [where wild animals live] provide our food."[38] Uru narratives frequently associate the Uru with water, lakes, bofedales (wetlands), and the biblical flood. The constant association between nature and the Urus formed part of an ecological discourse that Miranda would promote later in the haciendas.[39]

Miranda represented the Urus through the Aymara concept of qhuchapuchus (traces of the lake), a nomenclature already used in Uru oral history of the time.[40] A letter from Elisardo Moracio, the apoderado of the Qhutsuñ community, to Oruro's prefecture in 1912 repeatedly refers to the Urus to as qhuchapuchus and qhutsuñ people, meaning "vestige of the lake or flood."[41] In other words, the Urus considered themselves to be "first peoples" in relation to other indigenous peoples and the rest of Bolivian society. Miranda, like his predecessors, used this metaphor to request state support on the basis of this native identification and to defend Uru communities from the aggression of other ayllus.[42]

By the late 1920s Miranda was an important apoderado who was presenting petitions not only for Uru communities but also for many other communities and haciendas. For instance, the ayllus of Quntu, Laimi, and Charqas appointed him to be their apoderado by the early 1930s. Miranda's knowledge of Aymara, Quechua, and Uru, and the fact that he lived in the center of the Bolivian Altiplano (Puxpu, Oruro), were important to his ability to network, which allowed him to connect Indians from the southern Andes (Chuquisaca and northern Potosí) with northern Andean communities (La Paz). Although the Urinuqa apoderados rejected his leadership, his connections to Santos Marka T'ula helped him to emerge as an influential leader in other regions of Bolivia. Marka T'ula appreciated Miranda as soon as they were introduced by the influential Aymara Feliciano Inka Marasa, who was well connected and powerful in the ayllus of Chuquisaca during the 1910s.

Toribio Miranda drew on Uru narratives to represent the problems and perspectives of southern Andean peoples. He constructed his worldview from an interethnic frontier at the intersection of these three large communities. Miranda used the concept of puchus (vestige) from Uru oral history to construct the AMP's ideology. As ethnic identity at the time was defined by the language that people spoke, which changed frequently in this frontier region, Miranda's vision of a pluri-ethnic Qullasuyu spoke to the ethnic diversity of the region. This interethnic mingling can be seen with the Jalqas of Chuquisaca, who emerged as a new ethnic group in the second half of the nineteenth century as a result of the combination of Aymara and Uru communities. However, they defined themselves as Quechuas because that was the language they spoke.[43] Renovating the notion of Qullasuyu, Miranda created a new discourse that converted the multiethnic dimension of the region into a structured history: "We are the Qullasuyu . . . we are Qhuchapuchu, Montepuchu [vestige of the tropical forest people], and Chullpapuchu [vestige of the Aymara funerary towers], and we are in this land by the grace of the virgin Pachamama."[44]

The word puchu (vestige) forms an important part of this discourse, which refers to the Aymara as the vestige of the chullpa (the founders of the ayllu who are represented in funerary towers in some parts of the highlands). Meanwhile, montepuchus, meaning the vestige of the people who live in the forest, refers to the Quechuas, implying that they used to live in the tropical zones along the frontier with Amazonian indigenous peoples. Miranda adopted the notion of vestige from the Urus' specific way of looking at history and used it to explain the situation and status of Indians in Bolivia. He thus showed how narratives based on local histories could be used to frame indigenous demands, which became a new way of doing politics in the early twentieth century among indigenous activists. Until then, the dominant current among activists was to frame their demands in terms of the republican law. Thus, Miranda's use of colonial law became a "new" strategy that would powerfully attract other indigenous activists. In contrast to the republican law, which emphasized the role of the individual, the colonial law framework included special rights for indigenous peoples as the original inhabitants of the land. Other activists recognized the potential in this new way of framing their demands because it broadened the justification of their claims. Miranda also used the notion of Qullasuyu to embody a multiethnic perspective in this narrative, which became a powerful idea in his new discourse.

In the context of discussions during the 1930s and 1940s between liberals and leftists regarding the relationship between Indians and the nation-state, Miranda elaborated a jaqi nationalism in which montepuchus, quchupuchus, and chullpapuchus were seen as the "vestiges" of previous civilizations, the "remnants" who endured the "white invasion and four centuries of colonialism." During a time when Indians were considered minors under the protection of the state, and consequently had no rights of citizenship, Miranda's discourse revealed how diverse indigenous groups began to elaborate a discourse of earth politics in the context of hegemonic colonialism within contemporary Bolivia. In other words, Miranda and the AMP indigenous activists began to see themselves as a "republic of Indians" under white-mestizo domination. In the process of acknowledging the subaltern condition of Indians, Miranda developed a project of decolonization.

Miranda and the AMP network developed a discourse that was distinct from that of Santos Marka T'ula's network by directly connecting the idea of first peoples to nation making in Bolivia. Miranda frequently said that "when all Indians eat freely in the main plaza [in Sucre], . . . then we will truly be a human race, the montepuchus, quchupuchus, and chullpapuchus. And it would please Pachamama, the mother earth would be happy. That would be a great day."[45] This multiethnic discourse that highlights the importance of including the vestiges or first peoples in a harmonious vision of society became an important ideology of the subaltern classes, castes, and races during the 1920s and 1930s. Miranda wanted to unite the victims of a segregated Bolivia into a nation of subaltern groups that had previously been defined by the deep structures of internal colonialism in terms of cultural background and ideas about race. He rejected republican law because it could only be used to engage with liberal, "whitening," or segregationist policies. As a result of the rejection that Indians experienced in urban areas, Miranda adamantly defended the use of indigenous clothing and discouraged Indians from wearing other dress. He presented traditional garb as a religious duty, saying "we must honor Pachamama

de ocho Cantones. Provincia de Paria, Poopó de ocho cantones y Vice cantones y es tancias proyecto a que aún tenemos entre manos, pero hasta la fecha los señores párrocos no han conseguido ayuda de ninguna clase de parte de las comunidades. Concluímos exhortando una vez mas a los presentantes a fin de que procuren la asistencia del mayor número posible de alumnos a las escuelas existentes. Apoyados en el Canon 1379 del Código de Derecho Canónico, les rogamos que la cooperación que verbalmente, prometen, sea una hermosa realidad, para la fundación y sostenimiento de las escuelas rurales en proyecto, en los tres puntos indicados devuelvasé y pase una circular del presente documento a los señores parrocos, Abel Obispo.

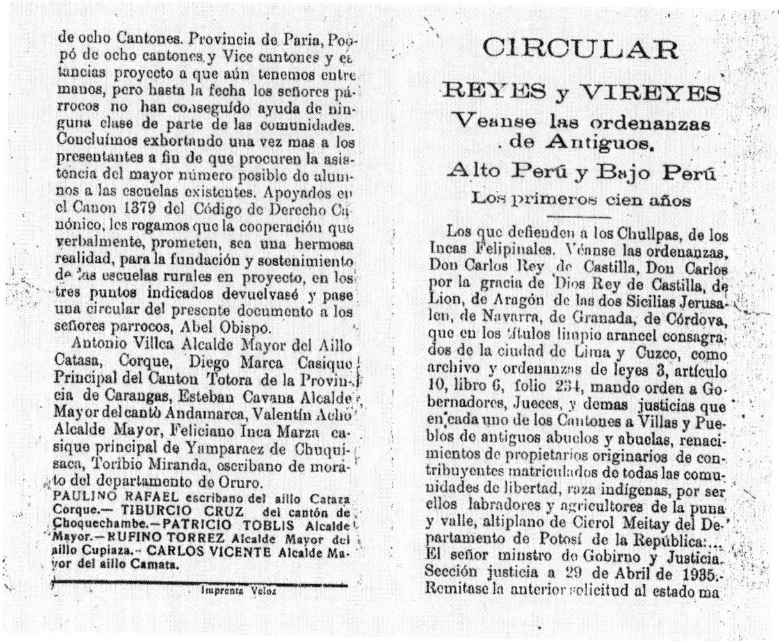

Antonio Villca Alcalde Mayor del Aillo Catasa, Corque, Diego Marca Casique Principal del Canton Totora de la Provincia de Carangas, Esteban Cavana Alcalde Mayor del canton Andamarca, Valentín Acho Alcalde Mayor, Feliciano Inca Marza casique principal de Yamparaez de Chuquisaca, Toribio Miranda, escribano de morato del departamento de Oruro.

PAULINO RAFAEL escribano del aillo Catara Corque.— TIBURCIO CRUZ del cantón de Choquechambe.— PATRICIO TOBLIS Alcalde Mayor.— RUFINO TORREZ Alcalde Mayor del aillo Cupiaza.- CARLOS VICENTE Alcalde Mayor del aillo Camata.

Imprenta Veloz

CIRCULAR
REYES y VIREYES
Veanse las ordenanzas de Antiguos,
Alto Perú y Bajo Perú
Los primeros cien años

Los que defienden a los Chullpas, de los Incas Felipinales. Véanse las ordenanzas, Don Carlos Rey de Castilla, Don Carlos por la gracia de Dios Rey de Castilla, de Lion, de Aragón de las dos Sicilias Jerusalen, de Navarra, de Granada, de Córdova, que en los títulos limpio arancel consagrados de la ciudad de Lima y Cuzco, como archivo y ordenanzas de leyes 3, artículo 10, libro 6, folio 234, mando orden a Gobernadores, Jueces, y demas justicias que en cada uno de los Cantones a Villas y Pueblos de antiguos abuelos y abuelas, renacimientos de propietarios originarios de contribuyentes matriculados de todas las comunidades de libertad, raza indígenas, por ser ellos labradores y agricultores de la puna y valle, altiplano de Cierol Meitay del Departamento de Potosí de la República: El señor minstro de Gobirno y Justicia. Sección justicia a 29 de Abril de 1935. Remítase la anterior solicitud al estado ma

FIGURE 3.1. This document shows the use of the Law of the Indies to portray the Indian struggle prior to 1953. It also shows the use of Uru historical narratives, such as the use of the term chullpas in the discourse of the Indian law. Toribio Miranda was among the people who authored this document, circa 1935. Archivo Privado de Jorge Córdoba, Potosí, Bolivia.

and the Achachilas by dressing proudly with indigenous clothes and never adopting the cholo style of dress."[46] As La Paz and other Bolivian cities doubled in size during the 1930s and 1940s, the use of cholo dress started to expand among Indians in urban areas. While Indian clothes had a positive meaning in Miranda's discourse, they were coded negatively in urban populations, becoming an emblem of an Indianness that Indians had to drop if they wanted to move ahead in the cities.

At the time that Miranda was framing this discourse, he also repositioned himself in respect to Santos Marka T'ula's indigenous network. Fighting for a common audience, Miranda used cultural means and colonial law to frame Indians' demands, while Santos Marka T'ula focused on the legal means of republican law as the only way to achieve Indian rights. Thus, far from internal conflicts among indigenous activists, what was really at stake was the inauguration of a new indigenous political strategy of challenging the coloniality of the state by using the very colonial law and cultural meanings that had in some ways shaped the modern Bolivian nation.

Disseminating Earth Politics throughout Bolivia

When he first became an apoderado in 1919, Miranda combined his work in petty trade and as a laborer with trips to Chuquisaca. To provide for his family's basic needs and earn an income to support his activism, Miranda carried agricultural products from the highlands to the valleys and various distant regions, including some micro-tropical areas. He traveled with his relatives and friends from the Quntu ayllu, taking dried fish, salt, and candles to Marawa (Chuquisaca) in exchange for peppers, peanuts, barley, and corn. The round trip took four months. Many of the ayllus belonging to the Qaranqas nation, such as Killaqas and Soras (Oruro), had community members in various regions of Chuquisaca, where the Aymara kingdoms had had land enclaves since pre-Inka times that provided them with barley and corn.[47] In the early years he only went to Marawa, but in the mid-1920s he expanded into other regions of Chuquisaca such as Ravelo, Tarabuco, Icla, and Tarwita. Miranda expanded his contacts by exchanging goods in the valleys of Phuxpu (Chuquisaca) and by working in the fields in return for goods, which he transported by llama to the highlands.[48] By the late 1920s he had visited most of Chuquisaca's valleys, including north and south Cinti, where he promoted his ideas to other apoderados. The dissemination of Miranda's political ideas and the construction of his network were profoundly shaped by ethnic alliances contracted through marriages to valley and Quechua women. His first marriage reinforced his links with the Quntu ayllu and the Qaqachaqas nation. When his first wife died in the late 1920s, Miranda subsequently married twice more.[49]

While serving as an apoderado in Oruro in 1928, Miranda met Manuel Andia, an extremely influential apoderado in the provinces of Campero and Misk'i (Cochabamba).[50] At this time Miranda also established connections with the leftist movement in Oruro and Sucre, as well as with the powerful anarchist Federación Obrera Local in La Paz. Although Miranda agreed with the Left's criticisms of the ruling elite, he felt that white and mestizo leftist and anarchist activists were trying to control indigenous peoples and the emerging working class by incorporating them into parties such as the Partido de la Izquierda Revolucionaria (PIR) and the

Partido de la Union Republicana Socialista (PURS).[51] Even though leftist intellectuals such as Tristán Marof held counter-hegemonic political beliefs, they were the children of the elite.[52] In Miranda's view the leftists were "only people who sought to hide Indianness and reproduce the entrenched paternal attitude about Indians, who were viewed as children."[53] Miranda also critiqued the cholo nature of the working class, condemning the fact that to be working class at the time basically meant to stop being Indian. Since Santos Marka T'ula continued to work very closely with working-class organizations and unions, a rift began to develop between these two influential activists.

In the early 1930s Miranda took up Manuel Andia's invitation to visit his native region, which was home to the peoples of the Bombo ayllu (Oruro) that held lands in Qalamarka and Miski'i (Cochabamba).[54] Activists during this era often invited jilaqatas and apoderados of other ayllus to teach about indigenous and land rights, and since Miranda was a well-known apoderado representing the Urus, the communities of Campero and Misk'i wanted to hear his ideas about the Indian struggle in the highlands.[55] On other occasions Miranda visited Chuquisaca and Cochabamba, where he met many Quechuas living on haciendas. There he became convinced that the apoderados should not only represent the ayllus and communities, as the Santos Marka T'ula network primarily did, but also combat the abuses suffered by peons.[56] Manuel Andia was one of few indigenous leaders in the valley of Cochabamba working for Indian rights in regions where haciendas dominated. People dubbed Andia as "Atahualpa" (the last Inka ruler), "Kollasuyu wawa" (the son of the Aymara nation), or "the Inka." All of these names called on imaginary notions of an amalgamation of the pre-Inka and Inka peoples. Andia's ideology was based in the traditions of the Aymara ayllus from the Altiplano because he belonged to a community that was originally part of the Qaranqas nation.[57] Thus, activists still used the links between highland ayllus (Oruro) and former "Aymara enclaves" in the valleys of Cochabamba and Chuquisaca as a channel to move from one region to another. In other words, AMP indigenous activists like Miranda used ancient ethnic links to try to reunify Bolivia's various indigenous groups in a struggle for rights and recognition.

Although the indigenous residents of Campero and Misk'i appreciated Miranda's efforts, they were reluctant to follow him in opposing the hacendados because he was from the highlands. It was especially difficult for the residents to trust outsiders because of their fear of eviction, which was a common punishment when landlords found out that a peon had associated with *cabecillas*, a derogatory term used for indigenous activists, from the highlands.[58] Because of these circumstances, Miranda, who by this time was a widower and was recruiting new people into his AMP movement, decided to marry Berna Andia, one of Manuel Andia's sisters from the community of Qalamarka, in an indigenous ceremony. With his new son-in-law status, reactions to him changed, and he could promote his political ideas more effectively in the region.[59] Peons told him that since "your wife is from here, you now have the right to speak in our name."[60] In the 1930s and 1940s he organized a total of forty-six cells in the Campero and Misk'i Provinces. These cells were called *escuelas particulares* and operated as clandestine schools to educate Indians in literacy and the Indian law discourse. In this context the Indian law, an indigenous worldview and interpretation of colonial law, was no longer used only by ayllu members, as it had been in the time of Feliciano Inka Marasa. Hacienda peons now used it to frame and organize their demands.

With his "native marriage" to Berna Andia, Miranda was converted into a "local." Residents of Qalamarca still remembered his presence in 1981, when they showed Fermin Vallejos the plot of land that had belonged to Miranda.[61] Well known for the production of *chicha* (corn beer), Qalamarca has three micro-climates that allow for the production of potatoes, maize, and sugarcane on the shores of the Caine River. After visiting that plot and talking with neighbors, Vallejos realized that Berna Andia had actually inherited the land from her mother's side.[62] Communities like Qalamarca had a very different system of land tenure than the vast majority of the haciendas that surrounded them; kinship and inheritance were traced both through the father's and the mother's side. In the Cochabamba countryside of the 1930s, gender relationships were understood as two different spheres, one for males and the other for females, with a clear division of labor between genders. However, the peasantry and the AMP perceived this relation to be complementary and considered women's participation in rituals to be crucial to their success. Accordingly, while Berna Andia held several ceremonies to worship Pachamama in the *apacheta of Raqaypampa* (site of rituals), Miranda spoke out against the absentee landlords of the haciendas. He also ordered a seal from Oruro that read: "Toribio Miranda—Berna Andia, Alcaldes Mayor, Mizque-Paria," the two regions they were originally from, as an emblem of the shared roles in leadership that Miranda and the AMP promoted.[63]

As local activists, Miranda and Berna Andia started to organize the AMP. In Qiwinal and Laguna (Cochabamba) Miranda argued in favor of "creating schools in the Indian way." During February 1941 in Quewiñal, Toribio Miranda appointed Indalicio Vargas as an alcalde particular, who, with the help of local peons, acquired a piece of land, built a two-room building for a school, and hired Macabeo Prieto as a school teacher. Prieto, who had a third-grade education and was originally from Quillaqullu (Cochabamba), gathered all the children of elementary and high school age to teach them reading and writing with works in both Spanish and Quechua. This type of local school used a Quechua writing style, based on the Aymara and Quechua alphabet developed by Protestant churches.[64] Indalicio Vargas used the building at night to hold meetings with the parents and talk about AMP philosophies and the Indian law. In response a strong resistance to the clandestine schools emerged among the landlords of Misk'i's and Aiquile's haciendas. An association of absentee landlords organized to repress the indigenous activists involved with this educational movement, especially Miranda and the Andias.

At that time the political class in Bolivia was just starting to discuss whether Indians and women should be granted citizenship.[65] While these issues were debated at the National Convention of 1938, the delegates eventually rejected such a possibility. Indeed, worried that these changes were too revolutionary and might cause a coup, the country's conservatives, reformists, and revolutionaries decided not to make major changes to the constitution in the area of civil rights for Indians and women. In some ways this occurred because of the strong influence of the conservatives in the public sphere, particularly on the radio and in newspapers. In the case of women's voting rights, the concern was that changes in the gendered order might threaten the stability of the family.[66]

The convention closed shortly after debating the abolition of personal service, known as *pongueaje*, which was a kind of domestic slavery. However, because *gamonales* (landlords who ruled through a kind of bossism)[67] were at the center of Bolivia's economic and political system prior to 1952, the delegates were not able to make any major decisions on this point. Shortly after the promulgation of the constitution, it was suspended by President Busch, who proclaimed himself dictator. The era after the Chaco War was marked by challenges to the balance of power between elite groups and the emerging Left; the status quo was also destabilized by the effects of the Great Depression.[68]

In November 1946 Manuel Andia was murdered in a crime master-minded by the hacendado of Laguna Grande. In response the entire region of Misk'i and Campero rose up in rebellion, joining the many rebellions between 1946 and 1948 that were sparked by abuses on haciendas.[69] Although the hacendados wanted to prevent rebellions, their repressive acts, such as assassinating Andia, actually promoted resistance. As a consequence of the social turmoil in the 1940s, a conservative regime reemerged in 1947 with Enrique Herzog as its new leader.[70] Manuel Andia's murder took place just months after the progressive President Villarroel was lynched in La Paz. At the time Miranda was touring the Uru and Aymara communities in the Oruro highlands. He did not return to Cochabamba for many years because the hacendados of Misk'i and Campero sought to assassinate him as well.[71] During his long absence, his wife decided to move to Tarata (Cochabamba) alone because being the wife of an activist was too difficult.[72] Although Miranda did not see his wife again, they did not divorce. During the years prior to the national revolution, Miranda focused his efforts on Chuquisaca, where he trained alcaldes particulares such as Juan Huallpa and Nicolas Abrigo. Huallpa and Abrigo would become influential leaders in the Icla and Tarwita region in the late 1940s.[73] He also got in touch with Melitón Gallardo, an up-and-coming alcalde escolar (indigenous education officer), with the purpose of fighting for autonomous indigenous schools.

Because Miranda had such a strong relationship with the indigenous peasants of many local haciendas and communities, they asked him to marry a woman from Chuquisaca in 1949. Within some Indian communities, unmarried people struggled to obtain full rights and could not hold leadership positions. Since Miranda had lost contact with his second wife by that time, he was married for a third time, this time to Manuela Quevedo from the hacienda Ch'uqi Ch'uqi, which was heavily populated with peons growing potatoes and barley on small plots.[74] His marriage to Manuela Quevedo was different from those to his two previous wives. About forty years younger than her husband, Quevedo's main reason for marrying was to "explore the world" with Miranda. In 1951 Tomas Quevedo, Manuela's brother, wrote to her saying, "I hope you fulfilled your strong desire to see other Indian brothers' communities and La Paz and to learn more about the Indian law."[75] Like his marriage to Andia, this union gave Miranda local legitimacy to act in the region. While promoting Indian interests there, he became a member of the Ch'uqi Ch'uqi hacienda

FIGURE 3.2. Toribio Miranda (right), the Uru-Aymara
indigenous activist who was a crucial actor in the AMP
indigenous network. Manuela Quevedo (left), a Quechua
speaker and Miranda's third wife, married him to signify an
alliance between not only Aymaras, Quechuas, and Urus but
also between ayllus and hacienda peons. Oruro, circa 1950.

and was an *arrimante* (peon's peon), with his wife in the *arriendo* (a par-
cel of land the peon worked for himself in exchange for free labor on the
hacienda), of Manuela's father Fermin Quevedo. Through the marriage,
Manuela received five sheep and one baby cow but no land. Manuela also
made many kinship connections by marrying and working with Miranda,
whose activism also benefitted from the marriage. For instance, Tomas
Quevedo became a strong advocate of Miranda's Indian law discourses,

and his relatives Nicolas Abrigo and Petrona Callisaya ended up being extremely helpful to Miranda.

Throughout his time as an activist, Miranda moved between the highlands and lowlands and worked among indigenous peoples whose economies varied from the Uru economy to hacienda labor. To forge allies among the hacienda peons, Miranda used Pablo Zárate Willka's strategy of forming networks based on kinship and marriage. In this sense his marriages to his second and third wives were both a political strategy and an enactment of his discourse about gender parity. Toribio Miranda's experiences provide an interesting opportunity to understand patriarchalism in the early AMP era. His actions show that although Andean patriarchalism is based on strategies of parity and complementarily between women and men, this clearly does not mean that there was complete gender equity. As for Miranda's wives, the case of Manuela Quevedo shows how an indigenous woman might have her own reason for getting involved with an older man who was from another region and probably had other customs. Basically, this type of marriage offered an indigenous woman a way to become involved with Indian circles of power that typically gave priority to men. Through marriage, women like Manuela were able to learn about indigenous activism and also exercise some of this power in their own favor. Manuela Quevedo was famous in Chuquisaca during the 1960s for transforming from a simple daughter of a peon into a woman who traveled extensively with her husband and eventually lived in Oruro and La Paz.

An Intellectual of the Peons and the Healing of the Pachamama in Sumala

A huge hacienda the size of New York City, Sumala had about five hundred peons, contained all of the Andean micro-climates, and was located in the Zudáñez Province (Chuquisaca), which was near the Chaco region. In the high puna the hacienda had alpacas and sheep and made chuño (dry potatoes). It produced maize in the high valleys, wine in the lower valleys, and sugar cane in the tropical islands.[76] Miranda found Sumala to be full of followers eager to hear his Indian law message. He believed that no Indians should be in servitude and was ready to work against it. He visited Sumala at least three times in the 1940s from his native Puñaca at the shores of Lake Poopó, coming with caravans of tatalas challxasiris (Indian petty traders). Traveling by foot and making several stops at other haciendas on the way, it took him four to six months to get from the shores of Poopó to Sumala. It was through visiting haciendas like Sumala that Miranda created a social movement, framing his discourse to fit the changing Bolivian world of the 1940s.

The evening of February 21, 1943, eighty peons from Sumala and apoderados from fourteen other haciendas, including Soroma, Candelaria, Marapampa, and Quinua Chajra, gathered in a remote area of Zudáñez so that hacienda managers would not notice. Mariano Qhispe from Sumala reported that since the new conservative government of Enrique Peñaranda had come to power, the manager of the hacienda had stopped allowing the clandestine schools to operate, saying that President Germán Busch "is dead, and those decrees were no longer valid." Quispe was talking about Busch's decree of 1936 that haciendas must help to establish schools for Indians. Since 1936 apoderados, alcaldes mayores, and jilaqatas had been using the Busch decree to found schools. Another participant, Atiliano Peñaranda, an AMP from Suruma, said that the building that they had been fixing up to host a clandestine school had been destroyed at the order of the hacienda managers, who said that "cabesillas should be picked out and deported from the hacienda." According to their AMPs, seven other clandestine schools in the area were in the same situation. Nicolas Abrigo reported that the army and the police had recently killed mine workers and their families by the hundreds in Catavi (Potosí). The meeting's participants all lamented the hard times Indians endured under the new government and that the absentee landlords were now more powerful than ever.

With coca leaves in his hand, Miranda brought the earth politics perspective to this discussion, arguing that "our Pachamama must be sick since she is not protecting us from such sadness. . . . Our Achachillas [spirits of mountains] should be hungry [for worship] and we must serve them [with rituals]."[77] Toribio Miranda asked participants to intensify their worship in the nearby *pucara falda* (site of worship) so that Pachamama and the Achachillas could "wake up and help us again." Despite the difficulties of the time, Miranda emphasized that "*pachacuti* [the time of great change] is coming" for Indians after centuries of colonialism.[78] Miranda also pointed out that continuing to pay dues to the hacienda would offend the very foundations of indigenous religion, which emphasizes that payments should only be made to Pachamama. Protection from paying dues, he stated, was part of the Indian law, and he began distributing copies. While the older order fell apart in Bolivia and the state, depending on who was in power, started to decree laws both in favor of and against Indians, the peons increased requests for copies of the Indian law to back them up the next time the hacienda managers came asking for dues. While the attendees of this large meeting started to organize for *pachamamar waxtañ* (to worship Pachamama in pucara falda), Nicolas Abrigo called for *ramas* (fundraising to support the cause). Various kinds of contributions were given: Felix Condori from Soroma gave five bolivianos, Felipe Calderon from Quinua Chajra contributed seven bolivianos, a woman from Candelaria brought ten pounds of potatoes, Hermino Vargas gave twenty-five eggs, and Justino Miranda provided one chicken. Twenty-five peons promised to give one *surco* (line of crop) in their fields to the cause, and five other peons said that they would each provide two pounds of *charque* (dried llama meat) the next week. Miranda was involved in many similar meetings. In 1939 he held meetings at various haciendas in Cochabamba, including Jaywayco, Anzaldo, and Misk'i.[79] In 1941 he and Luis Quevedo (alias Rumi Sunqu [Rock Heart]) participated in meetings held at the Carakollo haciendas, again spreading the idea that peons should not pay dues.[80] Quevedo was widely supported in the Oruro haciendas.

After the First National Indigenous Congress, organized by the government in 1945, Miranda again visited the Sumala hacienda, reinforcing the idea that peons should not pay dues to the hacienda, especially now that even the law of the whites had abolished servitude through the decrees of May 15, 1945. He toured thirty-three haciendas in the region between 1945 and 1947 and handed out Indian law documents. His work reinforced peons' resistance to paying dues in the haciendas of Sumala and the surrounding areas.

However, once the pro-Indian president Gualberto Villarroel was killed in 1946, a new conservative regime was installed in the country by the small mestizo-white ruling class that formed the electorate at the time. The new regime reinforced absentee landlords' rights by creating a rural police force that enforced laws that favored the haciendas over the peons. In November and December 1946 the houses of the AMP in Sumala were burned and many AMP activists were put in jail, where they tried to defend themselves by using Indian law documents. The rural police arrived at the request of the hacienda managers and gathered up five hundred of Sumala's peons in Chunca Cancha in order to force them to pay dues to the hacienda. The peons did not readily accept the return of landowners;

another rebellion started the next year when five hundred peons refused to pay rent in the Sumala hacienda. The landowner of Sumala called the peons to a gathering, and he requested that they resume sharecropping and give the required cash payments to the landowner. This sparked a new struggle against paying dues. During this renewed crisis Basilia Diaz and Justina Menacho pushed an army lieutenant in Chunca Cancha. He fell from a high wall, and the army responded by firing into the crowd. Two peons and the lieutenant died, and twenty-five peons were injured. This quickly turned into a rebellion that expanded to the provinces of Zudañez, Yamparaez, Azurduy, and the neighboring hacienda of Orunquta (Potosí), which was only fifty kilometers from Chunca Cancha. The regions of Chunca Cancha and Orunquta are divided by the Pilcomayo River, which marks the border between the Chuquisaca and Potosí departments (the provinces of Zudáñez and Azurduy on the Chuquisaca side and Cornelio Saavedra on the Potosí side). Some hacienda houses were destroyed in this process, and the hacienda manager was killed.[81]

To stop the rebellion from expanding and to protect the haciendas, the government called in the air force to bomb the region in December 1947. Don Teodoro Tellez from hacienda Sumala stated that "for three days the military aircrafts flew in and people were in a panic; they did not know where to hide, so they went to the caves close to Suruma."[82] Don Julio Rivera from Santa Rosa remembered that "people were planning to go to mass in Icla, and they heard a big bombing close to the big hill of Urunquta, and later we learned that people from Urunquta had crossed the Pilcomayo River at night" to avoid more potential bombing the next day.[83] This region had large haciendas around the border between Chuquisaca and Potosí, and Urunquta was an important producer of potatoes for the mines of Potosí.

After these events many AMP leaders were caught and sent to Río Cajon, a concentration camp opened by the Hertzog government for Indians and located in the rain forests of the La Paz department. At least three AMP activists died in Río Cajon, and many were not released until after the national revolution of 1952. During this period of repression arsonists opposed to Indian rights burned down the houses of eighteen indigenous activists in the Sumala region. Military aircraft were also sent to Ayopaya (Cochabamba), where a great peasant and indigenous rebellion erupted in February 1947.[84] While the Ayopaya rebellion has been widely studied, with scholars emphasizing the role of the working class in bringing new ideologies to the region, the rebellion of Chunca Cancha and Urunquta remains widely unknown.[85] In Urunquta and Chunca Cancha new ideologies arrived through indigenous intellectuals such as Toribio Miranda, rather than through working-class miners.

Funding a New Tradition

Like all activist intellectuals, Miranda produced his discourse through cultural politics. He promoted the idea that Indians are puchus (vestiges) and that they should rise up in the name of Pachamama and their ancestors to combat state policies and hacienda owners. Strongly influenced by Uru historical narratives and his own life story, Miranda's earth politics combined this vestige discourse with religiosity and faith in Pachamama as well as the importance of colonial law. As he emerged as an activist, he developed his own distinct discourse that was grounded in the networks of the Qaranqas and Killaqas tribal confederations that extended from Oruro to Chuquisaca. He combined multicultural puchus discourse with the idea of Pachamama to shape an imagined community based primarily on Uru ethnic oral sources.[86] In response to the state of colonialism in the 1920s and the 1940s in Bolivia, where Indians were excluded from citizenship and were forced to work under the gamonal system, Miranda sought to unify these excluded and marginal communities into their own nation.

During the 1920a and 1930s there were several indigenous movements in Bolivia, each of which had its own political emphasis and oversaw different activities. As the AMP emerged, the network of Santos Marka T'ula rejected the new movement. Miranda and his network were accused of just "talking" and of being overly ambitious and interested in achieving positions of power beyond the traditional ayllu political structure.[87] These opinions about Miranda and his emerging network must be understood in the context of the fact that Marka T'ula rejected a wider use of the colonial law and of course rejected the factionalism that resulted from Miranda's and Titiriku's ideas. Another competing movement was led by Eduardo Nina Quispe, who mostly focused on the urban sphere but also had a few cells in the ayllus and communities of La Paz. Miranda never met him, but he did know of him. Responding to the ideas of Marka T'ula and Nina Quispe, Miranda argued that the republican law did not go far enough to address indigenous issues and that education based in Spanish was also not the solution to Indian oppression. As activist intellectuals, Toribio

Miranda and the AMP "spoke truth to power"; in this case the power embedded in the racial system that ruled Bolivian society and from which the rule of the republican law also emerged.[88]

Labor historians such as Guillermo Lora have argued for the importance of the working class and unions in Bolivian history, ignoring the contradictions under which these movements developed and the importance of ethnicity and race to the Bolivian experience.[89] Their importance, however, is well chronicled in the story of the AMP, which emerged to complicate Bolivian indigenous politics during the 1940s. The AMP denounced the oppression of the "Indian republic," by which they meant a diverse group of indigenous ethnicities, by the "world of whites," which included mestizos and cholos. Based on a political conception of colonial law, this construction was also strongly shaped by Miranda's life experiences. His interactions with cholos in leftist parties convinced him that working-class cholos cared more about modernization and "whitening" than indigenous rights.[90]

Miranda's story also introduces us to another unique characteristic of the AMP's earth politics: the important role of women in the development and dissemination of the movement. Miranda's society had clearly different gender roles for men and women, and these even differed in the three regions in which he worked. In Qunto the Aymaras believed that men and women had different but equally important skills; they considered men to be gifted in public life and speech, while women were seen as the "chief" of the house and the keeper of traditional religions and rituals. In the haciendas of Raqaypampa and Palqa, on the other hand, women's and men's lives were strongly linked to work in the fields. But in all cases both men and women were under the hegemony of state officials, hacienda managers, or other whites and mestizos from outside of the Indian village. Most were excluded regardless of gender. Some men, however, could achieve a precarious inclusion in the state prior to 1952 if they were able to get an elementary education.

In Miranda's case he relied on his second and third wives to build kinship networks in Cochabamba and Chuquisaca. This was typical of rural Andean communities, where even the general imagination is represented in terms of chachawarmi, a worldview of gender that emphasizes reciprocity, harmony, and collaboration between the sexes. Miranda's case also demonstrates that while Bolivia was reinforcing patriarchy through discussions about women's participation in politics during the National

Convention of 1938, the AMP was trying to increase women's participation based on ideas of gender parity. Having wives from each region provided this intellectual activist with a decided advantage and demonstrates the importance of seeking local support and reinforcing interethnic links between Indians from different regions and languages groups. This practice also helped to create a new generation that was multiethnic and transcended local boundaries. In other words, this was an early nation-making project to create a new multiethnic community in the twentieth century.

Among the four indigenous activists studied in this book and among the first generation of the AMP, Miranda epitomizes grassroots work and an emphasis on unity and multiculturalism. His legacy is the development of a new discourse that combined colonial law and the worship of the Aymara gods, which clearly distinguished his activism from that of previous indigenous movements, especially Santos Marka T'ula's. His discourse was highly influential and would be continued, extended, and modified by subsequent AMP leaders. His contemporary Gregorio Titiriku further developed and disseminated the Indian law, providing additional leadership to the AMP and widening the activist network.

Chapter Four

Against Cholification

*Gregorio Titiriku's Urban Experience
and the Development of Earth Politics
in Segregated Times*

The morning of August 1, 1925, Gregorio Titiriku discovered that he could
not enter La Paz's main plaza because he was Indian. Accompanied by ten
Indian apoderados from Potosí and Chuquisaca, Titiriku was on his way
to meet with his lawyer about a lawsuit against the landlord of a hacienda.
A policeman stopped Titiriku on the old downtown Comercio Street and
told him that he could go no further because he was dressed as an Indian.
Titiriku explained to the officer that he was unaware of any new regulations, and furthermore, the Potosí Indians had traveled twenty days on
foot and by train from their local village to get to La Paz.[1] When Titiriku
insisted on continuing toward the main plaza, he was taken to the police
station on Sucre Street and charged with "attempting to break the law."[2]

It was not new or unusual for indigenous people in Bolivian cities to experience this type of harassment. The segregation of plazas had begun in
colonial times and continued throughout many towns and cities in postcolonial Bolivia.[3] In the 1920s municipal and national laws actually institutionalized this de facto segregation. President Bautista Saavedra—the
leader of the Republican Party—signed an executive order forbidding indigenous peoples from "walk[ing] in the main plaza," particularly because
he did not want Indians to be visible during the celebration of Bolivia's first
century of independence in 1925.[4] Alcides Arguedas, the most influential
pro-elite Bolivian intellectual of the time, argued that this type of segregation was the best way to "achieve modernity and progress."[5] The asso-

ciation of modernity with the segregation of the Indian population from the principal public spaces in the country became a powerful driving force among the Bolivian elite during the 1920s and shaped racial discourse in significant ways.

Through his work with the Alcades Mayores Particulares (AMP), Gregorio Titiriku worked against this type of racialization, which was prevalent in the era prior to 1952. In this chapter I illustrate how a man like Titiriku, who was born in the ayllus at the shores of Lake Titikaka, ended up coming to the city of La Paz to serve the goals of the apoderado and cacique movement in the 1920s. While Toribio Miranda and Santos Marka T'ula had developed extensive experience fighting against coloniality with legal means, Titiriku is remembered as "essentially being a 'political animal' and a man with strong faith in the Aymara gods."[6] Titiriku used the garantías that all apoderados, jilaqatas, and other indigenous activists did at that time, but he gave them a new, decolonizing purpose in the form of the Indian law. Through the garantías, he developed and spread an agenda that had political, economic, educational, and religious goals. From the 1920s to the 1950s, Titiriku concentrated on disseminating his ideas and building up the AMP indigenous activist network, along with Toribio Miranda and other dissidents from Santos Marka T'ula's network of apoderados.

Titiriku's struggle occurred during a time when segregation, whether institutionally enforced or not, acutely affected the lives of Indians in Bolivian society, and this became important to his development as an individual and as an activist. Since most Bolivians perceived themselves to be particularly marginalized in an already marginal region, the idea of modernity was strongly linked to the outside and the international, which stood in stark contrast to native cultures. While segregation was constantly contested and only supported in a weak form through state policies during most of the twentieth century, it was highly effective in shaping the lives of subaltern groups. In this sense the history of segregation in Bolivia points to some of the contradictions and ironies in the history of modernity in Latin America.[7]

Titiriku's story brings into stark relief how the reinforcement of segregationist ideas and the development of discriminatory practices were crucial to Bolivian society. This chapter explains the role of racial categories in the first half of twentieth century and provides a brief history of segregation in the cities of La Paz and Oruro. In recounting how segregation operated in La Paz, I highlight the role of Bolivia's celebration of the centenary of its independence to show how ideas about modernity, patriotism, and making a good impression on international visitors encouraged leaders to support segregation. Although Oruro followed La Paz's example, segregation there was also shaped by the business community's response to Indians migrating from the countryside, which led to the creation of municipal laws to protect elite interests. In contrast to the dominant idea that elite and educated people were better fit for modernity, Titiriku argued that modernity did not conform to a single model and that Indians should have their own modernization project, informed by the goal of decolonization.

An important aspect of Titiriku's decolonization project was his reinforcement of the notion of an Indian nation, which he referred to as a nation of jaqis (indigenous peoples or qullas), along the lines of the republic of Qullasuyu. Titiriku stated, "we should enforce the border of the Republic of Qullasuyu," suggesting that Indians had a special right to patrol the borders because, as aboriginal people, they "were in their own country" unlike the "q'aras [whites] who were there as guests."[8] For Titiriku, "Qullasuyu is the land of jaqis and because of that we have the right to speak and we should not let q'aras dominate us."[9] Holding similar views, Eduardo Nina Quispe thought that the republic of Qullasuyu would become a reality only when Indians empowered themselves to dominate Bolivian politics. To facilitate these goals, he created La Sociedad Indígena (The Indigenous Society).[10] The nationalism that Quispe and Titiriku promoted portrayed a struggle between jaqis and q'aras, between dominant and subordinate groups, in which racialization was a major front. Questioning segregationist policies, their work as activist intellectuals addressed, from the perspective of subaltern groups, the "racial regulatory system" embedded in Bolivian society.[11]

Titiriku insisted that Bolivia consisted of two republics: one of which, the "white republic," oppressed the other, the "Indian republic." This discourse contributed to the construction of a strong fraternity among the networks of the AMP.[12] Operating within the ideological context of the 1930s, the AMP mobilized a discourse of two republics based on ideas about Indian law and equality, both of which were already being widely used and discussed by Santos Marka T'ula's indigenous network and other indigenous movements, especially after the Chaco War.[13] Titiriku's discourse, however, was more explicit, using the idea of two republics to confront Bolivia's social inequality and to illustrate Indians' aspirations.

Like his predecessor Marka T'ula, Tititriku was interested in equality within an Aymara worldview. In opposing ideas inherent to the republican law, like individual property, the AMP made a clear choice to emphasize religion in the Indian law. Indeed, in a petition to the Ministry of Education and Indigenous Affairs, Titiriku asked indigenous communities to create escuelas particulares (autonomous indigenous schools) that taught in Aymara or Quechua to help them live well (vivir bien). Titiriku thus sought equality in the context of education and opportunity, but he also expanded it by emphasizing the indigenous notion of living well (sumaqamaña), which included justice, equality, and harmony with Pachamama and nature.[14] Titiriku thus combined the liberal notion of equality with the Aymara notion of collective well-being.[15]

As we have seen, for some AMP activists in the 1930s, legal title documents became a symbol of oppression because they legitimized the persistence of the colonial order. Deriding Marka T'ula's emphasis on searching for titles, Titiriku argued that Indians should not worship "legal paperwork" and insisted that qullas should worship the Aymara gods, such as Pachamama, the Achachilas, qixuqixu (lightning or, for others, the Apostle James), and the moon (the representation of mother water). In the 1930s Pachamama and Achachillas were considered solely Aymara gods, while Qixuqixu conflated with the Apostle James, in a hybrid representation, both Christian and Aymara in the AMP discourse. This new perspective sought to legitimize the AMP and the Indian law in a new way: through indigenous religion.

A Man Raised among Indian Chiefs and the Utawawa System

In 1890 Gregorio Titiriku was born in Jach'a Q'axiata, which is located on the shores of Lake Titikaka in the Department of La Paz. The indigenous peoples of this region of Janqulaimes (Umasuyus) sprung from the mixing of Aymara- and Uru-speaking peoples during the sixteenth century under Viceroy Toledo.[16] Titiriku is a common Uru surname. His family held a strategic position because of their good relationships with various apoderados; a fact that would profoundly shape his activism. Titiriku became aware of the crucial work of the apoderados during his teenage years. A jilaqata and apoderado of his own community, his father collaborated with the principal apoderados of Janqulaimes and, in 1905, sent the young Titiriku to live with and work as an *utawawa* to Juan Mamani, who held the important position of apoderado of the region of Janqulaimes.[17] In the 1920s an utawawa, which in Aymara literally means "child of the house," worked for both white and mestizo bosses, as well as for priests and powerful Indians, usually as a domestic servant or general helper.[18] Since there were no schools for Indians, Titiriku's father saw this as a good opportunity for his son to learn to read.[19] In the early twentieth century, utawawas worked temporarily for other families; they were often considered members of the beneficiary's family or adoptive children. During his time with Juan Mamani, Titiriku kept records and was surrounded by people who knew how to read Spanish. He always remembered this as the time when "he learned to recognize the alphabet" by deciphering what he described as "letters dancing with each other." He also had a chance to learn some Spanish during frequent trips to Jach'aqhachi, in which he helped the apoderado Juan Mamani with paperwork for the Janqulaimes ayllus.[20] It was through this process that Titiriku became aware of the problems the communities faced, especially the usurpation of the Zamora ayllu's lands by the white provincial elite.[21]

However, this education suddenly stopped in 1915, when Titiriku's father called him home to help with fieldwork. Titiriku married Santusa Mamani, who was originally from a community not far from his own. The wedding was arranged by the parents of both the groom and the bride, which was customary in the ayllus. Since his father could no longer serve in the local ayllu because of his age, Titiriku assumed his post, where his knowledge and understanding of the communities' problems were useful. Titiriku served for more than ten years at the local and regional ayllu levels, making frequent trips to Jach'aqhachi.[22]

By the early 1920s Titiriku had expanded his network beyond Janqulaimes and started to attend meetings in the city of La Paz. During this time the apoderados needed someone to stay in Chukiawu (the indigenous name for La Paz) more often to coordinate their paperwork with lawyers and escribanos and to "collect newspapers" and other legal resolutions. The apoderados of Umasuyus, among them Rufino Willka and Carlos Pantipati, requested that Titiriku move to La Paz, which he willingly did.[23] As compensation Dionicio Paxipati promised to help Titiriku find seasonal jobs, and other apoderados promised to bring him food and supplies. The original plan was for Titiriku to help for one full year and to return occasionally to his community, especially during harvest time.[24]

Chukiawu Marka, the Segregated City:
Streetcars and Public Places

The practices of segregation instituted by municipal and national regulations are crucial to understanding Titiriku's life. The history of segregation in La Paz is intimately tied to the regulation of streetcars. When streetcars, owned by the British-run Bolivian General Enterprise, started to run in 1909, Indians were not allowed to board them.[25] As part of elite policies to segregate cholos and Indians, the municipality of La Paz issued a regulation on the use of streetcars in 1925 that prohibited passengers from carrying bags in first and second class and exclusively reserved first class for *gente decente* (decent people, meaning mostly whites). The municipal resolution did not focus on Indians but rather on the maids, cooks, and other cholas who carried their bags onto streetcars. Ironically, not only were the maids and cooks working for the elite but also the bags contained groceries to feed their employers. In response to these orders, the cooks' and maids' unions demonstrated outside the municipal offices. The protests were led, in part, by Aymara cholas like Catalina Mendoza and Petronilla Infantes.

Despite the rules, Gregorio Titiriku sometimes took the streetcar to visit his lawyers in Sopocachi and Obrajes on Tuesdays, when it had fewer passengers. He was allowed to ride in the very back of second class because his wife was an acquaintance of the driver's wife. The streetcar driver told him, "we are breaking the law, go to the back and make sure no one sees you." Once when Titiriku tried to get onto a crowded downtown streetcar, he was told that "Indians do not take streetcars." Although he had the ten-cent fare, his indigenous clothing prohibited him from boarding. Though other apoderados often changed their clothes so they could circulate freely, Titiriku refused.[26]

Clearly, Indians were not welcome in the city or, as Titiriku used to call it, the "white country."[27] Restaurants were also restricted at that time; Titiriku could not eat lunch on Calle Chirinos, near the San Francisco Church, because the owner, Gumercinda Huanca, who was probably a chola, argued that "she [could not] accept an Indian sitting in her restaurant" because "Indians eat at the *tambo* [house for Indian travelers]."[28]

FIGURE 4.1. A streetcar and its passengers in La Paz, 1924. Streetcars did not allow indigenous people to board and had especially restrictive policies for urban Indian women, called cholas. Passengers were mostly white and mestizo. Courtesy of Dolores Mejia, Patakamaya, La Paz.

Despite these restrictions, Titiriku's strong sense of mission led him to resist and continue going to the city. He justified his persistence by arguing that "we [Aymaras] are in our land and we have the right to walk in the streets, the plaza, the parks, and take the streetcars, as well as to sit down on El Prado and watch the trucks and the streetcars. No one has to stop doing that because we are the owner of these lands. This place is an Aymara land. We are not guests like the Spaniards are in these lands, we are not whites."[29] At that time Titiriku refused to address middle-class lawyers as *wiraxucha* (lord) or *caballero* (sir), and he would not stand up and hold his wool hat in his hands—a sign of respect—while speaking to them. As a man faithful to Pachamama and the Achachilas, he refused to use the term *wiraxuchas* for whites because it referred to gods in the Aymara language.[30] He said: "We cannot call these people wiraxuchas because only achachilas [the spirits of wak'as] are wiraxuchas. If we call the whites wiraxuchas, we are insulting ourselves. These people came from Spain and they are Spaniards, not wiraxuchas." Although most of the lawyers understood Aymara, they refused to speak it and mostly answered in Spanish.

La Paz and Oruro provide excellent examples for understanding how segregation policies developed in relation to modernity and dress codes. Beginning in the early nineteenth century, some cholos had adopted Western dress, while others preferred various types of ethnic dress. In 1925, when Indians were banned from downtown La Paz, some cholos, such as construction workers and carpenters, faced police aggression when they insisted on wearing their ponchos and ethnic pants called *calzones partidos* in the main plaza, and Titiriku protested alongside them to defend the presence of indigenous clothing in the public arena.[31] The policemen tore off the cholos' vicuña-wool ponchos and encouraged the men to sew the lower half of their pants together to accommodate this policy.[32] Consequently, people from La Paz began to be known as "ch'uqutas, the people who sewed their pants."[33] Oral histories frequently portray this period as the time when "Saavedra civilized the Aymaras of La Paz" and the years when Paceños left their calzones partidos and started to wear "civilized pants."[34] Despite the fact that the state promoted and reinforced the de-Indianization of cholos, many in La Paz and Oruro resisted.

The banning of Indians from certain spaces in an attempt to "modernize" society stemmed from the long-held opinions of public intellectuals. One of the first to address this topic was Manuel Rigoberto Paredes, who believed that the Indian race could become a modern people if they wore suits or other forms of Western dress.[35] Other intellectuals, such as Alcides Arguedas, argued that the Turkish Revolution provided the best model for Bolivia to follow in terms of modernity and tradition, affirming that

> the . . . abolition of aboriginal clothing . . . shows a sign of local progress by making [Indians] wear "the modern dress" of the civilized peoples. In Turkey President Mustafa Kemal suppressed Arabic writing and he imposed Latin characters. Furthermore, the president himself traveled through the country, installing big blackboards in public plazas and giving public lessons on [the new form of writing]. A picture from . . . 1928 . . . showed this state dignitary [Kemal] dressed with the best London [Western] fashion and writing [Latin characters] in front of a group of military and civilians all dressed in the Western style. . . . This is admirable.[36]

This ban on Indian dress had the biggest impact in La Paz. Preparing to celebrate the centenary of independence from Spain in 1925, Bolivia's elite forbade Indians from participating in the public festivities. The pro-government newspaper La República started to campaign for a law that would ban Indian presence, arguing that

> now more than ever before, because the centenary celebration is get-ting closer, a municipal order must be issued to prevent nothing less than the aboriginal from walking in parks and amusement places downtown. If they are allowed, they should be prohibited from wear-ing the poncho and pants that . . . are purposely made with a gap in the lower area. . . . The purpose of this ban is to remove from the city this exotic, ugly, colorful, and ridiculous dress that . . . presents to the foreigners a city with ponchos, "calzones partidos," and other extravagant clothes that Indians like to use.[37]

La República was so enthusiastic about this proposal that it even suggested that it had massive public support, reporting that "all the citizenry will make sure that the municipal orders are accomplished, and in a short time, the city, although not completely changed, at least would improve in its exterior aspects."[38] Moved by such opinions, President Saavedra issued an executive order banning Indians from downtown during the official celebration of the Bolivian centenary and encouraging other municipal authorities to follow La Paz's example.[39] By pioneering the implementa-tion of modern segregation policies, President Saavedra nourished the idea that cities are not proper places for Indians. This perspective would persist long after the celebration.

When the municipality of La Paz constructed small indoor markets and issued another order prohibiting women street vendors from selling out-doors, chola street vendors, who complained about the lack of space in the new markets, continued to sell their wares in the streets. In the end the police had to admit that they could not completely control these women.[40] As a result, they were able to create the first women's union, the Fed-eración Femenina Local, which was based on anarchist ideology.[41] While socialism became widely diffused mostly among the cholo (men) work-ing class, anarchist activists spread their ideology more among cholas (women) who were cooks and flower sellers. Titiriku's second wife, Rosa Ramos, and her mother, Anastacia Cutili, tried to join the association, but the cholas did not welcome them. Rosa Ramos was told she should instead join the caciques tituleros group, meaning a group reserved for indigenous people. These experiences indicated to Titiriku that cholo labor institutions were not, in fact, open to any Indian who wanted to retain or reassert their Indian heritage.[42]

Restrictive policies that municipal governments applied to cholos were implemented mostly along gender lines, based on the idea that men were the keepers of civilization, while women were more associated with nature and tradition.[43] In cities like La Paz, cholas were allowed to keep their ethnic dress, which consisted of a wide skirt, a *mantilla* (shawl), and a derby hat.[44] Cholo men, on the other hand, were forced to give up ethnic dress and don suits and hats. Both male and female indigenous peasants were either kept outside of urban centers or restricted from downtown areas.

Oruro also developed racial segregation policies. Thanks to mining prosperity, by the mid-1920s Oruro was becoming a real city, with sixty-six international firms setting up offices there. Among them were automobile companies that imported Ford Motors and other car brands. The biggest store in town, Ford House, was owned by the Chilean Juan Durán Zenteno. Serafín Ferrufino owned the Gundlach Company, which carried automobile parts. Concentrated on Soria Galvarro and Ayacucho Streets, other stores, filled with Singer sewing machines and typewriters, bicycles, and musical instruments, thrived. Oruro also had high-end pharmacies, such as Botica Alemana Kummel and Harry O'Donnell's Farmacia Inglesa on Bolivar and Potosí streets. In early 1926 many of these business owners wrote a letter to the municipality requesting that Indians be banned from downtown because, as Serafín Ferrufino argued, "Indian llama drivers in the plaza and main streets are making foreign customers uncomfortable."[45] After lobbying municipal authorities, the shop owners finally obtained a municipal resolution on July 9, 1928, that, inspired by the earlier La Paz resolution, banned indigenous people from Oruro's downtown.[46] Based on these experiences, even mining towns like Wanuni restricted indigenous people from walking in the plaza in 1929, demonstrating that, rather than being a marginal or isolated practice, segregation was widely instituted in Bolivia.[47]

Antonio García, an associate of Titiriku's, experienced this segregation when, as a young man, he left the hacienda of Suroma (Chuquisaca) and went to work in the mines of Oruro. In 1928 García was not allowed to enter Oruro's main plaza while wearing ethnic clothes, and the policemen told him that he needed to dress as a "civilized man with a suit and hat."[48]

In other cases this discrimination had more serious implications, such as when María Mamani was accused, in a charge based on her Indianness, of defecating in the bushes of the main plaza. Maria, who later became an indigenous activist associated with the AMP and worked for several years with Titiriku, was incarcerated in the Wanuni jail, where the police raped her several times.[49] Abuse of Indian women accused of littering or defecating in public places and restrictions on men entering cities became common features of Bolivian life in the late 1920s.

The emergence of segregation based on modernity and race was ironic. Elites saw clothing as a strong signifier of Indianness, which they believed stood in opposition to modernity. Yet the colonial practice mandating that Indians and whites must occupy different physical spaces was reinforced in various Bolivian cities in the 1920s. Thus, by promoting the ban on Indians in downtown areas, elites reinforced the colonial idea of two republics. La Paz was most strongly affected by this segregation because it had the country's largest ethnic community. Despite Bolivia's profound regional variations at the time, the case of La Paz had an impact on various parts of the country. In the years to come, segregationist policies gradually spread to the rest of country, as the cases of Oruro and Wanuni illustrate.[50] Other regions also had their own segregationist traditions. For instance, Sucre had been restricting Indians' movement in the downtown area since the 1870s.[51] Although these ordinances were imposed and enforced at different times, they were all grounded, in one way or another, in ideas about separate places for Indians and Spaniards in modern Bolivia. This situation only partially changed after the Chaco War between Bolivia and Paraguay. By then, President Salamanca was so alarmed by the cholo labor movement that he sent many Indian and cholo leaders to the front as a way to eliminate Indian rebellions and working-class movements.[52] During the war at least fifty thousand Bolivians, mostly from indigenous peoples, died.[53]

Struggles between Subaltern Groups: Jaqis versus Cholos

Titiriku not only rejected the elite class but also cholos. As an Indian, during his lifetime he experienced almost the same discrimination from both groups, though most cholos were of Indian heritage, too. Ideas about race also shaped class categories in the Bolivian social hierarchy of the 1920s. In the Bolivian racial imaginary, q'aras—whites and mestizos who shared a common commitment to a universal modernizing process—were at the top of the social structure. Below them were cholos, who represented the working class, artisans, mineworkers, and others associated with urban blue-collar jobs. While cholos developed a strong class identity, they typically had a weak Aymara or Quechua ethnic identity (although there were exceptions). Ch'utas or new cholos straddled the frontier between Indian and cholo identities. The majority of the population consisted of Indians who had strong Aymara or Quechua ethnic identities and often organized around ayllu or hacienda peons' representatives.

Most cholos had lived in the cities for one or two generations by this period, had mostly Indian descendents, and frequently still spoke Aymara or Quechua as well as Spanish. However, in terms of racial discourse, during the 1920s cholos defined themselves as neither Indian nor white. Bolivian literature presented fantasies of cholas' love and sex lives with elite men (white and mestizo). These stories reveal how white and mestizo men perceived cholas and document the rise in inequality between different racial segments of the Bolivian social structure. In an unequal world where women had an especially precarious position, cholas who were involved with white men and mestizos were often able to empower themselves.[54]

Cholos comprised the majority of the emerging working class in the new urban economy, which was closely linked to the subsidiary activities of mining. In La Paz the cholo elite lived in San Pedro, their own exclusive neighborhood, where they owned restaurants and printing shops and also worked in banks. However, most cholos worked as carpenters, construction workers, tailors, shoemakers, maids, flower and street vendors, leather tanners, railroad workers, and print-shop workers.[55] In several parts of the country, such as Sucre and Potosí, a subcategory of cholos called ch'utas, recent arrivals from the countryside, were differentiated from other cholos because they mixed their Indian ethnic fashion with cholo elements. Ch'utas often came from the surrounding countryside to sell milk, fruit, and vegetables in urban areas. They were considered different from rural cholos and Indians because they wore shoes rather than sandals.[56]

Cholos' power varied significantly by region. The majority of cholos in La Paz and Oruro were of Aymara heritage, and through leading the labor movement, they were at the head of the counter-hegemonic forces of the country. In Sucre and Potosí, Quechua cholos were governed by their own

FIGURES 4.2 AND 4.3.
ABOVE: The photograph
shows the difference be-
tween cholos and Indians.
In the 1920s cholos and
cholas were educated, and
literacy had become one of
the key differences between
Indians and cholos. In the
photo a chola takes notes of
her business with an Indian
man. LEFT: A couple of
Aymara cholos. In the 1920s
La Paz had its own Aymara
elite that lived in the exclusive neighborhood of San
Pedro. Men wore full Western suits, and chola women
wore full dresses made of
imported fabrics. Cholas
also wore boots in 1920s.
From Antonio Paredes
Candia, *La chola boliviana*
(La Paz: Editorial popular,
1992), 51–53.

elite, but working-class cholos followed leftist whites in the late 1920s. One of these leftists was Tristán Marof, who was from Sucre and founded the Partido Socialista Revolucionario (PSR, Revolutionary Socialist Party), which was the country's first socialist party.[57]

In the 1920s La Paz and Oruro cholos created a vibrant labor movement that contested existing racial policies based mainly on anarchist ideology. In La Paz cholos had a strong sense of group identity within the larger society, which lead them to reject the leftist white elite and instead foster their own intellectuals. Luis Cusicanqui, who came from this milieu, defined himself as an urban "Aymara Indian," which was something unusual for a cholo during that time. Cusicanqui founded the most influential anarchist organization, La Antorcha, and the largest labor organization in La Paz, the Federación Obrera Local (Local Workers Federation).[58] As they slowly became empowered by the new anarchist and labor movements, cholos were continuously condemned by the Bolivian elite. The well-known writer Alcides Arguedas, for example, argued that the country was in a "terminally ill condition" because Bolivian society was becoming "dominated by cholos."[59] In Arguedas's view the hybrid role of cholos in history represented a struggle between "civilization" and "barbarism."[60] Similarly, while Franz Tamayo, a politician·and intellectual of this period, defended the Indian race, he was disturbed by the "pervasive role" of cholos in Bolivian society.[61] Thus, during the 1920s Arguedas and Tamayo expressed the white elite's hatred of cholos for breaking up the binary caste system in Bolivia and for following threatening and counter-hegemonic ideologies.

While Titiriku was attending to the apoderados' issues, he also worked in temporary blue-collar jobs at a slaughterhouse and a small bakery that put him in touch with the urban working class. However, he always returned to the countryside, especially during harvests, to work in his community's fields. Moving between country and city, he got the impression that cholos were largely anti-Indian. For instance, in 1931 a group of cholos at his work in the market told Titiriku: "If you want to stay among us, you have to become civilized, . . . buy pants, wear a hat, and get a shirt. You could at least buy chu'ta clothes. People from the other groups will ask themselves why we let you stay among us."[62] Because of these attitudes and their refusal to speak Aymara, Titiriku often clashed with the cholo working class.[63] In later years Titiriku recalled refusing to speak Spanish in response to cholos who did not want to speak Aymara. Titiriku eventually decided to leave his blue-collar jobs and concentrate on his activist work.[64]

During Titiriku's lifetime political parties manipulated literacy. Beginning in 1905 the Education Minister Juan Misael Saracho created a law that paid instructors three bolivianos for every *indígena alfabetizado* (literate Indian) they taught, which essentially meant someone who knew how to sign his name. Since every literate man in the early twentieth century counted as a citizen under Bolivian law, Liberals and Republicans competed for votes by promoting literacy for Indians and cholos. In the mid-1920s this became particularly important because candidates could sway the results of national elections by signing up just a small number of new voters. At one point the majority of the Republican Party was comprised of cholos, some of whom had recently become literate. This phenomenon was especially important in Jach'aqhachi, where the Republicans won in 1925 for the first time. However, the Liberal elite refused to acknowledge this new type of citizen, calling them the "sheep of Jach'aqhachi" for blindly following the Republicans.[65] The Liberals thought that because these new citizens were Indians and cholos, they could not have rational reasons for supporting the Republican Party. Their fears were confirmed by several cases in which cholos and Indians received cash to vote for the Republicans. Titiriku recognized this manipulative practice for what it was and condemned the client-oriented relationship that linked literacy with political participation. Some of Titiriku's Indian friends became cholos in the 1920s by moving to Jach'aqhachi, working urban jobs, and learning Spanish. In the 1920s ethnic identity was defined from a class perspective through work categories. Jach'aqhachi became known for its hat making industry, and it provided rural Aymaras with supplies for rituals in the vast region of the Qulla or Umasuyus Aymara nation.[66] By the mid-1920s Jach'aqhachi had a huge number of cholos or ch'utas, groups which Titiriku referred to as "whitened Indians" (*vueltos en blancos*).[67] In the late 1930s he frequently mentioned that "while Indians are dying in Paqajaqis and Potosí, here the Indians in Jach'aqhachi want to become white, and they dress like cholos."[68] The killing of Aymaras in the massacre of Jesús de Machaqa in 1921 (Paqajaqis) and the massacre of Indians in Chayanta (Potosí) in 1927 justified his rejection of both mainstream political parties, particularly the Republican Party, which had vast support among cholos. During this time President Bautista Saavedra was known widely as "cholo Saavedra" because of his background and his strong support among cholos. From Titiriku's perspective, cholos, mestizos, and whites could not be trusted and were all part of the "white republic." Titiriku became increasingly convinced of the merit of Miranda and Marasa's confrontational demand for a "republic of Indians," which sought a fully and exclusively Indian country, separate from white Bolivia.[69] At that time society was so unequal that he could not imagine an integrated nation that did not require Indians to "cholify" and reject their heritage. Titiriku's personal experience of moving back and forth from the countryside to the city made him aware of the whitening process that was taking place, so he devoted most of his life to denouncing it and to offering an alternate vision of the nation.

Not until the 1970s, long after the Bolivian National Revolution of 1952, did the Katarista and Indianista movements take up Titiriku's concerns and denounce the similar situation of discrimination that a new generation of Aymaras and Quechuas were facing. They promulgated the Tiwanaku manifesto, arguing that "a nation cannot be free if it oppresses another nation." While Titiriku's experience epitomizes racialization before the national revolution, in a broader perspective the conflicts between Indians and cholos belong to a larger story of the struggle for and resistance to "whitening," "modernity," and "civilization," where whites discriminated against mestizos, mestizos against cholos, and cholos against Indians. These racial dynamics drove Titiriku and the AMP to deploy the Indian law as counter-hegemonic discourse within the cultural framework available in the 1930s.

Documenting the Indian Law and Its Context

In response to the political turmoil of the 1930s and the effects of the Great Depression on Bolivian politics and the labor movement, Titiriku promoted the AMP's ideas about the Indian law and religion by emphasizing faith in Pachamama and the Achachilas. In 1926 Titiriku urged several apoderados, including Francisco Condori and Juan Iquiapaza from Laxa and Jach'aqhachi, to study the connections between the Law of the Indies and what was then known as the Indian law, which was already a point of reference before Titiriku and Miranda appropriated it. Indian law had a variety of meanings and uses: as an alternative way to refer to the Law of the Indies; as a name for the struggle to legislate Indian rights; and even as a term that referred to the Indian lifestyle or worldview.[70] But it is only with Miranda, Titiriku, and other AMP activists that the Indian law emerged as something separate or different from the Law of the Indies, that is, a discourse that addressed dimensions of racialization by responding to the dehumanization of indigenous peoples and by articulating an agenda of decolonization. And of all the AMP members, Titiriku was most involved in drawing up a more structured doctrine with political and religious arguments.[71]

Titiriku frequently brought multiple volumes of the Law of the Indies to apoderado meetings and tried to explain its contents in Aymara.[72] He was especially interested in the articles related to the protection of Indians and their possessions. Ideas for a special judiciary system for Indians, separate authorities, and penalties for abuses against Indians also appealed to Titiriku. They coincided more with the Aymara concept of sumaqamaña, which the AMP promoted in their discourse. This Aymara philosophical approach to life translates as "to live well," in the sense of being good and just, and is in opposition to market-oriented and consumerist lifestyles. It advocates living in harmony with Pachamama and emphasizes justice and peace. In this sense he saw that colonial law had the potential to be more beneficial to Indians than republican law because the ideas expressed in the Law of the Indies connected to and overlapped with religious aspects in the Indian law.

Indigenous peoples and activists who worked with them, especially the apoderados in southern Bolivia (Potosí and Chuquisaca), were eager to learn about the AMP and Titiriku's new interpretation of the republic of Qullasuyu, which differed from other contemporary conceptions, such as those of Santos Marka T'ula and Eduardo Nina Quispe. While Santos Marka T'ula also sought a law for Indians that incorporated some colonial law, it was primarily based on republican law. On the other hand, Eduardo Nina Quispe believed that education was the key to protecting Indians from colonial abuses and ultimately strove for the full incorporation, or assimilation, of Indians into Bolivia, calling this process the "renovation of Bolivia." Titiriku promoted the Indian law in a more holistic sense of sumaqamaña (living well) and grounded it in colonial law in order to explicitly reject the republican law, which, in Titiriku's opinion, was inadequate. He wanted to establish an Indian nation.

In the 1930s Titiriku intensified his activism by interweaving his religious views with his political perspective while he began to create his own AMP networks in different regions of the country. The fragility of Bolivia's political system, weakened by defeat in the Chaco War, was an important factor in this shift. The apoderado movement had been destroyed by the war since many of its leaders either were sent to the front lines or faced persecution. Supporting the ideas of Feliciano Inka Marasa and Toribio Miranda after the war, Titiriku tried to reorganize the movement; however, he argued that, instead of apoderados, indigenous activists should call themselves Alcaldes Mayores Particulares because this better expressed their goal of leading an Indian nation as an alcalde (a mayor) does.[73] Titiriku insisted, however, that the AMP should distinguish itself from the *alcaldes escolares* (school mayors) or *alcaldes del campo* (field mayors), cholos who worked with the government in rural areas. Thus, they became alcaldes particulares (particular mayors) because they had a "particular cause," namely to promote the Indian law.

By 1936 Titiriku was already a prestigious apoderado and was especially well known among the Indians and apoderados of Potosí and Chuquisaca because of his connections with Marasa and Miranda.[74] Although they were in many ways critical of aspects of Santos Marka T'ula's doctrine, both Titiriku and Miranda had been active in his indigenous movement of the apoderados mallkus for more than two decades. Since the mid-1920s Titiriku and his allies Miranda and Marasa already questioned Santos Marka T'ula's leadership, but they only started to write petitions separately from Marka T'ula in the mid-1930s. Titiriku did not publicly criticize Marka T'ula until a mass meeting of apoderados in 1937, when he said: "The spirits of [colonial] titles did not bring any result. The blood of Qullasuyu [the Indian nation] is still crying. We give our money, we give our time and our hope to this worthless endeavor."[75] These meetings became an arena for confrontations between the two bands of indigenous activists. Many apoderados who sided with Santos Marka T'ula did not accept Miranda and Titiriku's questioning of his work. Titiriku, however, argued that indigenous activists should follow the Achachilas and Pachamama rather than Marka T'ula's paper titles.[76] A serious breakdown was underway among the apoderados.

In 1936 Gregorio Titiriku began periodically reproducing a document that he and most of the AMP called the Indian law, but was also known as a garantía. Over time, this document came to symbolize the AMP's discourse. This does not mean that the Indian law was codified in a single document; it became more of a template for articulating indigenous rights and culture. The document contained selected passages from the Law of the Indies, the colonial legal code, and portions of Titiriku's own petitions to Bolivian ministers and Congress. Even though Titiriku was mostly illiterate, literacy had an important role in the AMP indigenous movement's decolonization project and, in fact, functioned as a way to legitimize his project because of the prestige that written documents already had in indigenous communities. In all of Titiriku's garantías, the essence of the text was the same; they referenced the Law of the Indies and enumerated certain rights based on their status as "first peoples." One passage, for example, states:

> We report in this present certificate that . . . we have read the Law of the Indies and by the way of it understand that . . . [you whites] should not take our lands away; we were here because of the will of the virgin Pachamama. We are Indians, the first peoples. . . . Our languages are Aymara and Quechua. The Law of the Indies said we should not be in the army, nor should we be punished. . . . We should be protected, we should not have the army on our land to exterminate us. Ladies and gentlemen [whites], please note this tradition and see how few Indians remain in this territory of the Audience of Plata [present-day Bolivia] because of this mistreatment. Indians should not be treated as animals. I have testified in the name of good spirits that Indians are victims of abuses and dispossessions. Consequently [I and the AMP] issue this certificate to request that Indians should be protected.[77]

Unlike the garantías that the apoderados in Santos Marka T'ula's network produced, this one was handwritten. Since Titiriku had strong disagreements with the cholos who mostly ran the working-class unions and print houses by then, he refused to ask for their help in printing his own garantías.[78] Instead, he copied the garantías by hand and reproduced them in relatively large quantities.[79] For this reason, versions of this document could be found in the 1980s in diverse indigenous archives held by communities in La Paz, Potosí, and Chuquisaca.[80]

Indigenous peoples used this document in many different ways. For instance, Juan Wallpa from the community of Churumumu (Chuquisaca) used the "Indian law document" against the local hacienda to argue that according to "this document I cannot be obligated [to work] or [be] punish[ed] because I do not pay rent. . . . According this document I am the owner because I am the blood of these lands, so no Spaniard [white

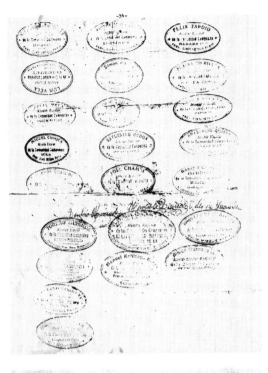

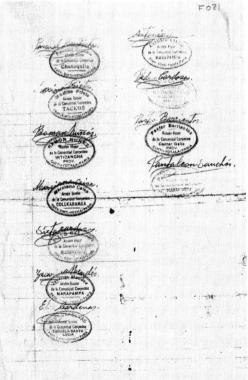

man] should punish me."[81] Like him, many other peons refused to pay rent; this situation led to widespread rebellion in 1947. Most of the AMP indigenous activists, including Melitón Gallardo, Toribio Miranda, and even many others in the later generation of Andrés Jach'aqullu, carried copies of this Indian law in order to contest the hacienda owners and the rural elite.

In another case Eustaquio Philly, an AMP activist in Wayllamarka (La Paz), rejected demands to provide free labor for the construction of another church based on the same garantía.[82] In addition, Philly used the Indian law to argue that they should not work for the church, which he said was the voice of Spain.[83] Titiriku used to argue at meetings that since they held indigenous ceremonies for weddings and baptisms, Indians no longer had to make requests to the Catholic Church.[84] Based on the same law, Pedro Ilaquita, in Santiago Pampa (La Paz), also refused to provide free labor on a new highway between Jach'aqhachi and Ambana.[85] People living in both ayllus and haciendas felt that this document was useful in their struggles. For people in the countryside and indigenous villages, the idea that Indians could no longer be subjected to "forced" labor was the document's principal message. Indigenous peoples were interested in the AMP's Indian law because it showed that Indians had some recourse and some sort of legal support during these difficult times. Titiriku's audience liked to listen to a translated version of the AMP's Indian law documents, which were originally written in Spanish. The idea that the AMP's activism was inspired by the Aymara gods and Pachamama was also attractive to his indigenous audience.[86] While there were many indigenous activists who presented their arguments in liberal, populist, and leftist frames, only the AMP and Titiriku based their ideas on indigenous religiosity and culture prior to 1952.

In 1945 the priest of Sacaca, Potosí, complained during the Sunday Mass that since the AMP were now in the region, some Indians were choosing not to marry in the church and were instead traveling to Oruro and Potosí in order to marry under false priests.[87] He was offended that these Indians would rather marry near the wak'as (Indian deities) instead of the church and asked that they be punished.[88] Soon after, Claudio Pacheco and Celso Paye were detained by the local police and their houses were searched for evidence of their connections to false priests.[89] The police found certain documents that Paye identified as garantías. Pacheco argued that "they indeed follow the Indian law" and complained that the Bolivian laws only teach people to follow Spaniards' laws, which meant "whitening laws."[90] Pacheco also admitted that they married and performed baptisms according to indigenous traditions. Implying that the AMP was helping them practice their culture, he added that with the "Indian law a time has come in which they are truly free."[91] After Pacheco and Paye had been in detention for eight days, the jilaqatas of the Saqaqa region pressured the authorities to set the men free.[92]

In another case, Antonio Garcia and his group of indigenous activists, apoderados, and jilaqatas from Chuquisaca and Potosí tried to enter the main plaza of Oruro in 1937 and were subsequently taken to the police station. The police told them that if they were so interested in using the main plaza, they should go as "a civilized man with a suit and hat . . . and follow the law."[93] Garcia responded that "we follow our Indian law," and thus they should dress according to their traditions and those of their ancestors.[94] These documents were not only used to address labor abuse and land issues but also to affirm the right to practice indigenous religion and to wear indigenous clothes. In some areas community members and peons organized fundraising meetings, or ramas, where indigenous peasants gave contributions, presented their views, and requested support for their causes. In return for their contribution, indigenous peoples would receive copies of the Indian law or garantías. Although most participants were illiterate, these texts were read during community meetings by the all-important escribanos and thus were orally transmitted for use as ammunition in confrontations with the white elite. According to the testimony of Juan Pari from Chuqurasi (Oruro), Indian law documents became handy reference tools when indigenous communities suffered different kinds of abuse from the state, the church, and the hacendados. For Titiriku, this was all part of a larger effort to decolonize the indigenous communities and unify them into a separate Indian republic, a nation of their own. Education, he came to believe, was also critical to this new Indian republic.

Religion, Indigenous Education, and the New Qullasuyu

Both the struggle for education and Protestant expansion took place in Titiriku's native Umasuyus during the 1920s and 1930s, which profoundly shaped his activism. Groups of Adventists and Methodists carried out literacy programs in Janqulaimes. Their work strongly influenced Titiriku, who joined the Methodist Church for a short time in 1926. Titiriku and other indigenous people did not find it difficult to embrace the church during this time because of their commitment to Christian beliefs and recognition of the benefits of combining aspects of Protestantism with traditional Aymara beliefs, such as the worship of Pachamama.[95] These churches either ignored or tried to control this syncretism. Although the Methodist Church, for instance, gradually changed its view about permitting indigenous peoples' belief systems, during the 1930s it encouraged commitment to official church doctrine.

In the 1930s the Methodist Church expanded into several communities of Janqulaimes and began prohibiting its parishioners from worshiping both Pachamama and the Christian God. Titiriku's brother Lorenzo Titiriku and his cousin José María Titiriku, who founded a Methodist church in the Lake Titikaka region, slowly stopped supporting the apoderado movements and the AMP movement in particular because of their personal adherence to the church. In 1935 Titiriku confronted them, arguing that they were "forgetting the good tradition of serving Pachamama, worshiping our lord lightning [qixuqixu wiraxucha] and our mother the water [uma taika]" and were "devoting themselves to the 'Evangelical God.'" Despite his initial involvement with the church, Titiriku strongly disapproved of the Protestant churches' teaching people to reject Aymara gods and goddesses. During August 1935, the month of special worship of Pachamama and the wak'as, he discovered, much to his dismay, that rituals such as the waxt'a (sweet offerings to Pachamama) and luxt'a (llama sacrifices to the Achachilas, the gods in the mountains) had declined in the region of Janqulaimes because the new converts to Methodism were no longer worshipping Pachamama.[96] One way to revive these traditional practices was to make sure that they were reincorporated into community teachings via indigenous schools.

A related factor that influenced Titiriku's activism in the 1930s was the dramatic transformation of the Warisata school that was located in his native Umasuyus. Founded by Elizardo Pérez, Raúl Pérez, and the local Aymara activist Avelino Siñani, Warista's administration and most of its expenses were in the hands of indigenous communities from 1934 to 1939. The founding of this first indigenous school was an act of disobedience against the white ruling elite, which perceived it as threatening the power of hacienda owners of the region.[97] Only the ayllus' defense of the school

FIGURE 4.7. Racialization and dress code in Bolivia. The people portrayed in the photograph are (left to right): Avelino Siñani (an indigenous pro-school activist), Elizardo Perez (the pioneer of the ayllu school), and Mariano Ramos (a mallku of the Aymara ayllu of Warisata). All three men were important actors in the formation of the Escuela Warisata, which, located in the La Paz Department, was the first large school run by Indians in Latin America. Avelino Sinani is dressed as a ch'uta, as signaled by his use of shoes and lack of poncho. In the era prior to 1953 he would have been seen as on the way to becoming a cholo. While Mariano Ramos is dressed as a full Indian, Elizardo Perez, a rural school teacher, was defined as mestizo in that era. Elizardo Pérez, *Warisata, la escuela Ayllu* (Buenos Aires: Burillo, 1962), 158.

and the firm decision of the apoderados and other Aymara chiefs of the region to support it allowed this project to survive. Titiriku thought that the Warisata experience could "help our race to flourish."[98] Because of his commitment to the network of Santos Marka T'ula, in the late 1920s he believed that the politics of literacy could help indigenous peoples. However, the failure of this strategy made Titiriku change his opinion by the late 1930s.

When Warisata became a clear success in 1939, the national government took over the school. This stemmed from a new belief, supported by the Left and later by President Gualberto Villarroel, who was in a political alliance with the Movimiento Nacionalista Revolucionario (MNR), that indigenous people should have state-sponsored education.[99] The Warisata school seemed like a good place to start, since the government argued that the communities could no longer support it financially. Under state sponsorship the school became a symbol of dependency on the state, making a mockery of its original purpose: to enhance communal autonomy.[100] This situation disappointed Titiriku, who compared it to "the colonial Spanish who came to rob our lands and nation. The public school will damage us in the same way."[101] He believed that the government was not providing public schools unconditionally and that it would later request that communities "pay back" their expenses. Urging indigenous communities to reject public schools, he argued that "Spaniards do not give anything for free. If you do not believe it, ask our grandparents. We are selling ourselves out. The whites will come back as owners of not only your lands, but also of yourselves."[102]

Titiriku saw the assimilationist policies that would put Bolivia under one school system as a mistake. He preferred a segregationist system of autonomous indigenous schools (escuelas particulares), which would be small, private, and experimental schools that would offer autonomy for Indians. As the idea of establishing schools became popular with indigenous people, Titiriku proposed that escuelas particulares should be created, that "they will prepare the people to achieve our dream . . . to organize the Republic of Qullasuyu. . . . The Achachilas and our Pachamama, the virgin, will rejoice in happiness seeing how we rise again."[103] Titiriku argued that the best way to promote this policy was to publicize President Germán Busch's decree of 1936, which ordered hacienda owners to promote education for Indians by founding and financially supporting elementary schools (escuelas particulares). Titiriku discovered this decree as soon it was published thanks to his frequent visits to the National Public Office for Information, known as the Gaceta Pública. Although the decree was vague and not widely disseminated, Gregorio Titiriku considered it useful for legally supporting community-controlled schools. In other words, for AMP indigenous activists such as Titiriku, escuelas particulares meant autonomous indigenous schools, while for the government the term meant elementary schools controlled by the state. Titiriku thus subverted governmental discourse and imbued it with his own meaning, to his own ends.[104]

In the 1930s the rural elite believed that the very the idea of escuelas particulares was dangerous. Hacendados were opposed to the idea of educating Indians, and earlier schools in the countryside had been considered "seriously subversive."[105] It was not until the 1940s that some white public intellectuals admitted that Indians should be educated; however, they believed this education should focus on the skills essential for fieldwork rather than on providing training that would allow Indians to become doctors or lawyers. These intellectuals argued that Indians would be good for industrial labor but not intellectual or professional endeavors.[106] Titiriku, on the other hand, used the decree of 1936 and the AMP organization to promote schools throughout the countryside and, in the process, to discuss the Indian law and faith in Pachamama and the Achachilas.[107]

Indeed, with the escuelas particulares, Titiriku sought to enhance Indian nationalism and to teach "the path of Qullasuyu peoples." Although Toribio Miranda, the founder of the AMP, started promoting escuelas particulares, Titiriku imbued them with a clear nationalist content, calling on them to "empower the blood of Qullasuyu." In contrast to Miranda, Titiriku did not just want the escuelas particulares to teach in native languages but also to promote Indianness.[108] In other words, Titiriku wanted the schools to teach the Indian law: "We should pray with faith and devotion to the Achachilas on the tops of mountains where the wak'as are, and say, Achachilas and Pachamama, give light to our hearts and fortify us with your will. . . . Only your will makes us strong. We are your children poor and crying . . . we are the blood of Qullasuyu."[109]

Titiriku believed that making requests on the top of the mountains to Pachamama and the Achachilas would "fortify" Indians to construct the "Republic of Qullasuyu" and confront the whites of Bolivia.[110] To lead the new schools, he started to appoint alcaldes particulares in different parts of the country. By 1944, 489 communities and ayllus throughout the country had founded escuelas particulares under Titiriku's sponsorship. While few of them really achieved the goal of teaching writing and reading skills, their existence reflected the impact of his discourse on indigenous communities and the way that the idea of two republics' separate educational systems made sense to Titiriku's audience in the communities. Based on the ideas of early Indian nationalists such as Zárate Willka, which he learned from Miranda and Feliciano Inka Marasa, Titiriku insisted that the Qullasuyu should be reorganized into nations. Using oral history as his source, he applied these ideas to the organization of the escuelas particulares, which were modeled on fifteenth-century Aymara nations. Although some "nations" were similar to current historical regions such as Umasuyus, he also reinvented others under nineteenth-century provincial names. For instance, the Qaranqas region was called Paria in his discourse and the historical Pacajes was called Inquisivi (Inqasiwi).[111] Disseminating these ideas, Titiriku required that every alcalde have a stamp that represented one of the nations of Qullasuyu. For example, the Umasuyus stamp had his name, his wife's name, and an inscription of the Umasuyus nation.[112]

The transformation of his native Umasuyus that emerged after the tumultuous Chaco War gave Titiriku a new audience. Based on Aymara oral history, his Qullasuyu nationalism gave the AMP an audience of indigenous ayllus and hacienda peons. Titiriku used his basic literacy skills, as well as his knowledge of city life, to enhance his nationalist perspectives and impact. He constructed an ethnic discourse that he used to counter the claims of the elite to power and organized a structure to promote it in the countryside. He actively associated ideas like "the blood of Qullasuyu," including qhuchapuchus, montepuchus, and chullpapuchus, with racialization. Whenever a group of alcaldes particulares came to La Paz, Titiriku liked to keep the group there for several days, talking with them about how to worship the Achachilas in the sites of wak'as and how to organize weddings and other acts that would promote Aymara religion. Titiriku told them: "We are creating escuelas particulares . . . to educate our people in the path of the *ley de indios* so that they can know our way of life, the Indian law, the *ama sua, ama llulla,* and *ama khella* [do not rob, do not lie, and do not be lazy]. They should not follow the path of cholos, the path that makes people Spaniard [white]. They should follow the Republic of Qullasuyu."[113] The ancient Andean moral code, what Titiriku refers to here as "the Indian law," was very much alive in the oral tradition of indigenous history and the culture of the twentieth century, and he thus incorporated into the Indian law discourse that he was developing and distributing. Also critical to the Indian law, both in terms of retaining or recovering Indigenous ways of life and in disseminating its ideas, were women.

The Roles of Titiriku's Wives in Constructing His Leadership

Titiriku's path again shows us how male leaders in the indigenous world depended on women's spheres of power, both in terms of access to land and the power of kinship in the Andean world. Titirikus' first wife, Santusa Mamani, was originally from Pacharia, which was a large ayllu; she belonged to a family with a great deal of land and whose members frequently achieved high community posts, which gave them considerable influence in the region. Pacharia was also an "original" ayllu, which meant it traced its history back to pre-Hispanic times. Within the Janqulaimes marka, Pacharia was considered to be *aransaya* (upper side), which meant it was a fully Aymara ayllu,[114] whereas members of the *urinsaya* (lower side) Qajiata were descendents of Aymara and Uru communities. Because his wife Santusa was an only child, Tititriku worked in a community post called a *cargo*. Community cargos were usually passed down from one man to the next in the Aymara community, unless there is no man in the household. This was important because it helped Titiriku build a larger web and hold leadership rolls in both communities, Pacharia and Qajiata. He started his work as jilaqata, then moved up to *segunda mayor*, which means the older brother of an ayllu faction of the region, and finally was appointed alcalde mayor, which was a regional post that commanded all the jilaqatas of Janqulaimes.[115] Santusa Mamani's networks reveal the importance of kinship ties for indigenous activists during this time, and they demonstrate women's role in the indigenous struggle as shapers of the networks and context in which indigenous men acted. Titiriku's story reveals a richly gendered history of how men in agrarian societies have the power of mobility and negotiate the construction of their masculine identity through a web of relationships with women and with other men.

After quitting the cholo workforce in 1930, Gregorio Titiriku worked as a mule driver, which was usually a job performed by urban Indians unwilling to cholify. Titiriku separated from Santusa Mamani, who remained in her village community with their three children, while he began to spend more and more time in the city of La Paz.[116] In the 1940s he married Rosa Ramos, with whom he had seven children. An Aymara from the ayllu of

FIGURE 4.8. Members of the AMP network during a visit to the president of the Universidad Mayor de San Andrés, La Paz, Bolivia, circa 1950s. Andrés Jach'aqullu and Gregorio Titiriku are standing. Archivo Privado de Tomás Quevedo, Chuquisaca.

Chukiawu, Rosa's father owned a small slaughterhouse near La Paz. Titiriku's ability to move smoothly between countryside and city increased over the years, since his close ties to his in-laws provided him with a strong hold in La Paz while he retained his leadership role in Qajiata. No other alcalde particular managed to establish such good connections in the city as Titiriku did in the 1940s, in no small part because Rosa owned several lots of land in the suburbs of La Paz. Titiriku bankrolled his activism by helping his wife with her work as a street vendor and petty butcher in the popular neighborhood of El Cementerio in La Paz.[117] His most important activism developed during this era, when his daily routine consisted of helping his wife and father-in-law Ezequiel Ramos set up their business.

After having breakfast in the streets of El Cementerio, he then visited officials to pursue issues related to indigenous communities.

Following Aymara gender norms, Ramos kept her economic and social independence by retaining her last name and her properties. Although she did not have a central role in the AMP, she provided food and shelter for many visiting alcaldes, participated in the movement's events, and provided financial support.[118] She sometimes appealed to her best-known customers in El Cementerio for help with her husband's movement. One of these was the Bolivian governmental official Luis Navia, who had worked on indigenous education issues and would later become known as an indigenista.[119] Ramos asked him to help Titiriku with his paperwork and to introduce him to public intellectuals such as Fernando Diez de Medina and Gamaliel Churata, a group of indigenistas that would later publish a magazine called *Kollasuyu*. Since Titiriku was only semiliterate and was inundated with paperwork, these connections and this assistance proved extremely helpful.[120] This complementarity between Ramos and Titiriku is representative of the Aymara view of gender roles, in which women and men share responsibilities and duties.

Perhaps because his two wives had played such a pivotal role in his leadership and in shaping his activism, Titiriku promoted women's participation among the AMP. While the leftist unions were mostly in the hands of men and Santos Marka T'ula's indigenous network did not attempt to include women, Titiriku insisted that women attend the AMP's meetings. In the early 1940s he changed the AMP stamp seals so that they included women's names. His own stamp was changed to read: "Gregorio Titirico–Rosa Ramos, Alcalde Mayor, Paria–Chuquiago."[121] In his years in La Paz, Tiritiku constructed indigenous networks through relationships with his wives, who provided him with kinship ties as well as occasional financial help. His first wife helped him initiate his activist career, while his second wife strongly supported him; these gendered relationships shaped his indigenous activism.

Among the subaltern groups in Bolivia, racial segregation worked differently for women and men. Cholo and Indian men faced strong pressure to reject their Indianness by changing their style of dress, while chola and Indian women were allowed to retain external signs of their Indian heritage. In the gendered culture of twentieth century Bolivia as elsewhere, woman is also a signifier of ethnic identity.[122] By emphasizing the suit and hat as the only appropriate dress for men, the elite implied that males had to be the bearers of modernity and power. In this sense the history of Indian men in La Paz differs from other cases in Latin America, such as Quetzaltenango (Guatemala). According to Greg Grandin's account, Maya K'iche' men were not pressured to change their dress.[123] On the other hand, the situation of Indian women in urban areas, including the Aymara cholas of La Paz and the Maya K'iche' women in Quetzaltenango, were similar.[124] They had to reproduce their subaltern condition in society by using ethnic dress to signify their ethnic identity.

The Role of Indigenous Religion in Challenging the System

Gregorio Titiriku confronted the conditions of coloniality in many ways, one being to advocate for the separation of Bolivian society. Titiriku worked within a system of segregation because it was all that he knew and because he saw aspects of it as beneficial to his audience. Living in La Paz in the 1920s, Titiriku saw the cholos as a group that was attempting to "become" white. He interpreted this as part of the nation-making process, which reinforced his decolonizing agenda of creating a separate jaqi nationalism. This decolonization project developed out of his grassroots upbringing and experiences in La Paz when he was sent there by the ayllus of Janqulaimes. As an activist intellectual, Titiriku crafted his discourse on Indian law in response to colonial conditions that were particularly linked to racialization. Titiriku experienced restrictions against entering the main plaza, boarding streetcars, eating in restaurants, and going to the cinema because he was an Indian and refused to shed the clothing that marked him as such. The emergence of legislated segregation in Bolivia represented a quest for modernity that was expressed through practices like prohibiting Indians and cholas from riding streetcars, banning Indians from the central plaza, prohibiting Indian street vendors, and controlling the overall circulation of indigenous people in the cities. Through such policies, the ruling elite attempted to domesticate the country's populace, the vast majority of which was Indian. The hegemonic elite developed an authoritarian version of modernity that denigrated Indianness and could be used as an instrument of domestication and self-empowerment for the white-mestizo minority.[125]

This was Titiriku's negative experience of urban life in La Paz; he was rejected by the city and saw other AMP activists and indigenous people being constantly degraded. La Paz, despite its mestizo roots, was deeply mired in the colonial legacy, which made it view the Indian population from a very hierarchical perspective.[126] As a response to racialization, Gregorio Titi-riku promoted worshipping Pachamama and the Achachilas and dressing in native style to express jaqi pride. Because religion was central to his decolonization project, the right to practice it freely was also critical. Ti-tiriku was thus a strong proponent of conducting Andean religious wed-dings and Indian baptisms. In 1939 he officiated at the wedding of Pedro Mamani and Cayetana Ikiapasa, both from Pukarani (La Paz), which took place at the site of one of the wak'as just outside the city.[127] After offering prayers to Pachamama and the local Achachila, the spirit of the grand-parents of the site, he declared the couple married.[128] That same month he organized seventeen weddings and gave the couples a "certificate" for the service. In December 1943 he celebrated another five weddings and twenty-one baptisms.[129] Marriage and baptismal ceremonies were cru-cial to Titiriku's activism because he believed that colonization was most deeply seated in religion and the church. Thus, celebrating these events with Aymara rituals instead was a critical step in decolonizing the lives of indigenous people.

Tititirku and the AMP also constructed a network of cells, which in 1940 numbered 489 throughout the Andean world. Many of these cells were organized in Chuquisaca and northern Potosí among the apodera-dos of ayllus and hacienda peons familiar with the AMP. In contrast to the other AMP activist intellectuals profiled in this book, Titiriku was much more involved in the urban public sphere. He visited newspapers, judicial buildings, lawyers' offices, and various state offices, such as the prefectura (governor's office), the Patronato de Indias (Indian Affairs Office), as it was called before the Chaco War, and, later, the Office of Indigenous Af-fairs in the Education Ministry. After his marriage to Rosa Ramos, Titiriku became a member of the Chamoco Chico ayllu, one of the urban ayllus of the suburbs of La Paz, where he worked one of the small fields that be-longed to his wife's family. This meant he did not need to negotiate an urban jaqi identity like other migrants. He could live there but completely retain his separate indigenous identity. First, he lived in a segregated rural space, then in an urban space that was segregated from white and mes-tizo neighborhoods such as Sopocachi or Miraflores. This is why the idea of two separate republics—one Indian, the other white—made sense to him and figured prominently in his decolonization project.

From 1936 to 1952 Titiriku mostly remained in La Paz and sometimes ran into members of the apoderados network led by Santos Marka T'ula. Occasionally the two factions encountered each other in the state offices while filing paperwork, sometimes exchanging confrontational words but not much else. Titiriku and Santos Marka T'ula's relationship was irreparably damaged, and the two leaders slowly lost contact, even though the two factions attended several of the same political events. Marka T'ula also slowly faded from the activist scene as he quickly aged and finally died in 1948. Titiriku was in contact with other AMP activists through *emisarios* (emissaries, or AMP local activists), so he very infrequently left La Paz after 1940. Still, he always went to Janqulaimes every year for the harvest season, except in 1947 and 1948 when the tense political situation in Bolivia forced him to stay in La Paz. He also organized the arrival of indigenous delegations from Chuquisaca and Potosí for the National Indigenous Congress of 1945, thus taking on a national leadership role. Melitón Gallardo, profiled in the next chapter, worked in southern Bolivia and provided critical regional leadership to the expanding AMP network through the idea of ethnic indigenous pluralism. His story helps us understand the relationship between the regional and the national leadership within the AMP.

Chapter Five

Between Internal Colonialism and War

Melitón Gallardo in the Southern Andean Estates

On the night of November 13, 1946, an assassin entered the *chuxlla* (a seasonal indigenous housing structure in the fields) in Icla where the clandestine indigenous activist Melitón Gallardo was sleeping hidden among the fieldworkers. The killer, who managed to stab Gallardo in the stomach, had been hired by Anselmo Cusolich, the administrator of Sumala hacienda. With one hand on his stomach to staunch the bleeding, Gallardo saved his own life by pushing the assassin away and running for help. The attack did not harm his digestive system, so Gallardo attributed his almost miraculous recovery to indigenous medicine and to the protection provided by the hacienda's indigenous peons. Although this assistance saved his life, he later received more medical attention in Tarabuco, where he denounced Cusolich for "trying to kill him."[1]

Between 1946 and 1951 the hacendados in various regions of Bolivia attempted to maintain control over the Indian population by eliminating indigenous activists like Melitón Gallardo. After the brief pro-Indian government of Gualberto Villarroel between December 1943 and July 1946, the conservatives, under Enrique Hertzog and then Mamerto Urriolagoitia, returned to power in Bolivia, repressing the labor and indigenous movements that had flourished during the previous years.[2] Most importantly, the hacendados tried to prevent frequent indigenous rebellions by eliminating their leadership.[3] In the case of indigenous activists like the Alcaldes Mayores Particulares (AMP), the hacendados resorted to racialized accusations about their activities. For instance, some Tarabuco hacendados decided that indigenous activists were not actually "Indians" but rather cholos or ch'utas from Sucre and Tarabuco.[4] These accusations were meant to justify the elimination of activist leadership and to delegitimize their role in indigenous peasant rebellions. In the late 1940s these accusations gradually spread to other regions of the country, including Icla and Cinti (Chuquisaca), Misk'i and Campero (Cochabamba), and Qaraqullo (Oruro). The hacendados also argued that the activists were not originally from the region and that the "only thing that they wanted was to raise money for their own benefit."[5] On other occasions these activists were accused of being "mine workers" or indigenous peasants from the high valleys of Cochabamba.

In the case of Melitón Gallardo, the hacienda manager Anselmo Cusolich argued that Gallardo was not an Indian and that he only wore "Indian costumes" to incite the peons when "actually he is a ch'uta,"[6] meaning someone who was making the switch from Indian to cholo. In fact, Gallardo had originally dressed as a ch'uta in 1939 when he arrived at Icla's haciendas with a group of indigenous peasants from Tarabuco who were seeking to rent grassland to feed their animals. Another accusation against Gallardo was that he made false promises to Indians, convincing them to rebel and demand "rights" that did not "correspond to the truth."[7]

Gallardo was not the only indigenous activist or alcalde particular who dressed like a ch'uta and was accused of not being Indian. Other indigenous activists had even worse experiences in other parts of the country. In Puqujatha (northern Potosí) Carlos Condori was hanged by the rural elite (vecinos de pueblo). They orchestrated his murder because they believed that indigenous activists such as Condori posed a danger to "civilized citizens."[8] To cite another example, Marcelino Mamani was killed by the hacendado Antonio Guide when he defended indigenous peasants by intervening in a conflict between the landowner and peons in Inqawasi (Chuquisaca).[9] In both of these cases, the activists were called either ch'utas or cholos and accused of engaging in subversive work among the Indians.

In this chapter I argue that caste, class, and race in the cities and countryside of southern Bolivia overlapped to form an internal colonialism that shaped the life of Melitón Gallardo, an AMP activist. Gallardo grew up on an hacienda, but he went through a series of personal transformations—from peon to soldier to chuta—and then on to strong identification with his indigenous roots. This history informed the way he used cultural translation to create a regional variation of earth politics in Chuquisaca. As in other regions, the elite in southern Bolivia tended to racialize and interpret Indians based on their regional or local ethnic dress and peasant status, so they did not usually consider urban Indians indigenous. Even for a local indigenous audience, indigenous activists with urban experiences, including Melitón Gallardo, had to provide racial markers to situate themselves in the Indian world. Without these markers their urban experiences cast them as cholos (which, in the first half of twentieth century, essentially meant not being Indian). When Indians left the countryside, they left their racial identity behind. The story of Melitón Gallardo, one of the most representative AMP indigenous intellectuals of 1940s, illustrates everyday forms of cultural translation and negotiation in the production of political discourse, and it shows how he drew on notions of race as a means to resist hacienda oppression.

The Rural Caste System in Chuquisaca

Although Melitón Gallardo was raised to reject his Indianness, he emerged as one of the key actors in AMP politics from 1940 to 1950. His mother, Dominga Gallardo, a young Indian woman from the community of Tapalilla (Oropeza, Chuquisaca), fell in love with Carlos Saavedra, a mestizo man of higher status, and Gallardo was born from their relationship. Dominga had to conceal who her child's father was, both because her own father would have been very angry to discover that she had been involved with a mestizo man and because Carlos Saavedra refused to accept paternity prior to Gallardo's birth.[10] Without the support of her widowed father, she felt ostracized from her community and had to deal with her pregnancy alone. Late one afternoon in 1915, Dominga gave birth while working as a shepherdess in the fields. Although she hid her baby for a few days, she soon gave him up because she could not face her kin and community as a single mother.[11]

Following the local tradition that the father's mother should care for an undesired child, Mercedes Calvimontes, Saavedra's mother, decided to take care of Gallardo. In order to avoid a public scandal for her son, and to leave him with a "clean" record in the eyes of the town and potential wives, she said the child was an orphan she had adopted to help her, since she was a *piquera*, a hardworking widow with her own small plot of land (as opposed to a hacienda peon).[12] Five years later Calvimontes finally saw her son married to a chola woman as she had originally wanted. Thus, she raised her grandson without recognizing his parentage, and Gallardo remained her *yanapaku*, or sharecropper, the entire time he lived with her. Although he knew from local gossip that he was her grandson, he never confronted Calvimontes about it until the year she died.[13]

Calvimontes and her son Saavedra were, in terms of racial background, mostly Indian; however, they very strongly identified as mestizos. Calvimontes's father was an indigenous peasant who had used his savings from working in northern Argentina to buy his plot in the 1890s from the hacienda. The family's mestizo identity dovetailed with contemporary local and national identity patterns, as only ayllu members or hacienda peons were defined as indigenous. Not wanting to be seen as indigenous, small holders and piqueros defined themselves as rural or new cholos and modified their dress to signify a nonindigenous identity.[14]

Although Gallardo was raised by his grandmother, his registration record from when he joined the army fifteen years later shows that he retained his mother's last name. Rather than dressing as a cholo like his grandmother, he dressed as an Indian to signify that he did not have a kinship relationship with her and to indicate servitude and dependency. As was common for servants of the era, Gallardo used to sleep with the dogs and horses. He understood that he was treated this way because he was born to an "Indian woman who belonged to an ayllu."[15] During his childhood, Gallardo helped his grandmother shepherd her animals, and she mostly fed him kitchen scraps, as cholos usually did with Indians. In his older years Gallardo said the fact that his father did not marry his mother because she was Indian was the most striking event of his childhood. Gallardo knew very little about his mother since he only saw her a few times in his life.[16] Although he was always thankful to his grandmother for raising him, he remembered his childhood as the saddest period of his life. Even his service in the Chaco War did not pain him as much.

As her father wanted, Dominga Gallardo later married a member of her own ethnic group. She had two other children while Melitón Gallardo was being raised by his grandmother, and she died in childbirth when he was still a boy. Gallardo did not meet his mother's relatives until many years later when he became an indigenous activist. When Mercedes Calvimontes died in 1933, her children, including Gallardo's father, came home to divide her possessions. His father neither recognized him legally as his son nor did he treat him as such, so Gallardo took his inheritance (two ponchos and one blanket) and moved to Sucre and dressed as an Indian *jalqa* (with long braids, colorful poncho, sheep's wool pants, and llama sandals).[17]

Relationships between people of different "races" were shaped by caste status during Gallardo's childhood. Dominga Gallardo's father did not want his daughter to get involved with a mestizo man because he knew that it was unlikely that a mestizo would marry his daughter; he wanted to secure her safety through marriage to an Indian man. On the other hand, Mercedes Calvimontes was worried that her son, by marrying an Indian, would lose the caste status that her father and family had taken such pains to earn. These concerns illustrate how cholos and mestizos racialized their caste relationship, which relied on Indians occupying a lower rung on the social ladder. We can see that in 1940s Bolivia race structured relationships in ways that reproduced colonial ideas of inequality. In the early twentieth century, these caste and race signifiers were especially reinforced in the marginal areas of Bolivia, such as the southern countryside of Chuquisaca. The preservation of caste status was of special concern to rural elites because it was crucial to maintaining their power and esteem in a highly racialized society. These were the structures of internal colonialism that shaped the lives of Melitón Gallardo and his parents. Consequently, eradicating these racialized forms of coloniality became central in Gallardo's life and explains why he so firmly embraced the AMP's project of decolonization.

A History of Internal Colonialism during the Chaco War

Throughout 1933, indigenous people were drafted for the Chaco War, and while many indigenous men resisted the draft, Gallardo actually volunteered because he felt that he had little to lose and that no one would miss him. He was sent to the front as a private and was promptly captured by the enemy. While a prisoner of the Paraguayan Army, he worked in the hacienda fields of the Paraguayan elite.[18] Among his fellow prisoners was the future president of Bolivia Gualberto Villarroel, who would later promote pro-Indian policies, including the abolition of servitude. Exposing Gallardo for the first time to discussions of social issues and inequality in

Bolivia, Villarroel made such a strong impression on the young man that when Villarroel became president, Gallardo tried unsuccessfully to visit him.[19]

During his imprisonment in Paraguay, Gallardo raised cattle and soon gained his supervisor's praise.[20] This conferred some power upon him in the eyes of the mestizos, who knew nothing about harvesting or irrigation. Gallardo's expertise meant that he occasionally received extra food and secondhand clothing as a reward for his hard work. At night the Bolivian mestizo prisoners talked about the need to change the Bolivian political system, and Gallardo gradually joined them in these discussions.[21]

When the Paraguayans asked Gallardo about his background, he told them that he was an Indian. Several, mostly Guarani-speaking, Paraguayans asked him, "Why did you come? This is not your war, why are you fighting?"[22] The Paraguayans believed that the war should not be a conflict between Indians, which inspired Gallardo to think more deeply about his place in Bolivian society. The Bolivian prisoners also discussed the fact that Bolivia had a caste system, that the country was ruled by a tiny elite, and that Indians were totally disenfranchised. These discussions made Gallardo recognize that, as an Indian, he was not even considered a citizen of his own country; instead he was more of a colonial subject, and this realization helped him to understand why he could not enter white areas of Sucre, such as the main plaza.[23]

After the Chaco War ended in Bolivia's defeat, the military staged a successful coup in 1936, and Gallardo returned to Sucre, where he realized that his status had changed. Veterans were highly respected in society and were thus able to cross some social barriers. In his military uniform, Gallardo was seen as a hero, and his Indianness became invisible.[24] Going downtown was an eye-opening experience for him:

> I went all dressed in my Chaco war veteran uniform to downtown Sucre, and went into a bar for whites near the main plaza. At the beginning I was afraid to be there, thinking that they would ask me to leave right away. But they did not; they even asked what I wanted to drink, and when I asked for a beer, the white owner brought it to me and served me. The Army had given me five bolivianos and I was happy to spend it in that place. . . . An older white gentleman came to me and said, "you men did a good job in the war," and gave me a hug. I really liked how people treated me and I thought people would

never treat me like that if I were to dress as a jalqa. My Chaco War uniform helped now.[25]

Gallardo considered his experience in the war to be a rite of passage. Contrasting his experiences as a common Indian to how he was treated as a war veteran, he decided not to dress as an Indian anymore because he felt that it was "limiting his advancement."[26] Dressed as a ch'uta (a new cholo), Gallardo secured a job in a bakery, where he soon recognized the limitations of his veteran advantages. He spoke Spanish poorly and with a strong Quechua accent, so when he applied for a job at the Chuquisaca Prefecture, he was rejected because of his poor language skills, despite the fact that the military regime of late 1937 wanted preference given to war veterans. Deep in his heart, he knew he was rejected because he was Quechua, particularly since the post was taken by a mestizo who spoke Spanish fluently.[27] He did enjoy some privileges as a ch'uta, however. When Presidents Peñaranda and Herzog restricted the circulation of indigenous peasants in the 1940s, but allowed ch'utas or rural cholos to travel freely, Gallardo took advantage of the opportunity.[28] Nonetheless, within this racial structure ch'utas were not able to get government jobs in urban services.

Like some other cholos and Indians, Gallardo joined the Escuela Ferrer, a continuing-education program in Sucre, which had workshops for workers interested in leadership and literacy and was run by anarchists linked to the International Anarchist Organization in Buenos Aires. The Escuela Ferrer, later named the Escuela Popular, was started by Estanislao Ari and Rafael Chavez. Opened in the 1920s, it had become an important place for workers and indigenous activists. There Gallardo learned about anarchist ideology and, in one session during late 1939, he met several apoderados and learned about Toribio Miranda and Gregorio Titiriku for the first time.[29] Several distinguished anarchists, such as Domingo Chumacero and Daniel Aru, also belonged to the school. It was through this forum that several indigenous activists from Tarabuco encouraged Gallardo to engage in petty trade in the Icla Valley. Community activists used these trade relationships to distribute anarchist and leftist flyers from the indigenous highland apoderados to the Icla hacienda peons; this combination of activities appealed to Gallardo.[30]

Gallardo processed the ideas he read in the indigenous handouts and framed them in ways that addressed the problems of Icla's hacienda peons, thus elaborating a regional AMP discourse. Gallardo was especially interested in learning more about the myth of the Achachilas, or the good spirits in the Aymara religion, who were believed to live in the high mountains of Saxama in Oruro. He had listened to these legends when he was a child in the hacienda of Palqa (Chuquisaca). Indigenous peoples of the communities of Porras and Marasa (Chuquisaca) told him that he should contact Toribio Miranda, who knew the myths of Qaranqas peoples, which he did when he visited Sucre in 1940.[31]

They did meet, but Miranda did not trust Gallardo because he dressed as a ch'uta, spoke Spanish, and was no longer considered Indian.[32] To avoid him, Miranda suggested they meet in his village in the Oruro highlands and then failed to show up. However, Miranda's rejection did not discourage Gallardo. In 1941 he went to La Paz and Oruro and visited not only Miranda but also other indigenous activists such as Santos Marka T'ula.[33] His trip to the Altiplano enhanced his activism because he learned the oral history of his ethnic community. Gallardo returned to the Icla region with the oral history of the Qaranqas, ideas about the Indian law, and many documents about activist work in the highlands.[34] Gallardo expanded his work with the Icla-Tarwita AMP, at which point Miranda finally accepted Gallardo and asked him to help organize the regions of Icla and Tarwita, where abuse against indigenous peons was rampant.[35] By this time Miranda already had a network of two hundred cells in haciendas and communities, and the ayllus consulted with him frequently about indigenous politics.

Gallardo's life demonstrates the radical shifts in identity that were possible during the early twentieth century and the racialized implications of each transformation. He went from being a jalqa Indian to a war veteran and then from a ch'uta to an activist. When he was a jalqa Indian, Gallardo could not enter the white areas of Sucre and was forced to live apart from the urban world, but in his military uniform he was suddenly welcome in white spaces. As a ch'uta, moreover, he was no longer considered Indian. These identities were externalized through dress codes, which were emblems of internal colonialism. Gallardo's life helps us to understand the changes in racial hierarchy during the 1930s and 1940s, when the ideas of race that strictly relegated all Indians to the lower strata began to break down, something that was almost impossible before the Chaco War. However, those barriers were not strictly determined by dress, as shown by the fact that when Gallardo changed his clothing, he encountered new bar riers: language and the association of Indians with the countryside and whites with urbanity and power. Indigenous veterans spearheaded the collapse of the caste system after the Chaco War, which prompted the restructuring of the racial system from segregationist to integrationist, meaning that cholos and ch'utas could gain some access to the working classes if their Spanish language skills were adequate.

Economic Change on the Haciendas and Chuquisaca's Indian Law

The AMP movement, his own life experiences, and his particular regional audience profoundly shaped Gallardo's politics. While Miranda focused on differentiating the AMP from the caciques apoderados of Santos Marka T'ula, and Titiriku spread and further defined the Indian law discourse, Gallardo emphasized Chuquisaca's ethnic connections with the highlands, especially the jach'a Carangas religious tradition. Indeed, during Gallardo's trips to Oruro and La Paz, he learned that the indigenous movement's strongholds were in the highland ayllus. Miranda gave Gallardo the mission of spreading the AMP movement among the peons of Icla and Tarwita.[36] And on Titiriku's orders Gallardo was to bring the Indian law (which Gallardo more pointedly defined as the message of Pachamama and the Achachilas) to the specific needs of the peons of Icla and Tarwita, reworking Titiriku and Miranda's discourse for the local audiences of the valleys of Chuquisaca.[37] Gallardo emphasized that the suffering that peons endured in the hacienda required a different focus than what he referred to as Titiriku and Miranda's focus on "laws and the government."[38]

Icla was an ecologically diverse region with the huge haciendas of Soroma and Sumala, where Gallardo already had connections. Peons from Icla were originally from both highland and lowland ethnic groups, as the region was a frontier for several Aymara ayllus, particularly the Qaranqas, Qillaqas, and Chichas ayllus, which had their nuclei in Oruro and Potosí. The lowland Indians were mostly Tuminas, a group that formed part of the Guaranís.[39] During the colonial era many other indigenous peoples from the highlands had moved to Icla haciendas to escape the heavy burden of service in the mines imposed on the ayllus by the mita servitude, from which the haciendas were exempt. In 1940 peons on all thirty-nine haciendas spoke Quechua but continued to be influenced by the ethnic heritage and oral history of Qaranqas and Quillaqas.[40] It was common to hear mention of myths from the Qaranqas and Qillaqas nations (Oruro) in the ayllu enclaves of Icla and Tarwita (Chuquisaca). In other words, the fact that they were Quechua-speaking peons did not keep them from being receptive to discourses based in Aymara religion and especially in devotion to Pachamama.[41]

In the 1930s Icla's haciendas fetched good prices on the real estate market in Chuquisaca because they were close to Sucre, connected by a relatively good highway, and produced a variety of goods such as grapes, oranges, barley, and potatoes.[42] These haciendas were owned by the most important members of southern Bolivia's white elite, among them the Arana, Argandoña, Zilvetti, Urioste, and Reyes families, who mostly lived in Sucre, La Paz, and Europe. Some of the owners sold property to the mestizo rural elite of Tarabuco, such as Mario Gorena and Ignacio Estrada, while others put the largest haciendas under foreign administration. Andrés Cusolich, an Italian citizen, purchased Sumala hacienda, and Suruma hacienda went to Mark Guide, a Dutch citizen that the Argandoña family had met in Europe. Gallardo and the AMP called all members of this group "Spaniards" and viewed them as the antithesis of the Indian peoples.[43]

These new administrators and owners instituted important changes in the hacienda economy between 1920 and 1930. In the Ch'awarani hacienda the Gorena family intensified the production of barley for sale to a Sucre brewery, while Guide and Cusolich increased the production of grapes to make wine called Vinos Soroma, which found a considerable market in Sucre and Potosí. These changes transformed labor relations, forcing peons to work more days for the hacienda and, in many cases, fewer days on their own fields. The peons were also forced to relinquish good lands for the hacienda to grow more grapes.[44]

It was in this context of intense economic change that Melitón Gallardo arrived in the late 1930s, carrying the AMP's message to the hacienda peons by using his prestige as a Chaco War veteran and his connections with the highland Aymara mallkus and apoderados, who were much admired by the peons.[45] Bringing food and other gifts, people came at night to hear Gallardo's opinions about the relationship between peons and hacienda owners. Because the Ch'awarani, Churumatas, Sumala, and Suruma haciendas had all had frequent labor confrontations since the 1910s, the peons were eager to listen to new ideas about how to handle these conflicts. The mallkus of the highlands were famous in Icla for supporting confrontations with highland haciendas and for their success in stopping hacienda expansion. When Gallardo started visiting the Icla region in early 1939, he went to the Churumatas, Suruma, and Cantar Gallo haciendas, where he met the activists José Chambi, Andrés Tik'a, and Luis Vela from the ayllus of Tarabuco, all of whom were closely associated with Toribio Miranda and Santos Marka T'ula.[46] According to a letter sent from Francisco Rivera to Toribio Miranda in 1941, Gallardo was presenting himself as "someone who speaks with the cabecillas of the highlands" and as "someone who knows how to solve the Indians' problems."[47]

Gallardo used Qaranqas's ethnic historical metaphors to construct his political platform in Icla. One of these myths argued that "Saxama Achachila [the spirit of Saxama mountain] is coming back to restore the unity among Aymaras and Quechuas. The power of Saxama is so strong that it will shake the world. [For instance,] the broken head of the Mururata Mountain will be restored, as the power of the Qullasuyus will be victorious and the blood of our land will be refreshed . . . and the domination of whites will end. . . . Then, Saxama will rest in peace and the [spirit] of the wak'as . . . will get relief after so much suffering."[48] Gallardo spoke about the Saxama Achachilas (Oruro) and the wak'as spirits because the memory of Saxama was still present among the peoples of Icla in the 1940s. The cult of Saxama spirituality was as important in oral religiosity in this region as it was in Gallardo's native Puxpu (Oruro). Gallardo had heard Saxama Achachila myths as a child and from his maternal family upon his return from the Chaco War; talking about Saxama helped him to legitimize his agenda in Icla. Through his new connection to Miranda, Gallardo learned more about the history and myths of Qaranqas and Qillaqas and began to educate himself about the jalqa, his own ethnic community in Chuquisaca, and its historical connections within the ayllus of Qarangas and Qillaqas (Oruro).[49] Gallardo discovered that his mother's grandparents spoke Aymara and that he had distant relatives in the highlands of Oruro. All of this reinforced his politics based on Aymara traditions from Oruro, even though he identified as a Quechua from Chuquisaca.[50] Gallardo's worldview connected the history of the valleys of Chuquisaca in the late nineteenth and early twentieth centuries to the colonial and pre-Columbian history of Aymara, Uru, and Quechua ethnicities, which had formed new identities, such as the jalqas.[51]

Gallardo used Qaranqas mythology in various ways to present his political ideas. In a letter to Andres T'ika in 1944, Gallardo used Saxama narratives to define his people as being from the "highlands and valleys," both "Aymara and Quechua," and to argue that "ayllus and haciendas should be joined as siblings." He said that these places of worship, the mountains of Saxama and Sawaya (Sabaya), were like two brothers and that the Quechua hacienda and Aymara ayllu peoples should behave as such, working together in brotherhood. The peons were desperately searching for political strategies to use against the haciendas to get their ancestral lands returned to them, and Gallardo's description of the highland ayllus' experience emphasized cooperation between ayllus based on a common historical background. By emphasizing the shared subaltern condition of different regions, ethnic groups, and individuals, and by infusing his discourse with both a local and an Andean flavor, Gallardo was able to promote his political leadership and expand the role of the AMP in hacienda-dominated regions.[52] This pan-Andean perspective emphasized the Indianness of Aymara and Quechua peoples, while the local dimension focused on the specific problems of the hacienda regions.

Referring to indigenous peoples as the "land's blood," Gallardo introduced the notion of jallp'a sangres to AMP discourse. Since the people of the Icla region did not retain memories of Aymara provenance, a discourse based on the Qullasuyu would not work there. Instead, Gallardo developed the idea of jallp'a sangres, a hybrid concept expressed in both Quechua and Spanish, to foster the peons' identification with the land and with the fact that they were its original owners. The term was an effective emblem of aboriginal peoples for both local audiences and outsiders. Gallardo's discourse promoted a nationalist message by connecting the idea of "Indian blood" with land rights. By representing a subaltern nation of Indians opposed to the dominant racial system, he racialized the content of his discourse but used race in a counter-hegemonic way. Gallardo's argument cast the hacienda owners and their administrators as Spaniards or whites who should return the land to the jallp'a sangres. In this way he used an earth politics to rebel against the powerful haciendas.[53]

Although Melitón Gallardo modified AMP discourse, he ultimately based his arguments on an Aymara heritage. The way that he tied Aymara gods such as Saxama and Sawaya to local ideas such as jallp'a sangres in the AMP narrative illustrates how earth politics was constructed in the Andes.[54] Studying the connections between religion and politics in ancient Israel, Steven Grosby argues that there is a religious element at the conceptual center of nation and that factors such as lineage (ethnicity) and territory are part of religion.[55] In the case of the AMP's earth politics, activists constructed an imagined community of jallp'a sangres under the protection of Saxama. In this sense indigenous religiosity represented the worldview of subaltern peoples living under enduring inequality.[56] The discourse and practices of the AMP incorporated subaltern perspectives to confront the colonial racial hierarchies that persisted in mid-twentieth-century Bolivia.[57]

This subaltern discourse was intended to confront the racialized system by unifying race and land in the notion of jallp'a sangres. It also presented an alternative to the idea of Qullasuyu presented by indigenous activists in La Paz and Oruro, which we saw in the previous two chapters. The idea of "blood" or race became more relevant in Chuquisaca because it helped Gallardo's audience understand the fact that the "Indian race" was strongly oppressed by the whites of the region. Indeed, while the peoples of Icla were also descendants of Chaco groups, they had a much stronger feeling of belonging to Andean society, especially after Gregorio Titiriku's investigations reinforced that the Andean tradition in Chuquisaca, especially in Icla and Tarwita, had deep connections with the Carangas Aymara tradition. Gallardo's audience in these haciendas knew several origin myths that discussed the big mountains, referred to as Achachilas, and that were widely told in many regions of the Qarangas ayllus in Oruro. These common connections and myths helped Gallardo use the Indian law to address the region's specific circumstances.

Gallardo's personal history uniquely qualified him to shape a message for this particular audience and to respond to their conditions. He was an insider who had been born in a hacienda and knew what it was like to live as a peon. His Indian law also expressed the shift that Indian identity was undergoing in this region, where Quechua identity was enhanced by Aymara, Uru, and other ethnicities.[58] By accepting his Quechua ethnic identity but also emphasizing his Aymara heritage, Gallardo was expressing an Indian identity in both a racialized and counter-hegemonic way. In Gallardo's discourse, to be Quechua symbolized an expression of pluralism, which was one of the goals of earth politics, but he also emphasized a specific way to be Quechua: to recognize one's Aymara descent and to be united against the whites. The AMP's earth politics emphasized that indigenous people were subaltern and it was this very condition that could unite Aymara and Quechua ethnic identities.

Promoting Earth Politics to Hacienda Peons and Highland Ayllus

When the Conservatives returned to power in 1939, restrictions on the circulation of Indians were reinforced in many parts of the country because Enrique Peñaranda's government was concerned about contact and collaboration between the ayllus and the urban labor movement. Labor organizations explicitly attempted to create peasant unions in the countryside, but Peñaranda prevented this by abolishing the existing labor organizational bylaws.[59] The importance of the bylaws can be seen in the case of the ayllus of Killakas and Sura Suras, which were incorporated into the agrarian branch of Oruro's labor organization (FOL-Oruro). Indigenous leaders showed the bylaws to government authorities when they encountered checkpoints around Sucre during their annual trip to the valleys of Chuquisaca. The highland ayllus of Killakas, Qaranqas, and Sura Suras had possessed lands in this region since pre-Inka times to complement their ethnic economy by exchanging maize and peanuts from the valleys for meat and potatoes from the highlands.[60] The increased governmental control and travel restrictions thus prevented them from easily reaching their lands. The ayllu members who traveled were usually part of groups of people called tatalas, llameros, or arrieros that engaged in petty trade with ayllu members and hacienda peons.[61]

Members of the Urqas ayllu, which was part of the Qaranqas ayllu in Oruro, traditionally had passed through the huge haciendas in Icla to reach their lands in Chuquisaca. The local elite, however, did not understand that historically there had been Aymaras in Chuquisaca, that Aymara ayllus had had territorial enclaves before the Inkas, or that most of the local Quechuas were descended from Aymara ethnic groups. Throughout the first half of the twentieth century, the white elite frequently argued that "Aymaras are foreigners in Chuquisaca [and their] tatalas [elders] shouldn't come to the region [because] they teach subversion and hate to the Quechuas. . . . The Aymaras are as rude as their language, [while] Quechuas are as sweet as their language."[62]

In June 1940 ayllu members loaded two hundred llamas with salt, sugar, candles, dried meats, and fish to trade with the peons of the region and to provide food and supplies to its enclaves in Marapampa and Urqas. When Icla's corregidor found leftist and ayllu handouts in their bags, he harassed the tatalas and sent their leaders to Tarabuco's prison, accusing them of "carrying subversive material" from "mining regions."[63]

Although the biggest mines were in Oruro, the Aymara ayllus of Qaranqas at the time were not specifically involved with any mining labor organizations but were rather part of Oruro's network of urban unions.[64] Mostly of Aymara descent, miners from Wanuni and Uncía emerged as the leaders of the mining labor movement in the 1940s and infused indigenous content into the labor unions' discourse.[65] In reaction to the jailing of the ta-talas' leaders, the Urqas ayllu contacted other highland Qaranqas ayllus and the apoderados of Quntu, among them Feliciano Inka Marasa and Pablo Espinoza Marasa, to request solidarity from the labor movement in Sucre.[66] These leaders also decided to organize the First Indigenous Congress of Quechua Speakers, which was sponsored by La Federación Obrera Sindical de Trabajadores de Chuquisaca.[67] The labor movement in Sucre and the leftist parties that emerged from the Universidad Mayor de San Xavier of Chuquisaca had long been trying to incorporate Indians into their movements and had enjoyed some success through the Escuela Ferrer. For the Left, this congress presented a unique opportunity to promote their goals of reappropriating land for the Indians and mines for the state.

On the other hand, the ayllus wanted to gain some power in the Chuquisaca region and, given the prevailing stereotypes, they sought legitimacy by presenting themselves as local. As a subaltern group, they did not want elites to think that they had set up the congress and then accuse them of bringing "subversion to the region." The congress, held from August 6 to 10, 1942, and presided over by Pablo Espinosa Marasa, was conducted in Quechua, since all of the indigenous peoples present were bilingual in Aymara and Quechua. The majority of the attendees were from ayllus in Chuquisaca, with others coming from ayllus in Oruro and Potosí. The congress discussed the need to request "free circulation," or unrestricted movement throughout the country, for "arrieros and llameros," as most of the audience belonged to that category.[68] For the local audience and the labor movement, this was considered to be an Indian-only gathering because it was held in Quechua. Presenting themselves as a language-unified group, they defied local elites, who still remembered the Aymara rebellions of 1899 and feared the group's potential power in Chuquisaca.[69]

Although most of the delegates were ayllu representatives, the congress focused on peon and hacienda issues. Marasa and other indigenous activists described how the ayllus in La Paz and Oruro had defended themselves and how various indigenous networks had worked to paralyze hacienda expansion. Some felt that the Indians from the valleys had been passive, while other activists argued that Chuquisaca had traditionally been a ha-cienda region and had not suffered new gamonal or hacienda expansion like the Altiplano had. Gallardo proposed using the Indian law as a way to address the region's problems.[70] After several days of debate and the en-couragement of labor leaders Estanislao Ari and Rafael Chavez, the con-gress agreed to promote strikes on the haciendas, using the model of the Bolivian labor movement.[71] The labor leaders hoped the region would join the strikes occurring in the mining regions of Wanuni and Uncía and on the haciendas of Qaraqollo and Cochabamba.[72] Among the people com-mitted to promoting the congress's resolutions were Carlos Condori, from the northern Potosí ayllus, Marcelino Mamani, from the ayllus of Inqawasi in southern Chuquisaca, and Melitón Gallardo on the haciendas of Icla.[73]

A second congress was organized in Sucre in 1943 to continue the same agenda and to organize strikes in Icla. This time a large number of peons attended the meeting, some of them arriving with Melitón Gallardo, who by then was known as a *ch'utita*, which means a "new little cholo" in the regional dialect. As one of the few ch'utitas attending the meeting, his presence was noted in the congress. Among the attendees were Francisco Rivera and Antonio García from Sumala, Mariano Qhispe from Suruma, and Nicolas Agrigo from Pasupaya.[74]

After the second congress Melitón Gallardo joined the ayllus of Tara-buco and Urqhas to promote their rights through strikes in the area sur-rounding the haciendas of Icla and Sopachuy.[75] They were unsuccessful in the beginning, but the situation changed when a pro-Indian govern-ment was installed in La Paz in 1943. President Gualberto Villarroel abol-ished servitude (pongueaje) during the National Indigenous Congress of 1945.[76] As more Indians started to believe that change was possible and that the discourse of Gallardo and other indigenous activists had a chance of succeeding, the Icla peons decided to strike on the haciendas of Sumala and Suruma. The hacienda administration reacted forcefully, burning the activists' houses. Mariano Quispe lost his home in late 1945 and had to find temporary housing in the ayllus of Urqha. In Churuma-tas Basilio Salazar not only lost his house but also his life in an attempt to save his property from arson. These assaults infuriated the peons of the re-gion, leading them to organize more strikes to demand respect and better treatment and to pursue the resolutions of the previous two indigenous congresses in Sucre.[77]

When Villarroel was lynched in La Paz's main square in July 1946, the Conservatives returned to power and gained control of the country within a few months. When Toribio Miranda and Gregorio Titiriku informed the newspapers that the hacendados were burning the houses of Icla peons, the journalists denounced these actions, but mainly because foreign administrators were in charge in Suruma and Sumala. Peons stopped working and paying rent to the haciendas, and the administrators eventually relented, leaving the region in early 1947.[78] In the meantime, regional rebellions and strikes continued in the valleys and highlands, including attacks on forty haciendas in Qaraqullu (Oruro) and the assault on haciendas by ten thousand peons who subsequently moved into other highland valleys in Ayopaya, Cochabamba.[79]

Melitón Gallardo, Mariano Qhispe, and Antonio García believed that the Indian law should rule in Icla, so they called for assemblies and meetings to pursue this goal.[80] In Wisanchis and Pasopaya the AMP promoted the Indian republic by using the Indian law to grant "land titles" to peons who were already working the land.[81] In the 1940s republican law did not recognize land rights for peons; only the colonial law had provisions granting special rights to Indians, so by invoking Indian law Gallardo used those clauses to justify the distribution of land to peons. Presenting certificos, which were documents that had extracts from colonial law, the peons argued they would no longer pay "taxes," meaning sharecropping obligations owed in work, service, and supplies to the landowner. Some of the plots that Melitón Gallardo gave out based on colonial laws were located on the Wisanchis and Pasopaya haciendas, which belonged to Armando Guidi and Crisologo Reyes.[82] New owners such as Armando Guidi, who was of Italian descendent, were more reluctant to acknowledge rights based on colonial legislation.[83] Similar actions were called toma de tierras (taking land) in other parts of the country, but in this region they focused on resisting traditional obligations since the peon was already in possession of the plot.

In order to better obtain plots of land, peons asked Melitón Gallardo to extend membership in the AMP to the peons of Sipiqani.[84] Mariano Qhispe in Suruma and Antonio García in Sumala made similar demands for concessions of land in the name of the Indian law.[85] Although the apoderados of Muru Muru (Chuquisaca) also made such attempts during the rebellion of Chayanta in 1927 for the return of plots of land to the ayllus of Killakas and Qaranqas,[86] the attempts in the 1940s represented a fundamental discursive shift because the AMP followed procedures in the name of the Indian law.[87]

Decolonization continued to be central to the Indian law, while the worship of Aymara gods and goddesses intensified during this period. In Pucara Falda, a pre-Inka worship site, peons of Churumatas, Churumumu, Jatun K'asa, and Ch'awarani gathered at the top of the hill to worship the Achachilas of the region and Pachamama.[88] According to Agapito Ponce Mamani and Atiliano Peñaranda, who attended these ceremonies at Pucara Falda between 1945 and 1947, the worship consisted of prayers and the sacrifice of white roosters, and Gallardo and other activists called for the protection of the Achachilas of Sabawa and Saxama. According to Ponce Mamani and Peñaranda, the prayers began with the following: "Saxama Achachila protect us, give us power and make us as big as you are. Pachamama do not eat us, [instead] feed us and sustain us with your energy."[89]

The rituals included the burning of symbolic "packages of sweet and other aromatic essences," called mesas, and offerings to Pachamama. During these rituals several peons, including Francisco Rivera and Atiliano Peñaranda, burned currency, birth certificates, and other documents to mark their passing from the white society into the republic of Indians and as a symbol of separation from whites.[90] These AMP rituals also symbolized the rejection of the dominant racial system and Christianity. Another sanctuary was Cantar Gallo, where white roosters were frequently sacrificed to Pachamama and the Saxama and Sawaya Achachilas. By the early 1950s such sacrifices had become Gallardo's favorite mode of worship, which he promoted as a way to mark the republic of Indians and to signify the fact that AMP activists were rejecting the dominant racial paradigm.[91]

Gallardo adopted the clothing style of Toribio Miranda and Gregorio Titiriku, abandoning his chu'ta dress in favor of a handmade gray suit like the one Santos Marka T'ula began wearing in the 1920s. Melitón Gallardo and Mariano Qhispe argued that under the new law of the republic of Indians, Indians should dress as Indians and worship their own gods. Gallardo suggested to the Icla peons that they emulate his style of dress.[92] In 1947 some groups from Tarabuco, including Félix and Luis Vela from Jatun Mayo and Candelaria, abandoned their colorful ethnic dress for the dress style that the Indian law designated as "right," believing the color gray was closest to Pachamama because of its similarity to the color of the earth.[93]

Meanwhile, the government intensified its suppression of various rebellions throughout the countryside in late 1947. President Herzog created a special army unit to suppress the rebellions and ordered the bombing of rebels in Ayopaya (Cochabamba), Inqawasi (Chuquisaca), and Urunquta (Potosí), as I described in chapter 2.[94] When the army arrived in December 1947, the leaders of the republic of Indians had to flee.[95] Melitón Gallardo escaped to Monteagudo in eastern Chuquisaca and only returned to Sucre several years after the national revolution of 1952. Francisco Rivera, a well-known Indian priest in the region, escaped to the Chaco; Ezequiel Orieta, who was Miranda's representative in the region, sought refuge among the Uru communities in Miranda's ayllu; and Juan de Dios Loayza, who led hunger strikes against the hacienda owners, fled to the ayllus of northern Potosí. Indigenous activists who could not escape were taken by government agents to detention camps in the eastern lowland regions of Chimoré and Yapacaní (Santa Cruz). Among the prisoners were Mariano Qhispe and Antonio García, both liaisons for Miranda and Titiriku with the leftist and anarchist parties and with unions in Chuquisaca and Oruro. Qhispe died in the detention camps, while García returned to Icla after the national revolution.[96] The AMP lost many of its most important members in this era of repression from 1947 to 1948. The pacification of the rebels proceeded slowly. Under strict police control, the administrators forced the peons to reinitiate cash rental payments in early 1948. The region was then under military control until 1949, and, very slowly, some peons began to pay their rent again. However, Sumala, Suruma, and Chunca Cancha continued to resist until the agrarian reform of 1953.[97]

The Construction of a Regional Interlocutor

As an AMP activist intellectual for over thirty years, Melitón Gallardo epitomizes the regionalization of the AMP's denunciations of the system of internal colonialism. Melitón adapted the discourse for Chuquisaca's indigenous audience by emphasizing Indian identity through the notion of jallp'a sangres and creating everyday forms of AMP discourse.[98] By using what was available in his social context, he created new signifiers of the Indian law. Borrowing ideas and terminology from the colonial-era republic of Indians, this discourse was a combination of politics and religion that encouraged the worship of wak'as.

Although Gallardo was part of the pre-1952 generation of the AMP, his role as a regional leader reveals some differences from the experiences of Miranda and Titiriku. His priorities were less focused on national issues than Miranda and Titiriku's, being more focused on how to reach his regional audience. His earth politics was grounded in the religious tradition of the Qaranqas Aymara nation of Oruro (and its enclaves in Chuquisaca) and based on blood, situating jallp'a sangres in opposition to the elite mestizos and cholos, who were lumped together under the terms *Spaniards* or *whites*. To take on the jallp'a sangres identity, followers had to perform the Indian law in rituals of worship to wak'as; they offered sacrifices and burned birth certificates, currency, and identification cards, which they considered to be signifiers of the white race and the hegemonic state.

Melitón Gallardo's case illustrates that the AMP was actually a collection of local and regional indigenous activists who necessarily differed in the ways that they constructed their discourse. Gregorio Titiriku and Toribio Miranda's Indian law played a central role in the general constructions of earth politics, but it was also adapted to account for local specifics. In Melitón Gallardo's case earth politics became a belief system that promoted uprisings against the hacienda and the racial system. It legitimized Indians' rightful ownership of land in places where the strategies of Santos Marka T'ula could not work, since those haciendas were long-established. The Indian law was an expression of the Aymara belief system that emphasized the worship of the spirits of the wak'as, such as Saxama and Sabaya, as a way to strengthen the republic of Indians. This framing was also critical for the second generation of AMP leaders, including Andres Jach'aqullu.

Chapter Six | # Against Whitening

Andrés Jach'aqullu's Movement between
Worlds in the Era of the Bolivian
National Revolution of 1952

On August 21, 1957, the AMP indigenous activist Andrés Jach'aqullu was one of seventeen indigenous people who arrived in Sucre to denounce the state-controlled peasant union in the community of Muxuquya. They claimed that union leaders had jailed them for twenty days with little food or water. Senon Galarza, Rafaelino Montano, Marcelino Gallo, Severo Navia, and Cecilio Colque said that they had been detained in an attempt to coerce them into agreeing with peasant union leaders. Andrés Jach'aqullu, a former policeman who was new to indigenous activism, explained that many similar cases had occurred over the past two years and that he was concerned that this type of problem was becoming engrained in many parts of the countryside in the late 1950s.[1] These accusations revealed a new face of the Bolivian National Revolution that began in 1952.

These events took place in the context of the changes wrought upon the elite sectors of Bolivia by the national revolution. The Rosca mining oligarchy was replaced by an emerging middle class that allied with the labor movement and rural indigenous people to nationalize the mines and institute an agrarian reform that would break up large unproductive haciendas into individual plots of land in the highland and valley regions of the western side of the country. This revolution was significant for Bolivia because it represented a "rite of passage" into the modern era. It was led by the Movimiento Nationalista Revolucionario (MNR) a political party that was mostly run by the emerging middle class and became a crucial actor in the complex and ever-changing alliances between classes and power players in Bolivia. To ensure their power after the revolution, the MNR instituted a one-party system that lasted for more than a decade and organized state-controlled peasant unions in the countryside. These unions existed throughout the national territory and tended to follow three patterns. Some peasant organizations, such as the one in Jach'aqhachi, were run primarily by Indians who were able to assimilate this institution to their needs, making these unions work according to the ayllu or community model. In other regions the unions conformed to the pattern of Ucureña, becoming associations of ex-peons. In other regions, however, such as northern Potosí and some parts of Chuquisaca, the rural middle class appropriated the peasant unions to serve their own needs. This was the case in 1957 when Andrés Jach'aqullu and his group denounced the cholo- and mestizo-run unions.[2] Jach'aqullu and the AMP found an important audience among people who were being dominated by this third group of unions, and their work reinvented the AMP social movement in the era of the national revolution.

By preventing women's participation within the peasant unions, promoting education only in Spanish, insisting that Indian men not wear traditional clothing, and empowering the mestizo provincial elite in some regions of Bolivia, the national revolution reintroduced racial assimilation discourse at a local level. The new revolutionary state, with its emphasis on Westernization, also considered many of the ayllus' ritual practices to be uncivilized, superstitious, and leading to alcoholism and coca addiction, and it resolved to combat them with what it considered "scientific" education.[3] Furthermore, because of their failure to support the peasant unions that were controlled by the rural middle class, the ex-peons were accused of opposing the modernizing ideas of agrarian reform and the national revolution. The revolutionary party, the MNR, gradually became a populist party with a middle-class agenda, developing a discourse of mestizaje that purported to end the caste system.[4] Integration interested them as a way to promote their version of Bolivian nationalism; however, their integrationist vision differed from the leftist version that emphasized unions and dreams of a socialist state.[5]

In the Muxuquya case Sucre's Radio La Plata broadcast a public denunciation of the peasant union leaders' actions, and Attorney General Gerardo Córdoba agreed to hear the case. Andrés Jach'aqullu, who was fluent in Spanish, described to the attorney general how the ex-peons from the ex-hacienda Rodeo Chico in Muxuquya had escaped from captivity by traveling for four days by foot. Jach'aqullu emphasized that the indigenous ex-peons only moved at night because they were afraid of getting caught by the peasant union and jailed again. They wanted the attorney general in Sucre to give them a guarantee of protection from Celedonio Reina and Agapito Peña, the leaders of the peasant union of Muxuquya, Chuquisaca. Jach'aqullu argued that since the national revolution a group of mestizos from small towns had organized *centrales agrarias* (peasant unions) and *comandos revolucionarios* (revolutionary committees) that had co-opted structures meant to represent the indigenous population, thus suppressing the true indigenous voice. Indeed, as in other parts of southern Bolivia, these peasant unions forced indigenous peoples to participate in pro-MNR activities. The ex-peons, with Jach'aqullu acting as translator, said that they were not followers of the MNR and that they did not want to participate in the union run by the mestizos because it did not represent their concerns. This group of former peons stated that their autonomy and right to practice their native religion was of utmost importance to them, and they announced that they were part of the group known as Qullasuyus, which belonged to the AMP network and had been confronting peasant unions in various parts of southern Bolivia.[6]

In the meeting on August 21, Jach'aqullu cautiously argued that the Qullasuyus were not part of the peasant unions, which were supposed to represent indigenous concerns, because these entities would not allow them to argue for autonomy and to "worship their cults," by which he meant perform ceremonies to honor Pachamama and worship their ancestors. During this legal process, the unions accused the Qullasuyus of not wanting "to be civilized" and instead wanting to "stay as they were in old times." Responding to these accusations, Jach'aqullu said that "Julian Zenteno, just as many other caudillos [leaders] of the pro-state peasant union and the revolutionary commandos, thought that his job was to punish the people who disagreed" with the MNR's vision of modernity and to make sure that people obeyed the dictates of the national revolution, using any means possible—including violence.[7] Consequently, a critical analysis of the goals of national revolution and its ideas about modernity emerged from these hearings. Former peons rejected state- and middle-class-controlled unions, and the AMP took the lead in denouncing the unions' coercive methods and despotic actions.

This type of violent imposition was frequent, especially in southern

Bolivia, where the rural middle class successfully co-opted the revolution, and Indians did not directly feel its effects on their daily lives.[8] Groups of peasant indigenous intellectuals like the AMP began to speak out against revolutionary policies. In Tipampa (Cochabamba), for example, ex-peons complained about how peasant union leaders from Chinguri and Tinta persecuted those who did not follow their orders. Common punishments included jailing, hanging offenders *al chancho* (upside down), and making them stand *al plantón* (in an upright position for a long time); the first and second were most often applied to men and the latter to women and older men.[9] In Tipapampa the leadership imposed arbitrary obligations based on personal whims, making ex-peons provide food for the sindicatos' meetings and take care of farm animals belonging to the central agraria's leaders.[10]

The unions were an important part of the MNR's modernizing project, and not all of them were tolerant of indigenous people. In Sutalaya, La Paz, the peasant union forced indigenous men to cut their long braids "as a way to incorporate them into civilization," and in Tarabuco, Chuquisaca, the peasant union encouraged people to abandon their indigenous dress in order to become "civilized."[11] The peasant unions and other revolutionary institutions were part of a new hegemony in the countryside. Intolerant of dissent, they conceptualized civilization and modernization as a way to "de-Indianize" the country. Framing indigenous worldviews as "uncivilized and primitive," they encouraged peasants to abandon Indian dress and tradition and commit to revolutionary rhetoric.[12] The worldview underlying the peasant unions' racialized policies toward Indians and their goals for transforming the countryside were still colonial.

In contrast to Miranda, Titiriku, and Gallardo, Andrés Jach'aqullu's case epitomizes the work of an AMP activist during the time of the national revolution. Andrés Jach'aqullu's used the Indian law as a way to challenge the discursive emphasis on nation making through "whitening" that was prominent in Bolivia during the era after 1952. As a second-generation AMP leader, Jach'aqullu also adjusted and re-elaborated ideas about the Indian law. Jach'aqullu and the second generation of the AMP were the bridge that connected the work and ideas of the broader movement of apoderados with the modern Katarista and Indianista movements that emerged in the 1970s.

Jach'aqullu's experiences of racialization in his daily life in Wanuni and Oruro, especially in his relationship with working-class miners who mostly spoke Quechua, represented a larger process in which segregationist and assimilationist discourses were simultaneously at play in the years after the Chaco War. In the 1940s the process of nation making also shifted, as Bolivian society changed from defining itself by race to defining itself by class—a middle ground promoted by many populist groups and parties. This transformation was not only discursive; it left behind people like Jach'aqullu and movements like the AMP that did not have their own peasant unions or fit into the discourse of equality emphasized by the new populist state that emerged after the revolution. Indeed, the indigenous peoples of the southern Andes still suffered abuse at the hands of the rural middle class—now represented by the peasant unions—and, in this context, they articulated a postrevolutionary AMP program. Jach'aqullu became a spokesperson for the AMP after he reassumed his indigenous identity and embraced the AMP's decolonization project. As the older generation died or retired, Jach'aqullu expanded the AMP's agenda to include new regions such as Wanuni. Jach'aqullu and his generation reworked the agenda of decolonization to fit the new conditions that reigned after 1952, rejecting the liberal policies of land tenure through agrarian reform, power for the rural middle class through peasant unions, and the need for the indigenous population to obtain birth and marriage certificates and national ID cards. In regions such as Icla and Tarwita, Jach'aqullu also supported the resistance to agrarian reform. In an era when Indianness was seen as antiquated and ethnic dress was rejected as backward in the cities, he insisted on wearing AMP ethnic dress. Since he was fluent in Spanish and, in the racialized stereotypes of the time, was considered to have "light skin," he broke many stereotypes about Indianness.

In promoting his agenda of decolonization, Jach'aqullu also took his discourse to a national and even international audience by contacting the International Labour Organization, which worked on the first international legislation for indigenous populations in the late 1950s. Jach'aqullu also associated with the Bahá'ís and traveled internationally while building indigenous activism in the cities. These efforts would result in the emergence of the Katarista and Indianista movements. During this period many indigenous peoples moved to the cities, where their experiences of rejection and frustration led them to embrace these new movements' ideas.

Jach'aqullu was part of the last generation of the AMP, thus this chapter also narrates the fall of the AMP in the early 1970s. In contrast to Miranda and Titiriku, who mostly confronted segregationist polices, Jach'aqullu had to confront the assimilationist or integrationist context that followed the national revolution. Jach'aqullu passed through many worlds by the time he joined the AMP. I mostly focus here on the years after the national revolution had consolidated its goals, which limited the ways that Jach'aqullu could conduct his struggle and forced him to depend more on kinship strategies.

Racialization in International Mining Zones and Aymara Ayllus

Wilaqullu, a village that belonged to a large Aymara ayllu and in the jurisdiction of the corregidor of Wanuni, was the breeding ground for a second generation of AMP activists who re-created the discourse of Indian law, but they created this discourse only after first rejecting their indigenous roots in the first half of twentieth century. A singular relationship emerged between the working class and indigenous peoples in Wilaqullu and Wanuni that would shape Andrés Jach'aqullu's life story. Wilaqullu was part of the Aymara Chullpas nation, which was located between southern Oruro and northern Potosí in the area where the most famous Bolivian mines of the twentieth century (Uncía, Q'atawi, Wanuni, Llallawa, and Siglo XX) were located.[13] Although these mines produced tin for the international economy, the region was also home to the country's largest ayllus, which depended on a long-standing agrarian economy based on exchange in kind between ayllus and other regions.[14] The wealthiest of these mines — Wanuni, Llallawa, and Q'atawi — belonged to Patiño Mines, the largest mining company in Bolivia. Wanuni and Uncía benefited from the mining boom; from the 1920s to the 1940s, Uncía had the best medical specialists in the country, some of whom were Americans brought in to attend to the company's management. As enclaves of the international economy, Wanuni and Uncía were, for a time, the largest tin producers in the world.[15]

Andrés Jach'aqullu was born into an Aymara family in 1921. His father, Domingo Jach'aqullu, wanted his children to be educated, so Andrés, the youngest of five, walked five hours from his village to the elementary school in Bombo, which was the main village of the Chullpas ethnic group. On weekends he went with his parents to sell dried potatoes, meat, and corn in the street market of Uncía, where they also bought sugar, bread, canned food, and school supplies. When Jach'aqullu and his mother sold goods in

Wanuni, they traded frequently with working-class housewives (Quechua-speaking cholas) who wanted to buy Indian goods at very low prices, but Jach'aqullu's mother often refused. These exchanges frequently resulted in the working-class women insulting Jach'aqullu's mother as an "ignorant Indian" since she did not speak Quechua or Spanish. Most cholos and cholas in Uncía and other mining towns did not speak Aymara during this time and defined themselves as superior to the Indians.[16] They were originally Quechua speakers from the Cochabamba valleys and were often ex-piqueras, who had worked in Chilean mines in Antofagasta and Tarapacá in the 1920s before moving to the Bolivian mines.[17]

Since 1890 Quechua-speaking miners from Cochabamba had migrated to the mining towns of Llallawa, Uncía, Qatawi, and Siglo XX for work, but the towns also contained enclaves of Aymara speakers.[18] Later, Quechua not only gained full hegemony in the mining towns but also gradually spread into the Aymara ayllus of the entire region. Over the course of several decades, the region's ayllus became bilingual in Aymara and Quechua; in other regions Quechua became consolidated as a new language in one or two generations. Spanish also became more widely spoken in these regions, complicating language use in ayllus and mining towns.

The miners, defined as cholos in the racialized language of Bolivia, working in Llallawa, Siglo XX, Uncía, and Catavi organized some of the world's most powerful mining labor movements between 1920 and 1940. The labor unions of these centers confronted the mining companies, demanding housing and an eight-hour workday; the unions organized several general strikes in the 1920s despite severe repression. Through the powerful Federación de Trabajadores Mineros de Bolivia (FTMB, Bolivian Federation of Mine Workers), the working-class people of these towns provided a coherent political agenda for the Bolivian working class. They created La Tesis de Pulacayo (The thesis of Pulacayo) in 1946, which advocated for improved labor conditions, promoted the state's takeover of mines, and defined Bolivia as a primitive capitalist country. The document was one of the most radical in Latin America, and its spirit impacted Bolivian politics for many years.[19] The FTMB would later play a key role in creating the Central Obrera Boliviana (COB), an umbrella organization that would become one of the most unified unions in the world. Frequent confrontations between the emerging labor movement and conservative governments resulted in the constant repression of workers between the

1920s and the 1940s.[20] Jach'aqullu came of age in this context of strife. His uncle Zacarías Jach'aqullu was one of nearly one hundred miners who were killed when the army and police repressed a strike at Uncía in 1923.

Literacy was a long-standing obsession in the Jach'aqullu family. His grandfather was a nephew of Felipe Beltrán, who had promoted education in Aymara and Quechua in the 1870s. Although he had some schooling, Jach'aqullu's father was only partially literate because he did not practice his reading and writing skills, but he wanted his son to be fully literate. In a time when few Indians from the ayllus had access to schooling, this family's focus on formal education was unusual.[21] For two years in the early 1930s, Jach'aqullu attended the public school of Uncía, where both the teachers and the students subjected him to jokes about the Aymara language. People in the mining town considered Spanish to be the most cultured language and Quechua to be acceptable, but they had no tolerance for Aymara since it was associated with the indigenous people of the surrounding ayllus. Jach'aqullu's teacher told him that "Aymara is a primitive language," while "Quechua is sweet and the language of the Inkas."[22] Quechua was considered the language of the working class who identified themselves with the Inka elite.[23] From Jach'aqullu's perspective, however, these cholos were also Indians; the only difference was that they spoke Spanish and Quechua and lived in mining towns. The cholos, though, considered themselves to be mestizos rather than Indians.

After finishing elementary school in 1932, Jach'aqullu returned to his village of Wilaqullu to farm and accompany his father on trips to trade dry goods for corn and wheat in the lowlands of nearby Misk'i (Cochabamba). In 1940, when he was nineteen, he sought employment with the police department of Uncía. However, when filling out his application at the police enrollment, he had a challenging decision to make.[24] Jach'aqullu gave his real name, but the policeman in charge of IDs encouraged him to change his last name, telling him that since his "skin was too light to be Indian," he did not need to "carry such an Indian last name, which was hard to pronounce." Jach'aqullu thus decided to translate his last name into Spanish; as it meant high hill, he became "Cerrogrande." In 1939 he got a national identity card that reflected this new name.[25]

Between 1939 and 1942 he was posted in Uncía, where he learned that a policeman's job frequently involved abusing indigenous members of the community. In 1942 Jach'aqullu as Cerrogrande was sent to reinforce a police squad that was protecting the Patiño Mining Company from widespread strikes. He saw twenty people killed and one hundred others wounded—an experience that affected him profoundly. He became critical of the white elite's power and requested a transfer to another post. Although he would have preferred to leave his job with the police, he needed the money.[26] Late in 1942 he was sent to Wanuni, where he witnessed a woman being gang raped by a group of policemen.[27] At other times he observed police forcing indigenous women to pick up garbage that they had not dropped and accusing them of defecating in the main street of Wanuni. This exposure to the constant humiliation of indigenous peoples and the working class laid bare the deep inequality in Bolivian society, and it slowly changed the way that Jach'aqullu saw the world.

During this time he met Matilde Qulqi from the Parapiani community, which was part of his own ayllu. Matilde shared Jach'aqullu's budding perspectives on indigenous politics and was familiar with local oral history. Her father was an indigenous priest, and she was faithful to the Aymara religion as practiced through highland indigenous spirituality and rites. She persistently attempted to convince Jach'aqullu to leave the police force and return to the community. Although she refused to move with him to Wanuni for this reason, the couple finally married in December 1942.[28]

Earlier that year Jach'aqullu as Cerrogrande was sent to Oruro, where he was appointed to a police station on Camacho Avenue. It was there that he met detainee Toribio Miranda in 1943. Miranda's thoughts and political ideas had a transformative effect on Jach'aqullu, convincing him to leave the police in late 1944 and return to his community, where he started to organize for the AMP. To demonstrate that he had adopted a completely different worldview, he not only abandoned his police uniform but also adopted Indian dress as Toribio Miranda required, donning a gray poncho and handmade pants.[29] In addition, he started to encourage long hair among AMP members and let his own hair grow below his shoulders, according to ancient Aymara customs.[30]

From 1945 to 1957 Jach'aqullu and his wife advocated the ideas of the AMP in the region surrounding Wanuni, building on the work that had already been done by people like José Willka and Eusebio Quyu. In 1952 Miranda and Titiriku suggested to Jach'aqullu that "he should help the activists in those regions" because he was traveling to Chuquisaca and Misk'i. Since these areas were mostly under the hacienda system, Titiriku and Miranda thought that Jach'aqullu's experience in the mines and with the labor movements in Wanuni would help the AMP in Chuquisaca.[31]

FIGURES 6.1 AND 6.2. Andrés Jach'aqullu's historical trajectory as an Aymara leader of the second generation of the AMP indigenous network. LEFT: Andrés Cerrogrande when he was a policeman in Uncía (Potosí), 1942. RIGHT: Andrés Jach'aqullu in Oruro when he revived the cult to the wak'as and used native dress as a signifier of identity, circa 1956. Courtesy of Eusebio Quyu, Qala Qala, Potosí.

With Matilde's support, Jach'aqullu not only organized the ayllus of northern Potosí and southern Oruro but also worked with the activists of Chuquisaca. His initiative came from living in a region with a powerful labor movement that had taught him the importance of activism. Jach'aqullu had confronted racial subordination when he had to translate his last name from Aymara to Spanish in order to obtain a working-class job as a policeman. Similarly, he had a long history of having to confront negative reactions to his Aymaraness from the cholo working class, who considered him a backward Indian. His marriage to Qulqi, who was a devout follower of Aymara religion, and his exposure to AMP ideas shaped the path he would forge in the crucial years of the 1950s.

The emergence in the 1940s of a new generation of ex-Indians and ex-cholos connected to class paradigms rather than the caste system had a profound influence on Jach'aqullu's story. The caste system slowly disintegrated after the Chaco War, which had brought Bolivian men of widely disparate backgrounds together for the first time. The concept of de-Indianization became more popular as many cholos adopted a leftist discourse and focused their energies on class struggle. Crucial to de-Indianization, integration started to affect ethnic and racial identities. Influenced by the labor movement, the ethnic category of cholo was abandoned in favor the term *obrero* (worker), which privileged class over ethnic identity for urban male Aymaras. Cholo artisans during the 1940s and 1950s in Jach'aqhachi (La Paz), for example, strongly preferred the designation obreros over cholos.[32]

Some cholos' daughters adopted "full Western dress" and became *birlochas*, which implied that they were of plebeian origin and no longer cholas.[33] Ana Paredes, an accountant and the daughter of a prosperous vendor in the Camacho market, provides a good example of this tendency. Because her family was originally from Oruro, they were acquaintances of Jach'aqullu, who, when he was in La Paz for his work as an indigenous activist, often rented a room in the home of Ana's mother Mercedes Mamani.[34] He was personally affected when Mercedes Mamani died in 1941. Ana Paredes then wanted to sell her mother's market stall, but the other vendors opposed the sale, arguing that it was collective property. The market cholas had a verbal confrontation with Ana and used the fact that she had changed her surname from the Aymara "Colque" to the Spanish "Paredes" to bolster their argument that she was no longer one of them. Ana Paredes took them to court for libel, explaining that one had said: "Birlocha, *refinada* [refined woman]. You have forgotten your mother's *polleras* [indigenous skirt] and now you act like any other white. You are a refinada. . . . You are Paredes, go to the Paredes. Do not come back here."[35] Ana believed that she should be treated with greater respect because she was a lady and not from the same class as the market vendors. She argued that she only wanted to sell her mother's market stall as soon possible and that she had changed her last name with the permission of both parents. But the street vendors' association prevailed, preventing the sale and assigning her mother's stall to another member. Although Jach'aqullu helped Ana Paredes by serving as witness in the libel case, he did not want Aymaras and other indigenous communities to feel as if they had to take the path of whitening or reject their identity as Ana had and as he had also done in the 1930s. Cases like Ana's reinforced his commitment to work against whitening by promoting the Indian law as a project of decolonization.[36] Despite Jach'aqullu's views, this case demonstrates how class identity trumped ethnic identity for a second generation of cholos, like Ana Paredes, in this period.[37]

Ethnic rejection also affected other dimensions of social life; most notably, a paternalistic vision of needing to protect Indians reemerged. As a consequence of a law passed by President Saavedra in 1925, Indians' land could only be sold through the prosecutor's office. In the legal sense of the term, Indians were to be considered *minors*, which strongly encouraged them to abandon their Indianness.[38] Although Saavedra justified this decree by arguing that it would protect Indians from being exploited by lawyers, the measure reinforced the idea of Indians as powerless. As a result, Indians in the 1940s no longer had the freedom to sell or buy land. Jach'aqullu believed that land tenure in Bolivia needed to undergo a major transformation and proposed that the Indian law structure the system.[39]

Adopting the elite's hegemonic strategies and ideas about race, cholos also assumed a paternalistic attitude toward indigenous peoples in the countryside. They largely internalized their own struggles against the elites and did not recognize the vibrancy and power of ethnic organizations such as the Aymara ayllus nor the way in which the indigenous peoples as a subaltern nation had been systematically attacked by the Bolivian state. Instead, they argued that the struggle against the traditional elite should only be addressed from a working-class perspective, which, they asserted, embodied Indian concerns. By the 1940s cholos and their labor movement had adopted a vision of Indians as a "problem" and, rejecting the term *Indian*, insisted on referring to indigenous peoples as *campesinos* (peasants).[40] Their labor organizations argued that Indians needed to "modernize" their forms of protest, from rebellion to "union organization, hunger strikes and Marxist organization."[41] To this end, they promoted unionization in the Aymara regions from the 1920s to the 1940s, creating the Federación Agraria Departamental de La Paz (FAD) in 1946. Although at first FAD counted important Indian leaders, such as Santos Marka T'ula, among its ranks, in its later years, it advocated cholification for Indians.[42] By this time the Federación Obrera Local was no longer in the hands of anarchists but was controlled by less radical leftists. Jach'aqullu emerged from this world of the ex-cholo labor movement, which was influenced by Marxist literature and contemporaneous social movements in Latin America. As a way of advancing their social struggle, this ex-cholo labor movement attempted to re-elaborate the past in terms of class. In other words, liberals and leftists wanted Bolivia to "Westernize," while Jach'aqullu and the AMP not only wanted to retain their Indian heritage but also had their own modernization project.

In Bolivia's racialized history of nation making, 1943 to 1945 was a period in which the government emphasized integration. The MNR and its ally and military president Gualberto Villarroel initiated this process by organizing the first National Indigenous Congress and promoting the incorporation of indigenous people into political parties. The congress in May 1945, which was the first one organized by the Bolivian state in the twentieth century, brought together three thousand indigenous people, mainly Aymaras and Quechuas. Although the congress attracted many grassroots indigenous groups, the government marginalized indigenous radicals by jailing them in the days and months leading up to the event. Despite these circumstances, this was a momentous event in terms of Bolivia's history of racialization; for the first time, a president attended an Indian gathering and addressed them.[43] According to *La Calle*: "Something extremely unusual happened yesterday . . . the inauguration of the National Indigenous Congress . . . with the assistance of the whole executive branch [of the Bolivian state], . . . the national army, . . . the diplomatic body, . . . all with the highest form of dignity to inaugurate an indigenous gathering. . . . This shows a break from the norm [of the country]."[44] Following the lead of other populists in Latin America, Villarroel signed a decree at the congress that abolished servitude.[45] The MNR later used this as a means to attract new militants to the party, arguing that an MNR government had made that possible. These actions reflect how the party had begun competing for hegemony among indigenous peoples by incorporating representatives from the Indian world.[46]

Augusto Céspedes, who became a key ideologue of Bolivian nationalism in the 1940s and 1950s, emphasized the central role mestizos played in the making of the new Bolivian nationalism. He believed that *el pueblo*— the cholos—and moderates among the elite were mixing to create a mestizo identity that would become the ruling ethnic and racial category in opposition to Indianness.[47] In this context the cholo (meaning working-class Indian) started to be absorbed into this new mestizo identity, in which Indians were represented as ancestors rather than as living social and political actors. In other words, mestizaje became a discourse of whitening or de-Indianization that would become crucial in the era after 1952. This whitening would also become central to how colonialism would operate in this new era, and it is what an activist like Jach'aqullu had to resist.

During the 1940s and 1950s, the core of the racialized Bolivian caste system was deconstructed and racial ideologies were transformed. Although Indians remained at the bottom of the hierarchical system, they were there for a different reason. This transformation took place in the context of an intense political struggle between the Left and Right in Bolivia, between groups that wanted to retain colonial privileges and those that wanted a new order. The assimilationist ideas and policies that emerged from this conflict were the dominant force that the AMP would address after the national revolution.

The Impact of the Bolivian National Revolution on the Indian World

Segregationist Bolivia regained the upper hand in the revolution of July 21, 1946, when a mob of cholos and elites overthrew President Villarroel and hanged him in La Paz's main plaza. They were outraged by his attempts to end segregation and wanted to punish him severly for attending the National Indigenous Congress as an official representative of the Bolivian state. The policies of his government were an affront to Bolivia's general whitening trend. Despite these efforts, however, the ruling elite failed to stay in power and largely disappeared from mainstream Bolivian politics during the 1950s. When the national revolution began on April 9, 1952, it could have been just one more coup in Bolivia's complex and turbulent history, except for the massive popular participation that quickly developed. The leaders of the MNR, which the Bolivian social theorist René Zavaleta Mercado refers to as an emerging "middle class that was originally the poor relatives of the white and tiny [traditional] elite,"[48] soon found themselves running one of the largest Indian countries in the hemisphere.[49] Herbert Klein has described these middle-class leaders as "reluctant revolutionaries" who were forced into many of the choices that they made.[50] Most of the progressive measures undertaken by the revolution were prompted by strong pressure from below. The nationalization of the mines came in 1952, and universal suffrage occurred for the first time during the elections of 1956, which meant that the indigenous population and women voted for the first time. Many indigenous peasants in the valley of Cochabamba and in the highlands of La Paz began to take over lands, and the government had no other option but to sign the agrarian reform bill in 1953. With these important reforms pongueaje—the old system of absentee landlords and Indian servitude—finally collapsed.[51]

The national revolution completed the process of integrating indigenous peoples into mainstream Bolivian society that had started after the Chaco War. This was reflected in President Paz Estenssoro's pronouncement to a crowd of two hundred thousand Amerindians during the national land reform celebration in 1953 that "from now on you will no longer be Indians, but rather peasants."[52] This speech represented the national revolution's strong championing of de-Indianization as the culmination of the long evolution of integration discourse. As integration became official state policy, indigenous communities had to shift, at least in legal terms, from being Indians to being peasants and accept a process of domestication that the new elite had designed from the top down.[53] Astenio Averanga, a key policy maker and intellectual of the national revolution during this time, argued that "the problem [of the government] was to transform 63 percent of the national population, which is indigenous, and make them modern economic types[, which] . . . is like repopulating the country."[54] Averanga's words reflected the perspective of the early twentieth-century intellectual Alfredo Guillén Pinto, who used to lament that, although public schools were so few among indigenous communities, he was pleased with those that existed because they made "more Bolivians."[55] Both intellectuals saw integration as reproducing mainstream nationalism and ignored subaltern forms of nationalism. During the 1950s the revolution essentially defined Indian integration as the complete elimination of Indian culture.

Revolution shaped people in a very heterogeneous way; instead of only focusing on its effects at the national level, it is also important to look at what happened at the local level. Indian participation in the national revolution varied regionally, with the core and periphery participating in different ways.[56] These regional variations profoundly shaped Jach'aqullu's life story. The core of the indigenous world, such as the Aymara area of Jach'aqhachi (Achacachi) and the Quechua region of Ucureña, were the most populated regions and were better linked to the Bolivian economy of the 1950s. The Indian periphery consisted of less-populated regions that were poorly connected to the official Bolivian economy, such as the Aymara regions of Wilaqullu, Oruro, and the valleys of northern Potosí and the Quechua regions of Icla and Misk'i. In the core areas indigenous peasants supported massive unionization because they saw it as a way to achieve empowerment. In places like the haciendas of Ucureña, peasants had already started to organize sindicatos in the 1930s; the first sindicatos in Jach'aqhachi's haciendas were founded during the 1940s. In both regions, but especially in Ucureña and in other parts of Cochabamba, ex-peons used violent methods to take control of several haciendas and enforce the agrarian reform of August 2, 1953. Some sindicatos achieved full autonomy, which helped to empower indigenous peasants and became an important source of peasant organization in the ex-haciendas. For a time, the Ucureña sindicatos were under the Trotskyist leadership of José Rojas, Crisóstomo Inturias, Borio Orellana, Carlos Montaño, and Napoleón Chaco, who were all politically independent from the government and shaped the measures of the land reform of 1953.[57] On the other hand, the ayllus and ex-haciendas of Jach'aqhachi imbued the peasant unions with ethnic discourse. Although known as sindicatos, they functioned as ayllus to a large degree. Jach'aqhachi was able to achieve this because their community ran its own organization and had powerful leaders like Toribio Salas, known as "willasaku," and Laureano Machaca.[58] Not satisfied with partial and local autonomy for the sindicatos, Machaca sought to create a "República Aymara" on the shores of Lake Titikaka by ensuring, often violently, that Aymaras were not expelled from the region.[59]

Jach'aqhachi and Ucureña achieved some control as a result of the national revolution but could not avoid cultural domination by "white" and "mestizo" Bolivia. The state mobilized the peasant unions for both large and small conflicts, calling to action massive waves of the sindicatos to express opposition to traditional modes of political power, especially against the hacendados and the whole power system of the old regime that had supported them in the countryside. The government also manipulated peasant unions to support different factions of revolutionary leaders. For instance, during the early 1960s the confrontation between Clisa and Ucureña in Cochabamba embodied not just MNR factionalism but also Cold War relations of the time.[60] This confrontation was known in Bolivian history as *ch'ampa guerra*, meaning the localized war. In spite of this, the peasant unions were able partially to control the homogenization process and to construct localized everyday forms of revolution. For instance, in Jach'aqhachi the peasant union gradually took control of state institutions and expelled landlords and hacienda administrators. The Cold War polarized contradictions among the new national elites, creating regional and factional conflicts. These conflicts often meant that local issues were left in the hands of indigenous peoples, opening a space for a fragmented empowerment of indigenous peoples in some regions.[61] However, local schools, which heavily promoted the national revolution, remained in the hands of the central state. This created generational differences in the local impact of the revolution. While the older generation of indigenous peasants kept and gained power, education ensured that more of the younger generation would speak Spanish and assimilate to the new version of the nation-state. Consequently, Aymara organizations, especially in core areas like Jach'aqhachi, started to decline as the revolution became widespread.

In contrast to this experience of relative autonomy, Indians in the Quechua-speaking regions of Icla (Chuquisaca) and Tomata Palqa (northern Potosí), where the AMP and Jach'aqullu had a wide audience, resisted the unions.[62] Icla's powerful provincial elite, mostly composed of ex-hacienda overseers and members of the local government prior to 1953, maintained their leadership positions during the revolution. Mariano Malpartida, who became the leader (comando campesino) of the MNR regional party and corregidor of the town in 1950, was a former overseer of various haciendas in the 1930s and had been corregidor of Icla in the 1940s. He used these positions to control the peasant unions during the land reform.[63] On the other hand, Tomata Palqa's new provincial elite were former members of the mining community of Uncía and former laborers in northern Argentina who had gained power by acquiring land and creating unions in indigenous communities. For instance, Anselmo Vargas, a leader of the peasant sindicatos of Tomata Palqa, was a former mine worker of Llallagua who obtained community lands by cheating Indians.

These examples may point to why the AMP was able to retain some of their audience and even gain new followers: Both the old and new provincial elite reproduced traditional patterns of domination over Indian peoples, and the peasant unions in Icla and Tomata Palqa served to maintain dominant groups because the national revolution did not have a comprehensive policy on Indian representation in the sindicatos. This type of provincial elite developed an unequal relationship with Indian people based on their imagined ethnic differences and class conditions. Rural corregidores often forced indigenous people to produce agricultural goods in the communities and ex-haciendas of some regions. Although many indigenous peasants resisted forced labor for the revolution, those who did not follow the directions of the so-called peasant union were often punished, jailed, and tortured. To exercise additional power over the movements of people in his region, Mariano Malpartida, the corregidor of Icla, required indigenous peasants to use national ID papers and other documents whenever they wanted to travel outside of the region.[64] Checking IDs in the region was a good opportunity to keep out any "subversives" on his blacklist.[65] Malpartida became an enemy of the AMP's goals and worked to combat Jach'aqullu's influence in Icla.

In the peripheral regions where the revolution was led by the provincial elite, daily life was shaped by elite hegemony. For instance, the establishment of public schools provided new fields for the empowerment of the dominant group in the indigenous world of communities and ex-haciendas. The MNR was not interested in maintaining the private school system that had been run by indigenous associations prior to the revolution, such as those run by the AMP in Tipapampa and Jatun Mayo. Instead, the national revolution promoted its discourse of integration in the public schools and pursued tightly controlled educational programs. In Chunca Cancha, Sumala (Icla), and other areas, the government mandated teaching in Spanish rather than Quechua, which made the AMP audience unhappy.[66]

Bolivian literature of the 1950s and 1960s depicts the new conceptualization of Indians that the AMP and Jach'aqullu rejected.[67] By employing the term *peasant community*, many writers and intellectuals denied whitening and attempted to claim that race and caste were irrelevant. On the other hand, the word *Indian* assumed pejorative connotations, implying that indigenous peoples were dirty. The winner of a municipal literature prize in the years after the national revolution, the Bolivian author Mario Guzmán Aspiazu wrote: "women with dirty blouses and long sleeves identify the Indian with the dirtiness that became its signifier."[68] This popular conception of Indians was also tied up with ideas of progress, industrialization, unionization, and the peasant community. Indeed, for the most part, individual Indians did not matter to the revolution, as Indians were seen as a mass of people represented in the idea of the peasant community. The author Oscar Gomez wrote about a peasant worker: "How the times have changed! Jesús does not work with a plow and bulls . . . he learned to work machines that now cut the land. Jesús is a tractor driver and he is indeed in the [peasant] union."[69]

After the agrarian reform of 1953, gender relationships also changed in indigenous communities as the spheres of power reserved for women in rituals collapsed in some regions. Before the national revolution the perception of gender and power in indigenous communities was very different from that in urban elite society. In Jach'aqhachi, for instance, the jilaqata (chief of the ethnic community) was elected with his wife, and they held office as a couple. However, with the national revolution this practice was abandoned.[70] Jach'aqhachi's peasant unions only enlisted male peasants as members and only considered male candidates when delegating community duties. Among the local sindicatos, those who included wives' names on the list of offices were told that they needed to stop the "ancient practice" of including women and "adjust to work in the civilized way."[71] In this sense the peasant union was not totally in the hands of Indians, and many levels of government used them to emphasize that the peasant must follow rather than lead. Not only did the rule of the *mama t'alla* (the jilaqata's wife) collapse but also the political participation of women declined dramatically during the time of the revolution. In addition, the revolution began to shape Indians' daily lives in other ways, demonstrating how much the Indian world of communities and ayllus had changed. For instance, during the 1960s members of the peasant unions no longer wanted to take their lunch wrapped in Andean textiles and instead insisted on taking it in "white pieces of cloth" because traditional textiles were seen as too old fashioned for men to carry.[72] In rejecting this process of whitening, Jach'aqullu actively encouraged women to participate in AMP meetings and believed that both men and women should be indigenous activists.[73]

Indian Law and the Wak'as versus MNR Assimilation Programs and Agrarian Reform

After the national revolution Andrés Jach'aqullu and the leadership of the AMP still promoted the Indian law, but it was modified by the revolution, which rejected Indian clothing and insisted that Indians were simply peasants. In response the AMP reinforced the dress code as the core of its indigenous identity and argued that wearing Indian clothing symbolized better communication with Pachamama and the Achachillas. Jach'aqullu believed that militant ethnic dress was necessary to differentiate indigenous people from cholos in all spheres of life. To him, cholo or Western dress was evidence of coloniality.[74] While this emphasis on Indian clothes was obviously not new in the AMP, Jach'aqullu reemphasized and revised the tradition by encouraging people to wear Indian clothes in all colors rather than only gray tones, as Titiriku and Miranda had done.[75] Jach'aqullu also placed more emphasis on the Aymara religion and the resumption of widespread and open worshipping of local deities, or wak'as, in Wanuni, a mining region in Oruro. He described the purpose of this in a letter published by a local newspaper in 1953: "Gaining an understanding of the Qullasuyu heritage, the true link to nature . . . [and] to recuperate, restore, conserve, and protect the wak'as."[76] The AMP and Jach'aqullu earned the nicknames Qullasuyus and *bayeta camisas* (referring to the fabric their clothing was made from) because they promoted an Indian dress code and talked about the revival of the Qullasuyu; in so doing they were rejecting the whitening path that Bolivia was following.[77]

Jach'aqullu also began to discourage indigenous people from getting married in the Catholic Church and instead urged them to celebrate their baptisms and death rituals outside of the church.[78] In September 1950 he and his wife Matilde Qulqi performed one of their first marriages between AMP members Julio Cutrina and Isabel Wari in Wilaqullu (Oruro) next to a wak'a on the top of the hill known as Waraq Achachilla.[79] They performed four other weddings from December 1950 to May 1952, and Jach'aqullu became known as the "Indian priest in Wanuni." As a result, the local Catholic priests and the corregidor of Bombo accused him of being a "false priest" and argued that "he was working against the government" by promoting an officially unrecognized religion. Church officials in Wanuni argued that he did "not follow the Catholic religion" and that he wanted to establish schools "to gain influence among the Indians."[80] These denunciations landed him in Wanuni's municipal jail in December of 1951, but since his accusers could not prove their case, he was released in February 1952.[81]

In the months to come, Jach'aqullu continued celebrating weddings, death rituals, and baptisms, leading to his jailing in August 1952 and again in April 1953.[82] During his last detention, Jach'aqullu was jailed along with his pregnant wife and four of his children. Matilde Qulqi did not want to leave her husband alone, and since she was also accused of being a "woman priest," she was imprisoned as well. As the children did not have

FIGURE 6.3. Andrés Jach'aqullu, his wife, Matilde Qulqi, and their children, circa 1951; the picture was taken once they were liberated from jail, after having been accused of being "Indian priests." The media called Matilde Qulqi *mama cura* (women priest). The idea of priesthood in urban Bolivia was so associated with men that Qulqi was presented as a curiosity by the racialized media. Courtesy of Fondo Privado de Agapito Ponce, Chuquisaca, Bolivia.

anyone else to care for them, they were allowed to be with their parents in jail. The mining unions of Wanuni hired a lawyer who helped to end the family's detention based on the children's welfare.[83] Although labor and indigenous organizations had moments of collaboration and support, as demonstrated in this case, after the national revolution they had clearly different agendas. Labor organizations were focused on the needs and concerns of the working class, so whitening was not an issue for them; on the other hand, Indian organizations such as the AMP focused on ethnic and religious components in their agenda of decolonization. Meanwhile, a new political atmosphere developed throughout the country as a result of the national revolution. Peasant unions started to organize in indigenous communities and haciendas. But, in regions such as Icla where the AMP was strong, unions were mainly led by mestizos and therefore did not represent indigenous people. In the mid-1950s requests for Toribio Miranda and Gregorio Titiriku's support increased dramatically in the ex-hacienda regions of Cochabamba, Chuquisaca, and northern Potosí. Peons and ayllu members from Icla, Muxuqhuya (Chuquisaca), and Misk'i (Cochabamba) engaged in bitter conflicts with the MNR peasant union, and some AMP members ended up in jail.[84] Since Miranda was over eighty years old and ill, he could no longer march on the front lines of activism as he had in the past. Titiriku also needed to stay in La Paz to denounce abuses on the haciendas to newspapers and international organizations. Under these circumstances, Miranda asked Jach'aqullu to tour these regions of conflict and support the AMP cells there.[85]

In August 1956 Jach'aqullu started the long trip from Chuquisaca to Cochabamba, finding conflicts with peasant unions and MNR cells everywhere he went. His clothing marked him as an Indian activist, which helped him gain acceptance in the region very quickly. In the Chuquisaca countryside, ethnic fashion was a signifier of Indianness, and Jach'aqullu took advantage of this to promote the AMP's goals.[86] In Icla Mariano Malpartida, a former administrator of the hacienda of Churumatas, had assumed the leadership of a new peasant union, the central agraria of Icla. He forced indigenous people to attend demonstrations in support of the MNR cell in Tarabuco.[87] When AMP members Ezequiel Urieta, Francisco Rivera, and Eladio Padilla refused to follow this order, Malpartida jailed a total of thirteen people, saying "all of them are in a conspiracy against the national revolution [for] not collaborating in the production of food supplies for the markets in Sucre."[88] Indeed, the national government assigned production quotas to the region of Icla, and the unions were responsible for reaching these goals between 1953 and 1958.[89]

In Muxuqhuya, Chuquisaca, the community's situation was also very difficult in the mid-1950s because of the power of the state-sponsored unions. The mestizos from the town led the central agraria of Muxuqhuya and were hungry to exercise their new power over the ayllus of the region.

In 1955 Pedro Quispe and Andrés Mayta, both from Qullachiwanway, had a dispute over a piece of land. Mayta did not agree with the results of the mediating ethnic authorities, and his godfather Claudio Peralta, a mestizo from the town of Muxuqhuya, persuaded him to seek "the justice of the peasant unions." The ayllus of the region rejected this recourse and resisted the arrival of Peralta and his people in the village of Qullachiwanway. At the next Muxuqhuya Sunday fair, Peralta attempted to detain all the leaders of the ayllus, many of whom were AMP members. They were all detained and imprisoned in Tarabuco.[90]

In Misk'i, Cochabamba, the unions led by mestizos entered into similar conflicts in 1958. In Quiwinal, Tinta, and Tipapampa the influence of Zenón Ibañez, a rural teacher and a leader of the regional peasant union that had a vast network stretching from Misk'i to Aiquile, helped expand the renting and sharecropping of ex-piqueros' land, essentially turning landowning ex-peons back into landless workers.[91] The unions used this type of arrangement to dominate indigenous people and took on an abusive hacienda-like role. Similar relationships developed in Saqaqa (northern Potosí), where Pedro Qarita, a regional chief of the central agraria of Saqaqa expanded his farm holdings in various indigenous communities.[92] Despite their disputes over ethnic ceremonies, the AMP used their connections to the Catholic Church in order to respond to these tactics. At the AMP's request, in 1962 Cardinal Maurer wrote a letter to the Indian communities in Sucre urging them to "try to respect each other."[93] This letter stemmed from the good relations that the AMP's Tomas Quevedo from Chuki Chuki (Chuquisaca) had with the church due to his sister's marriage to Elias Sacaca, who was a deacon and became a close assistant of Cardinal Maurer. In the letter of support, the cardinal did not address his differences with indigenous religiosity but instead emphasized his concern regarding the violence that had occurred in Chuquisaca. Frequently this type of letter was used as protection against the repression of unions and revolutionary orders. Given the hegemonic nature of the MNR in Bolivia during the late 1950s, the Catholic Church was often the only refuge for dissidents.

In this context Jach'aqullu intensified his activism and discovered a receptive environment in which to promote his ideas. He visited the Icla region in June 1957, Muxuquya in December, and Tipapampa (Cochabamba) in April 1958.[94] Throughout this tour he strongly denounced the political situation, arguing that "we should follow the Indian law [Ley de Indios] and worship for the protection of the wak'as and Achachilas. We should beg Pachamama, the lighting and the water [uma kankaña], and the Achachilas especially for protection against forced participation in peasant unions."[95] Jach'aqullu believed that a return to Aymara religion would liberate Indians from the suffering that had continued under the peasant unions after the national revolution. He argued that these regions were having problems because their regional wak'as were not worshipped as often as the wak'as in the highlands. He advocated worship on the hills and using appropriate Indian dress as the most effective way to solicit the intervention of Pachamama and the wak'as. Jach'aqullu also called on everybody to act as "good children" of Pachamama and the Achachilas.[96]

However, an incident that led to controversial rumors about the AMP marred Jach'aqullu's tour of Chuquisaca in late 1957. Two AMP men from Sipiqani, Claudio Villca and Teodoro Martínez, died in Pucara Falda (Icla) when they fell into a ravine that they did not see while they were climbing the hill on a dark night to worship their local wak'as, wearing militant ethnic dress and long hair.[97] Emilio Estrada, the Icla corregidor, charged Jach'aqullu with promoting ideas that "caused death in the region," a charge to which Jach'aqullu never responded.[98] As a result of these events, the rural elite of Icla declared that: "Jesus punished the idolatrous worshipers, [and that the] 'Qullasuyus' were the weirdest people [they had] ever seen." They pointed out, for example, that "the 'Qullasuyus' do not send their kids to school, nor do they want to invest time in building public schools."[99]

But believers in indigenous religions had a different interpretation of the events. According to them, Martínez and Villca had not been truly faithful to Pachamama and the "rites of Qullasuyu," so Pachamama and the Achachilas of Pucara Falda had punished them for their lack of faith. These indigenous adherents urged people to worship and devote more energy to Pachamama, or other punishments might be doled out. Indeed, the poor harvest between 1956 and 1958 was associated with the people's lack of faith in Pachamama and the Indian law's lack of power in the region. The AMP urged widespread worship in the hills and more prayers to Pachamama to end the "bad times that the revolution brought to them."[100] As a result, worship in the name of the Andean gods increased. Cantar Gallo and Nasaqani emerged as new centers of worship in the Icla region. From Icla, the worship of wak'as and Pachamama expanded to Poxpo, Muxuquya, Poroma, and Inqawasi.[101]

The death of Martínez and Villca fed myths about indigenous peoples, eventually leading to a belief in the existence of a group of Chuquisaca Indians who were phawayrunas, or "flying men." According to this myth, these men wore strange clothes that were not proper for the peasants of Chuquisaca, did not send their children to school, and died when they tried to fly. The Chuquisaca media's focus on this and other myths shaped the urban collective imagination about indigenous peoples. For instance, when some AMP leaders converted to the Bahá'í faith in the mid-1960s, the Bahá'ís had to issue a public statement clarifying that the idea of flying men was "misleading" and that the myth predated the Bahá'í faith in Chuquisaca. This collective imagination was racialized, with urban denizens ready to believe that Indians could do strange things. Although the media later argued that this was only a fantasy, this perception of differently dressed Indians helps illustrate how people could believe that Indians were able to fly and disliked schools. Indeed, urban Bolivians were ready to accept such myths because they dehumanized Indians and represented them as opposed to modernity.[102] In the context of these racialized myths, the Icla region had a mixed response to the application of agrarian reform. Since Jach'aqullu kept promoting adherence to the Indian law, he was accused of opposing agrarian reform. In late 1958 the peasant unions of Muxuqhuya denounced him as having said that the "true law is the Indian law and that if Indians followed it ex-peons would not need more laws because as 'jallp'a sangres' we are the true owners of the land." Based on these alleged comments, the peasant unions concluded that Jach'aqullu "encouraged the rejection" of the implementation of the National Commission of Agrarian Reform.[103]

Icla's mestizos were among the strongest supporters of the agrarian reform because it helped them consolidate land acquisitions. Therefore, some indigenous activists organized a boycott of land measurement, a process in which topographers visited every peasant plot and measured the lots in order to distribute private property titles. Francisco Rivera, Agapito Ponce Mamani, and Teodoro Cabezas urged the communities on the ex-haciendas of Wisk'anchis, Suruma, and Sumala to reject these measurements because the AMP believed that indigenous persons were already the legitimate owners of the land. Felix Vela Ortiz and Claudio Paye also organized similar protests.[104] During one such protest in Marapa, indigenous participants also burned national ID cards, state-issued birth certificates, marriage certificates, and some currency as an expression of their rejection of the type of modernity that was arriving in the region, based on ideologies of whitening and consumerism.[105] As these ideas spread, the topographers encountered resistance and often failed in their efforts to measure boundaries between lots. They reported that "it was only on the third attempt that we could measure the properties of this region . . . but Marapampa could not be done because of the opposition of indigenous peoples. . . . [At] the last moment the indigenous peoples brought a list of people from the region and they requested collective property [instead of individual property]. They did not understand the agrarian reform law."[106] In the villages of Redención Pampa and Quinua Chaxra, the commissioners in charge of the application of agrarian reform encountered similar problems; references to the Indian law occur frequently in the records of their efforts.[107] Peons rejected agrarian reform, arguing that as followers of the Indian law, they should not follow other laws. They believed that the Indian law embodied all their rights to land, so they did not need titles from the Bolivian state. This widespread attitude shows how embedded the AMP discourse had become in Icla.

Jach'aqullu's discourse and activism helped to disseminate the notion of the Indian law in the context of the national revolution. His handling of religious rituals such as weddings and his calls for people to worship the Aymara gods confronted the challenges brought by agrarian reform. As in Miranda and Titiriku's time, the ideas of the Indian law gained support because they dovetailed with local issues, such as the abuse of state-sponsored unions. Jach'aqullu thus helped to reshape the AMP's Indian law in the 1960s.

Speaking Out and Subverting Racial Stereotypes in Postrevolutionary Bolivia

In the mid-1960s a new political context began to emerge in Bolivia. After twelve years of the national revolution, the MNR disintegrated and a succession of military regimes governed the country. Some ideas initiated by the revolution, such as private ownership of land, peasant unions, and the right to vote, finally coalesced and were appropriated by the indigenous peasantry in many parts of the country. A new generation of grassroots leaders emerged at the local level of the peasant unions and gradually replaced the mestizo ruling elite at the head of peasant unions in Chuquisaca, northern Potosí, and southern Cochabamba. This new generation was more sympathetic to Jach'aqullu and ideas of the Indian law. Thus, by the 1970s the peasant unions had stopped working against the AMP in Sumala and Cantar Gallo (Chuquisaca). As had occurred in the Aymara highlands, these regions gradually came under the control of their own people. This process started on the most productive ex-haciendas and gradually extended throughout the entire area.[108] In 1964 the sons of ex-peons in Churumumu took control of Icla's largest peasant union the central agaria of Uyuni. By 1967 most of the peasant union of Icla was under grassroots control, but the top positions still remained in the hands of mestizos.[109] Confrontation accompanied this process of change elsewhere in the Bolivian countryside. In the valley of Cochabamba, a power struggle emerged between Clisa and Ucureña. However, it was not until the Katarista movement of 1979 that the national leadership of the peasant unions landed in the hands of an indigenous person.[110]

After Miranda died in 1959, the AMP started to go through a crucial change, and Jach'aqullu was asked to remain in La Paz. Although Titiriku was still active during the 1960s, he could not perform many duties, and by the early 1960s Jach'aqullu had emerged as a central figure in the AMP. Little did he know that the end of the AMP was drawing near.[111] Jach'aqullu saw the rural elite, made up mostly of mestizos, as a central problem that would be very difficult to confront. Although Jach'aqullu was very active in the countryside of Cochabamba and Chuquisaca during the 1950s, he stayed away from the regions of greatest activity in the early 1960s because different MNR cells and centrales agrarias had obtained warrants against him. In 1961 a judge in Icla issued a warrant against him for the accidental deaths of Vilka and Martinez in 1957. A judge in Aiquile issued another warrant in 1963 for "cultivating uprisings." And the subprefect of Misk'i Province accused him of "giving the wrong ideas to the peasants of Laguna Grande [by] telling them [that] the revolution was not good for them [and] that they should follow the Indian law."[112]

Like Miranda and Gallardo who distributed hacienda lands in late 1940s in the name of the Indian law, Jach'aqullu used the Indian law to contest the liberal and populist program of the agrarian reform. However, Jach'aqullu and other AMP were not the only ones in the late 1950s and early 1960s to resist the problems caused by the agrarian reform in the region of Lake Titikaka. Laureano Machaca, who was one of the leaders of the new peasant unions in Escoma, distanced himself from the progovernment peasant unionist agenda and called for regional autonomy and the creation of an Aymara republic on the shores of Lake Titikaka.[113] While Machaca's project was an Aymara nationalist one, it was totally secular and centered on creating an Aymara republic run by indigenous peasant unions. In Escoma the mestizos retained the municipality and exercised power from there, while in Icla and Tarvita, Jach'aqullu's hometown, mestizos also ran the peasant unions.[114] Machaca and Jach'aqullu were both opposed to the way that the national revolution kept the mestizos in power and perpetuated racialized systems in the countryside. However, Jach'aqullu and the AMP's project emphasized cultural and religious transformation, while Machaca's project lacked these components. Indigenous resistance to the projects of the revolution was strongest in areas where mestizos had clearly different priorities and where exclusion and racialization continued long after 1952.

Although Jach'aqullu gained some new followers in Marapampa and Ch'ikitayox, his audience began to decline in southern Bolivia, and he had to find other ways to carry out his political agenda. La Paz was quickly acquiring an Aymara majority; however, most Aymaras were cholos who had adopted Western, working-class dress. Jach'aqullu's handmade woolen clothes and long hair allowed him to represent himself as a "true" Indian in the urban imagination. Because he appeared to be from a very remote indigenous community, he shocked people when they learned that he was literate or heard him speak Spanish fluently. For example, Dr. Luis Monje, one of the lawyers of the International Labour Organization, wrote the following in 1967: "We had a labor discussion [meeting] at the University of La Paz and [an] Indian from Oruro, Andrés, came and he, surprisingly, spoke Spanish well and he was literate, he was very smart."[115] During this time Jach'aqullu broke all the racial stereotypes established after the national revolution, contradicting ideas that anyone dressed as an Indian was an illiterate person from the country who only spoke native languages. Due to his command of Spanish, his literacy, and his experience working as a policeman, Jach'aqullu would have been considered a cholo in La Paz if not for his clothing.

In 1958 Jach'aqullu focused on defending indigenous rights by requesting the support of Bolivian intellectuals and international organizations based in La Paz, specifically writers such as Dr. Juan María Salles, Gabriel Gosalvez, Enrique Baldivieso, José Espada Aguirre, Waldo Belmonte Pool, Juan Cabral García, Fernando Díez de Medina, and Fausto Reinaga. This group of intellectuals frequently wrote in national newspapers about indigenous issues. José Espada helped Jach'aqullu connect with international organizations such as the United Nations. Gabriel Gosalvez wrote frequently in defense of "indigenous culture."[116] Because Jach'aqullu spoke Spanish, could give them firsthand information, and could attend meetings in La Paz, he was a crucial source of information and inspiration about indigenous issues and identity for these intellectuals and international dignitaries. During this time Jach'aqullu advocated the right to worship native religions, denounced the abuses of MNR unions, and declared the Indian law to be the best path for indigenous people to regain their rights. Jach'aqullu's ideas had an especially powerful influence on Fausto Reinaga and Fernando Díez de Medina. In the 1970s Reinaga was the most influential writer on Indian nationalism, and he remained prominent until the end of the twentieth century, inspiring different indigenous movements.

The relationship between the AMP and their audience changed in the new political context that emerged after 1964. As Steve Feierman has asserted, activist intellectuals must perform and speak for a specific audience because their representations are meaningless without such a link.[117] The AMP activist intellectuals advocating subaltern nationalism lost their audience in the 1960s and 1970s because ex-peons and their children were gradually empowered as they gained influence in the peasant unions. These unions ceased to be foreign organizations, and indigenous peasants gradually appropriated the revolution's ideas. Activist intellectuals such as Jach'aqullu continued to insist on subaltern nationalism through their mode of dress and their faith in Indian gods, but they became increasingly powerless as their audience diminished.

In a radio broadcast in Aymara and Quechua in November 1973, a man using the name Andrés Tikuna called all Indians to a meeting in Tiwanaku.[118] Tikuna was actually Andrés Jach'aqullu, who had taken his mother's maiden name in the 1970s because his clandestine indigenous activism had become dangerous under the Banzer dictatorship, which persecuted activists of all kinds. Additionally, Tikuna (Jach'aqullu) had become a Bahá'í preacher in the mid-1960s, and the Bahá'ís strictly forbade its members from political activity. These circumstances forced Jach'aqullu to handle his activism with extreme care.[119] Preaching for the Bahá'ís provided Jach'aqullu with income to support his family and allowed him to travel widely as an international preacher and visit Indian communities throughout the Americas, such as the Mapuche in Chile, the Navajo in the

United States, and the Maya in Mexico. By the late 1960s, he was the most famous Indian in the Bahá'í international arena, even visiting the Bahá'í World Center in Israel. However, while Jach'aqullu might have developed a hybrid religiosity, there is evidence to indicate that his faith in Pachamama and the good spirits embodied in the wak'as remained strong.[120]

The AMP refused to join the leftist parties because they were too secular, rejected Indian nationalism, and condemned the Aymara religion. However, some AMP members decided to become Bahá'ís because the religion offered them legal protection against the abuses they suffered at the hands of the state-run peasant unions. When the Bahá'ís focused on Latin America as part of their strategic plan in the early 1960s, the AMP were in desperate need of legal aid. As Andrés Jach'aqullu searched for support, he found the Bahá'ís, whom he convinced to give legal support to AMP activists. Over the years, Jach'aqullu and other indigenous activists became believers. Several of the AMP activists joined the Bahá'ís because the religion's syncretic vision did not condemn the Aymara religion as did the Catholic and Protestant faiths. The AMP was naturally attracted to this more open position.[121] Recounting his conversion to that faith in the late 1960s, Teodoro Tellez remembered that Andrés Jach'aqullu had told several AMP in La Paz, "I met a group of very good people and their religion is good, let us get into this religion, they will help us [with our legal problems], and they will became our allies." The AMP responded by completely rejecting the idea, saying "our religion is the wak'as, our path is the Indian law, and we worship Pachamama. The Bahá'í comes from the whites and it is for the Spaniards."[122] When Andrés Jach'aqullu insisted on his proposal and brought the Bahá'ís to Chuquisaca, several AMP did enroll, though many others never accepted it. When those AMP who did join asked the Bahá'ís for their opinion on Aymara religion, the response was, "your religion is good, is truth." According to Tellez, after that various AMP groups decided to "get into that religion to get protection against the sindicatos that persecuted us."[123]

Indeed, when the AMP used the phrase *to get into* to refer to conversion, they meant that they were using the organization as a resource to maintain their counter-hegemonic views. However, many left the Bahá'ís after just a few years. The rupture came during a international Bahá'í meeting in 1974 that was held in Sucre, with more than two hundred AMP members attending from the valleys of Chuquisaca.[124] They all came wearing the AMP dress and congregated in the main cinema of Sucre, where the conference was being held. The AMP was particularly interested in speaking to Hooper Dunbar, one of the Bahá'í leaders who had come from the World Center in Israel. Agapito Ponce Mamani asked to speak and was turned down, probably because the conference's leaders knew that he would raise controversial topics. Other members also tried unsuccessfully to speak during the first day of the meeting. The second day, Francisco Rivera finally had a chance.[125] He asked if the Indians who had converted to the Bahá'í faith should follow the "ley de los españoles," which meant the current Bolivian law (liberal, conservative, or populist), or if the Bahá'í faith would enforce the Indian law. The response he got from Hooper Dunbar was that the Bahá'ís should honor the Bolivian law and obey the government, whatever its political affiliation. After his response was translated into Quechua and Spanish, the two hundred AMP members stood up and started speaking loudly in Quechua, and then they left. That night, this group congregated on the Killa Killa hill and decided to found their own official religion, which would allow them to practice without persecution. This resulted in the founding of the Hermanos Espirituales (Spiritual Brotherhood), which passed bylaws in 1969 and was legally recognized by the government, thus becoming the first institutionalized native religion in Bolivia.[126]

Despite this break in 1974, Bahá'í and Protestant churches had shaped the AMP, and the Indian law had transformed over time. The Hermanos Espirituales remained a branch of the AMP that followed its dress code, created its own bible that narrated the suffering of the indigenous people in hacienda times, and incorporated the AMP's early messages. They remembered Toribio Miranda, Gregorio Titiriku, Feliciano Inka Marasa, and other AMP members from the time of the haciendas as sacred people with a special message from their God. At the beginning they spoke about a God called the Sun, but by the 1990s they called that being only God or the angel Gabriel.[127] In 1970 the Hermanos Espirituales built a temple with colonial and modern elements in Ruditayox, Tarwita, Chuquisaca. The religion still exists today, albeit in a much reduced form, in the region of Tarwita. Its adherents are still opposed to participation in national elections, unions, development projects, and municipal government. They believe in the Indian law but in a millenarian way that contains more Christian elements than before.[128] The Hermanos Espirituales in Cantar Gallo are not the only ones who directly trace their roots to the AMP. There is a small group in Culpina, Chuquisaca, who invented their own language using a system similar to kipus, the ancient Inka and pre-Inka recording devices,

and they also practice a form of native religion. The other Hermanos Espirituales in Tumata Palqa, northern Potosí, emphasize indigenous medicine
and religion. Thus, in going from being a political conception of society
to a type of religious utopia, the Indian law lost its power to transform
people in the name of the wak'as, as it had in the 1940s and 1950s, and
with this shift, the AMP began its decline.

Despite this, Jach'aqullu's role among the indigenous population, although clandestine and precarious, was quite important and influenced
the development of Katarismo in the 1980s. In 1973 different groups of
Indian intellectuals, students, and Indian peasant organizations gathered
in a meeting called the Congreso de Tiwanaku in La Paz. Jach'aqullu, using
the name Tikuna, was one of the main organizers of the meeting, along
with Constantino Lima, Jaime Apaza, and Luciano Tapia.[129] Jach'aqullu
held very well-attended discussions about Gregorio Titiriku and Toribio
Miranda's work within the AMP. Based on these talks, the congress produced the *Tiwanaku Manifesto*, a founding statement of Katarismo and one
of the most important documents in the history of civil rights in Bolivia.
Referring to the relationship between non-Indian Bolivians and indigenous peoples, the manifesto states that "a nation oppressed by another
cannot be free."

The congress asked Jach'aqullu to assume a position on the permanent board it created, but he refused because he would have had to give
up his work as a preacher. Instead he proposed placing his son, Rogelio
Cerrogrande, on the board of directors.[130] He followed a similar strategy
in 1977, when he helped organize the first Indian party in South America,
the Movimiento Indio Tupak Katari (MITKA), an Indianist party. Again,
he was asked to serve on the board of directors but could not risk losing
his source of income as a preacher, since he had three children in col-
lege. This time, Jach'aqullu proposed his wife as a member, so Matilde
Qulqi became responsible for MITKA women's affairs.[131] Matilde Qulqi
also stood as a MITKA candidate for the Bolivian Chamber of Deputies
from the Oruro Department in the election of 1978—the first in Bolivia
following military rule. At the time the idea of Indians running for office
and the very notion of an Indian party was considered more fiction than
reality. Although Matilde Qulqi did not get the post, she was very involved
with the media and party activities.[132]

Other indigenous activists of the AMP followed similar paths during
this time. In the 1960s and 1970s, many AMP members worked silently

with Fausto Reinaga and helped form the Partido Indio de Bolivia (Bolivian Indian Party), which disbanded shortly after the election of 1978.[133] The interrelationship with the AMP helped Reinaga to produce a large number of books that developed the ideology for the modern phase of the indigenous movement in Latin America. Among the movement's leaders were Julian Ugarte, Agapito Ponce Mamani, Celestino Peralta, and Matilde Qulqi.[134] In the early 1970s this group of activists even raised money in the communities to publish the first edition of Reinaga's *Revolución India*.[135] Reinaga also installed a facility in his house for indigenous people who came from other parts of the country.[136] Some of the people who spent time with Reinaga were Bahá'ís, Methodists, Adventists, or involved in earlier versions of community-based Catholic groups in La Paz, Oruro, and Sucre. In 1970 many of the Indians from Potosí and Chuquisaca who came to La Paz to attend the Bahá'í meeting, which paid for their travel expenses, also attended a meeting with Fausto Reinaga to learn about the new ideology called Indianismo.[137]

The Katarista movement of the 1980s emerged out of this experience of Indianismo. The Katarista and Indianista movements are in dialogue with the history of liberal, leftist, and populist thought in Bolivia. While the Indianistas argue that oppression as a nation should be the only focus of the Indian agenda, the Kataristas argue that Indian peasants are oppressed as a class and nation. Thus, the Katarista struggle is basically an ethnic and class struggle. Katarista activists used an ethnic discourse that strongly condemned racialization when they spoke to the recently formed Confederación Nacional de Trabajadores Campesinos de Bolivia, a national umbrella organization of Bolivian peasants. Katarista ideology also influenced two political parties that had some clout in the late 1980s: the Movimiento Revolucionario Tupak Katari Liberación (MRTKL), a Katarista party, and MITKA, an Indianist party. In fact, Víctor Hugo Cárdenas from MRTKL became the first Aymara vice president of Bolivia in 1994. Additionally, Felipe Quispe, an Aymara from La Paz who placed fourth in the election of 2002, brought the notion of two republics to the national arena. Quispe was closely aligned with the last generation of AMP in Chuquisaca and organized the Ayllus Rojos, a guerrilla Indian organization led by the AMP's descendants in the 1980s. While J'achaqullu and the AMP's notion of two republics was used to express differences between Indians and mestizos following the national revolution, Quispe used the same idea to express political and ideological differences between the white power structure and the indigenous movement in the Banzer era (1971–1978).[138] In contemporary Bolivian language, this contradiction is often expressed as mestizos versus originarios (native peoples).

Forging an Agenda of Decolonization in a Time of Revolution

Jach'aqullu's history shows how indigenous activism changed in the decades after the consolidation of the national revolution, during which the AMP became a dissident voice, as the cases of Icla, Tarwita, and Wilaqullu demonstrate. After the revolution the vast majority of the population was still in a subaltern condition and ruled by a minority of whites and mestizos, who promoted whitening in the national discourse. In this new era indigenous people still felt the sting of racism after they migrated to urban areas, and this became the context in which the nationalism of jaqi peoples, or Indians, reemerged.[139]

Assimilation discourse promoted a form of de-Indianizaton during the stage of Bolivian modernization that overlapped with the national revolution. Assimilation was the leftists' main goal in the 1940s, and the populists considered it to be their greatest achievement after the national revolution. In 1953 Víctor Paz Estenssoro, the leader of the national revolution and three-time Bolivian president, told an indigenous crowd they were "no longer" Indians, but "peasants."[140] Astenio Averanga, an intellectual and policy maker of the revolution, argued that the national revolution would essentially repopulate the country by transforming people's pre-modern Indianness. Paz Estenssoro and Averanga perceived this "transformation" as "profoundly meaningful" because, for them, it meant that Indians could become modern. As state policy after the national revolution, de-Indianization through the removal of Indian signifiers was an alternative and supposedly nonviolent way of practicing ethnic cleansing.[141]

After the national revolution, ex-peons in possession of land in regions like Icla and Tarwita turned to the Indian law because they were worried that the agrarian reform was empowering the rural mestizos, who controlled state-oriented peasant unions and reinforced racialized practices against Indians. As such, the Indian law became a way to articulate an agenda of decolonization that spoke to the contradictions created by the national revolution of 1952. Postrevolutionary indigenous activists developed their own nationalism based on faith in wak'as and a narrative of the

Aymara past, and they promoted this project through a network of cells in the western part of the country. The enactment of this indigenous network also called on gender relationships in strategic ways. Matilde Qulqi, Jach'aqullu's wife, represented him politically at several points over the years, and she acted as co-priest in various indigenous ceremonies. In both religious and political contexts, Jach'aqullu and Qulqi's relationship fits the Aymara world's notion of gender complementarity and was an essential part of their struggle. The Katarista and Indianista movements still incorporated issues of gender in their work, but there was less emphasis than was present in the AMP. In the end, from the 1950s through the 1970s, the AMP had a major, though at times indirect, effect on the modern Bolivian political system. It helped not only to invigorate a new type of activism in the late 1970s but also provided more contemporary indigenous activists with historical context and concepts with which to fight late twentieth-century coloniality.[142]

| Conclusion | The AMP's Innovations and Its Legacy in Bolivia under Evo Morales |

When they separated from previous activist networks, the four AMP leaders that I have studied in this book drew on memory, understood as the capacity to form historical interpretations based on the impact of past experiences on the present, in order to renovate the indigenous movement of the 1930s and then to respond to the changed historical circumstances after 1952.[1] Gregorio Titiriku and Toribio Miranda emphasized the political and cultural importance of worshiping Aymara gods, advocated for an end to segregation in public plazas and streetcars, worked to secure autonomous education for Indians, and rejected symbols of white and mestizo hegemony. This generation based its activism in part on the previous generation of indigenous activists that had participated in the civil war of 1898–1899. For instance, it was crucial for them to draw on the direct participation of Toribio Miranda's stepfather in the early network of apoderados, mallkus, jilaqatas, and segundas. The AMP's later adherents, such as Meliton Gallardo and Andrés Jach'aqullu, were in turn inspired by the memory of men like Miranda and Titiriku. They also reaped the benefits of their predecessors' organizational structure of ayllus and ex-haciendas, which I have defined here as a network. They used this network grounded in memory to oppose the agrarian reform in 1953, reject state-issued identification cards and the civil registration of weddings and births, and resist public Spanish-speaking elementary schools. These leaders faced an urgent need to reinterpret the past, given the events of the agrarian reform and the national revolution. They responded by using memory to elaborate and re-elaborate a political discourse in terms of these new historical circumstances.

The AMP sought actively to shape memory by producing documents such as testimony or memoirs. For instance, in the era of the national revolution and agrarian reform (1952–1964), members of the first generation of the AMP made sure to create notarized versions of their testimonies in order to project their "lives and experiences" onto the next generation. Indeed, through the narrative of Andrés Jach'aqullu's life, I show how Indian activists such as Fidel Wanka and Radio Mendez were especially influential in transferring this memory to what later would become the Katarista and Indianista movements as they, along with some members of the AMP, confronted the challenges of living under military dictatorship.[2]

The idea of memoria corta, or historical interpretation concerning the previous generation (short-term memory), helps us to understand the relationship between the first and second generations of the AMP because the second generation elaborated a political discourse based on their collective memory of the first generation.[3] The notion of memoria larga (long-term memory or historical interpretation regarding two or more generations earlier), however, explains the reasons why the AMP emerged as a separate network of cells in this story, starting with Santos Marka T'ula. In other words, memory helped the AMP to articulate an indigenous political discourse in 1936 and then rearticulate it after 1952. However, memory's use, role, and impact were different in these two eras of the AMP. The AMP's work in producing and circulating counter-hegemonic memory prior to 1952 focused primarily on the liberal state while the post-1952 AMP focused on the populist state. More than a half-century later, their decolonization agenda still resonates in twenty-first-century Bolivia. Consequently, the story of these four men is also the story of the production of an Aymara and indigenous memory.

Baud and Rutten identify three important types of activist intellectuals: innovators, movement intellectuals, and allies.[4] I consider the AMP to be innovators because they carved out a new discursive space and developed the political program most commonly known as the Indian law through the conscious construction and deployment of memory, in addition to other strategies. While Santos Marka T'ula built an indigenous movement based primarily on using legal documents and colonial documents, Miranda and Titiriku based their ideology on faith in the Indian gods, religion, and some elements of the Law of the Indies, all of which they combined to call the Indian law. The second generation of AMP, with the help of Melitón Gallardo, trained several "movement intellectuals" in Sumala and Tarvita in the 1940s, along with the Mizque peasants who resisted the unions in southern Cochabamba in the 1950s and 1960s. Jach'aqullu continued the work of the AMP in the era of the Bolivian National Revolution and confronted new challenges such as the agrarian reform and mestizo-led peasant unions. Although these men were fairly heterogeneous in personality and leadership style, they all shared a belief in the importance of the Indian law. Instead of allowing their network to fracture, they were able to create a cross-regional, multiethnic organization. Despite their differences, these activists reached an ideological consensus that rendered those differences insignificant. To conclude this history of the AMP, I look at the main points of the AMP discourse as it evolved over the course of its fifty-year development and identify its traces in contemporary Bolivian indigenous politics.

Framing Earth Politics and Coloniality

During the fifty years that the AMP operated, its leaders were exposed to several imported religions as well as Marxist and liberal ideas, all of which shaped and reshaped these four life stories and the production of their memories. For example, imported religious ideas fundamentally influenced the lives of some of these men. Indeed, Gregorio Titiriku adhered to Methodism for many years and benefitted from it, as long as it did not interfere with his goals. Andrés Jach'aqullu, however, joined the Bahá'í faith in times of the AMP's retreat; among the Bahá'í, he and other AMP members found some legal support and religious tolerance, at least in the 1960s. The involvement of Gregorio Titiriku and Jach'aqullu with imported faiths can be explained by understanding that ecumenism is like a "nutrient" in Andean religions.[5] Imported religions could sometimes serve to enrich the Andean pantheon, without losing the goals of earth politics in the AMP narrative. Because of the role of indigenous memory, both generations of AMP remained fervent believers in earth politics although with different emphases and priorities. Earth politics, unlike other philosophies or political frames, incorporated the worship of nature and

Pachamama. The AMP linked ideas about Pachamama, the Achachilas, and the worship of qixuqixu (lightning) and uma kankaña (water) to fighting the colonial structures that imposed dehumanization on many indigenous people in mid-twentieth-century Bolivia. The AMP organized around local concerns regarding nature and Pachamama, and the movement argued that Indians had the right to practice their own religion, baptisms, and weddings, apart from Catholic or Christian rites. These four intellectuals grew up in close contact with the beliefs of their constituencies; they shared a "common sense."[6] These leaders thus became the transmitters of assertive local, indigenous sentiments and articulated counter-hegemonic discourses.[7]

However, as Tilly argues, repertoires of collectivity are not only based in local history and context; translocal mimicry and exchange also take place, with activists adapting borrowed forms to their specific conditions, just as the AMP incorporated aspects of their program borrowed from different traditions.[8] From the Catholic tradition they appropriated the notion of using baptismal and wedding ceremonies to express their religious beliefs; from the Left they took the idea of class struggle; from liberals, their emphasis on legal institutions; all of which they used to construct their Indian law ideology. These activist intellectuals thus incorporated a range of discourses for local adaptation, convinced their peers and wider audiences that their ideas were worthy of consideration, and strategically positioned themselves within relevant communication networks.[9] They effectively connected their prospective constituency to new sources of ideas and to new networks of activists and allies. This task eventually became institutionalized under the name of the AMP.

The AMP leaders' ability to speak and write Spanish and their connections with the urban world played an important role in the formation of their movement, which interpreted Bolivia as a colonial institution, a world divided between "Spaniards" and "Indians" (see chapter 4). These activist intellectuals strategically used this dichotomy to express the racialization that indigenous people, including themselves, faced in Bolivian society. Their knowledge of the colonial legacies of the Andean world, such as the memories of land usurpations and their systematic study of Aymara language, religion, ritual sites, and cultural codes, directly informed their political ideology and strategy. The AMP was one of the first indigenous activist groups in the twentieth century to essentialize racial and ethnic differences and put them to work in favor of their own goals. The conditions that they were resisting would later be termed *internal colonialism*.[10]

Unlike the collaboration between indigenous and Marxists activists in Ecuador,[11] the indigenous activists of the AMP operated very independently. They did not rely on intermediaries from the Left or Right, and they were focused on their own agendas. Their goals and independence reveal the complexities and radical nature of the Bolivian indigenous agenda in the early and mid-twentieth century, which stands in stark contrast to the integrationist and Indigenista narratives. These four indigenous intellectuals were able to organize hacienda peons under a set of ideologies that were primarily based on the indigenous gods. Although the AMP also worked closely with the Left at some points in their history, over the course of fifty years they were able to construct their own networks, keep their independence, and elaborate sophisticated political discourses based on the idea of the Indian law. Also unlike the other movements during this time that have been studied by Laura Gotkowitz and others, the AMP was actively involved in the revival of indigenous beliefs, religion, and spirituality in Bolivia.[12]

While Toribio Miranda and Melitón Gallardo mostly worked within the AMP network, one of Titiriku and Jach'aqullu's greatest assets was their range of audiences. These leaders were able to speak with rural communities, hacienda peons, and international delegations. Jach'aqullu, however, also sent letters he wrote himself to international organizations. Both leaders followed what was going on with other indigenous networks both inside and outside of Bolivia, and they knew many lawyers, politicians, and public intellectuals. They communicated with these audiences in both Spanish and Aymara.

Between 1920 and 1960 state institutions and media (newspapers and radio) primarily reached urban areas and played only a minor role in the Indian public sphere. Given that the vast majority of the Indian audience was illiterate, the AMP leaders mainly communicated with their audience orally, a strategy that is still extraordinarily important today in Bolivia. As their ideas were disseminated, heard, and debated, Indians' concerns slowly moved from the private to the public sphere by word of mouth. Strategies of language were thus crucial for their popular audience; in their vocabulary and concepts, the Aymara, Quechua, and Uru languages retained the feelings and history of the relationship between whites and

Indians. For instance, the idea of the opposition of contraries in the Aymara language are expressed through oppositional pairings, like Indians versus Spaniards, which in pre-Hispanic times was communicated in the concept of *alaxsaya* ("the ones on the top," *la parcialidad de arriba*) versus *mank'asaya* ("the ones on the bottom," *la parcialidad de abajo*). These conflicts and contradictions embedded in the language also usually included the participation of the gods. Interweaving these concepts in their discourse, the AMP broadcast their national ideas and diagnoses from the highlands to landless people in the hacienda regions. While many Indians in the highlands joined peasant unions, Jach'aqullu and the AMP found an engaged audience in the haciendas and used oral resources to organize them.

Toribio Miranda, Gregorio Titiriku, Melitón Gallardo, and Andrés Jach'aqullu were formed by the same experience of coloniality that shaped the lives of many Latin American Indians during most of the twentieth century. Miranda belonged to the Uru people, an Indian minority in the highlands. He focused on elaborating a decolonization project that used traditional patriarchal structures to create a social movement around its anti-colonial agenda.[13] Titiriku went further than Miranda by unifying people through their beliefs in Indian gods, clearly articulating an Indian agenda and vilifying the ways that the Bolivian state dominated Indians. These two men were the main elaborators of the Indian law, while Andrés Jach'aqullu and Melitón Gallardo promoted it in a new era and context. Jach'aqullu brought these ideas to new audiences and continued the work of AMP during the challenging post-1952 era. Melitón Gallardo, for his part, adapted the AMP's Indian law to the specific circumstances of the hacienda regions. Despite their different roles, all of these leaders embodied the Indian law.

Religion, Ethnicity, Politics, and Social Movements

In order to promote their agenda and discourse, the AMP had grown to 489 cells in the highlands and valleys by 1949; each cell worked for the larger goal of the network: the Indian law. According some moderate estimates, each cell had an average of twenty to fifty adherents or members in the 1940s, depending of the size of the surrounding haciendas, ayllus, and communities. The estimates indicate that while a few ex-haciendas had even more members after 1952, most of the cells in ayllus and ex-haciendas had dwindled to only a dozen members. Although their network had grown far more fragile as they began to focus on the new, populist state of the revolution, the AMP cells were still held together by the goals of the Indian law.[14] Prior to 1952 many of the adherents were peons, arrenderos, arrimantes, and community and ayllu members. Many of them were seeking colonial titles and advocating for legislation that would protect their rights. After 1952 new adherents included ex-peons and ayllu members who did not really benefit in any significant way from the outcomes of the revolution.

Adherents of the AMP referred to the working class (cholos and ch'utas) as "converted Spaniards" and to the elite (whites and mestizos) as the "thieves of the Republic of Indians."[15] Indigenous activists also strongly condemned cholos' and ch'utas' rejection of their Indian heritage. Many AMP leaders had confronted issues of dress code in their own lives, changing their style of dress at turning points in their personal histories. From their point of view, becoming a cholo or ch'uta implied crossing a racial frontier at the point of no return. Therefore, Indian fashion became a signifier of this difference in both the cities and the countryside. AMP activists envisioned the republic of Indians as resisting the whitening of the Bolivian racial structure. In their earth politics the AMP called all de-Indianized people (including the white elite, mestizos, cholos, and chu'tas) "Spaniards."[16]

The AMP sought out Indians living in ayllus, communities, and haciendas to bolster their earth politics. Their program of a republic of Indians subsumed all of Bolivia's ethnic groups under the category of Indians, presenting them as united against the rest of society. In addressing their varied audience, indigenous intellectuals need to establish credibility as spokespeople, inspirers, or intermediaries who consolidate their legitimacy. The moment popular intellectuals connect to a social movement they become susceptible to the same kinds of dynamics as the movement itself. As their position changes, so do the political impact and significance of their ideas and interpretations. Social movements emerge, articulate demands, find audiences, have their demands granted or repressed, and then are either institutionalized or disappear. In the course of such historical cycles, the position of popular intellectuals—and their ideas— may be strengthened, marginalized, or contested. Such processes are understood, as we have seen throughout this work, by focusing on the social and historical dynamics of the activism of such intellectuals.[17]

The AMP's earth politics grounded itself in Aymara religiosity, the radical spirituality of the Bolivian Andes. The dominant Bolivian culture of the mid-twentieth century assumed that Aymara spirituality was based on superstition, and adherents mostly practiced it clandestinely. As the AMP refined its discourse, both the cult of Pachamama and the worship of wak'as on the mountaintops became central to its followers. As we saw, Melitón Gallardo sought to practice a spirituality based on the Saxama Mountain in Oruro, one of the great spiritual centers of the Aymara world, and Jach'aqullu expanded the role of religious rites by creating new ones, such as weddings and death rites.

Indigenous spirituality proved fertile ground for the production of counter-hegemonic texts because it provided the AMP with an oral tradition that allowed it to build an ethnic social movement based on previous movements.[18] The AMP elaborated new notions of Indian fashion as an external representation of the jaqi religion that exemplified their radical perspectives of opposition to the de-Indianization represented by ch'utas and cholos. They created their own dress code as a signifier of the republic of Indians. Miranda emphasized the restrictions faced by qhuchapuchus (Uru), montepuchus (Quechua), and chullpapuchus (Aymara) during the 1930s and 1940s in Bolivia.[19] Titiriku spoke from the core of the Aymara world in favor of what he called the "Qullasuyu blood," in other words, the Indian race.[20] In Chuquisaca, Gallardo used a regional perspective and ideas about jallp'a sangres to elaborate a discourse on the notion of Qullasuyu. As the movement spread, these diverse ideas merged through the use of the term jallp'a sangres to inspire ethnic pride and religious devotion to Indian deities. These ideas about Qullasuyu and jallp'a sangres came from the AMP leaders' experience with the oral tradition of the highland mallkus and apoderados in the early 1920s, among whom fragments of the Law of the Indies as well books written by leftist intellectuals circulated. In this sense the republic of Indians incorporated notions of ethnicity into its social movement by referring to an imagined community of people directly linked to the pre-Inka heritage.

For the AMP, the Indian law was not a remote colonial legacy but rather a contemporary tool to articulate indigenous activists' anticolonial discontent with racist policies throughout the mid-twentieth century. The AMP activist intellectuals were thus able to use the discourse of the Indian law to facilitate indigenous peoples' incorporation into an imagined community. Fighting for the Indian law kept this movement alive through the two generations. Because the AMP indigenous activists and their audience envisioned a community with common religious elements that also incorporated a racial factor, their efforts can be considered a social movement of earth politics: the jaqi gods intervened in Bolivian politics.

Earth Politics and Its Resonances in Bolivia under Evo Morales

Earth politics is a discourse that encompassed ideas about land, territory, nation, faith, religion, rights, and Indianness—all issues that strongly resonate in contemporary Bolivia. After the era of the national revolution, Bolivia underwent a long period of dictatorships and military administrations from 1964 to 1982, during which little progress was made in terms of equality for indigenous peoples and furthering an earth politics agenda. Since many indigenous women did not participate in elections in the 1980s, democratic regimes in Bolivia from 1983 to 2006 worked to expand the electorate by getting women out to the polls, which had an enormous impact on political change in Bolivia.[21] Evo Morales, an Aymara from Oruro who represented coca growers in the Chapare region in the east of Cochabamba, emerged as an important politician in Bolivia in the elections of 2002, when he nearly won the presidency. He would go on to be elected president in 2006. His thinking is inspired, in part, by Fausto Reinaga, who was himself inspired by the AMP in the early 1960s.[22] Felipe Quispe, a contemporary of Evo Morales, more clearly expresses the notion of two republics elaborated by Titiriku and continued by Jach'aqullu, while Morales represents the legacy of the AMP in less direct ways.

When Evo Morales was elected president in 2006, with 54 percent of the vote, an unprecedented number of indigenous activists were voted into the Bolivian Congress. These changes have created a new political context that resonates with the AMP's earth politics. Indeed, while most of the Americas celebrate Columbus Day on October 12, Bolivia now celebrates the Day of Decolonization instead.[23] Bolivia under Evo Morales has written a new constitution that emphasizes the country's indigenous heritage and requires that women constitute 50 percent of the federal, state, and municipal legislative branches.[24] Indeed, women make up 49 percent of the current Bolivian Congress, which is the highest representation of women in a legislative branch in the western hemisphere.[25] These ideals of women's participation in government echo the idea of parity that the AMP advocated in the years after the national revolution and serve as a testimony to its resonance in today's Bolivia. Other policies include an agrarian reform that benefited Guaraní Indians in the southeast of Bolivia, where the labor system still resembled slavery.[26] On May 1, 2006, Morales announced his intent to nationalize the oil and gas industry. The subsequent nationalization of gas and power companies has brought increased income to the state, which has allowed the administration to provide welfare for the elderly and a subsidy for families with toddlers and children in school. These social programs in turn have helped to reactivate the economy.[27] The government implemented an education reform that addresses diversity and includes ideas about indigenous religion and decolonization in the curriculum. In October 2010 Morales signed the Law Against Racism and Any Form of Discrimination, the only one of its kind in Latin America, that attempts to prevent and punish racism.[28] In December 2010 Bolivia's Plurinational Legislative Assembly passed the Law of the Rights of Mother Earth (Ley de Derechos de la Madre Tierra), known as Law 071, which gives nature the same rights as humans and defines the earth as a collective subject of public interest (see appendix 2).[29] To highlight this as an important issue, the government promulgated the Mother Earth and Holistic Development for Living Well Framework Law (Ley Marco de la Madre Tierra y Desarrollo Integral para Vivir Bien), also known as Law 300, on October 15, 2012. Consisting of 259 articles, this law contains far more specific content than the previous short Law 071.[30] Another piece of legislation called the Autonomy and Decentralization Framework Law (Ley Marco de Autonomía y Descentralización) provides indigenous communities the opportunity to declare autonomy and develop their own norms, procedures, and institutions. These laws have also generated class tensions in the last six years, gaining strong political support from most Aymaras and Quechuas and encountering resistance from some mestizos and the elite in the western and eastern regions of Bolivia.

Racialization continues to be a problem, but in a new context.[31] For instance, as in the AMP era, Indian dress code is still a crucial emblem of race in the era of Evo Morales. While Bolivian society and the place of Indians in it are evolving, racism persists. Today, however, there are laws in place to prevent and punish racial discrimination; however, they are not yet regularly enforced. In a similar sense, which I will elaborate on more below, when it comes to protecting the environment, the Rights of Mother Earth have not halted the destruction of natural resources, but they have provided indigenous environmentalists with a legal foundation to make

FIGURE CONC. 1. In this picture, a policeman stands in front of the Presidential Palace in La Paz burning a poncho that he violently tore away from an indigenous transient a few minutes before. Dressed in civilian clothes, the policeman burned the poncho as an expression of his rejection of the Aymara and Quechua who support Morales. Despite the law against racism, this incident occurred during a protest in June 2012 in La Paz in which police were demanding a salary increase from Morales. Since the protester is most likely of indigenous descent, this picture is also an example of how deeply ideologies of "whitening" have penetrated Bolivian society. Photograph by Walter Aduviri, La Paz, Bolivia.

certain claims, though they may not always be successful. Furthermore, the visibility of indigenous people in different offices, serving as supreme justices, members of Congress, and municipal officers, is helping to establish a new perception of the place of "Indians" in society and, with it, more tolerance and pluralism. These laws are not only symbolic. It is, indeed, more difficult to practice racism and to ignore indigenous rights in Bolivia than it was before, including in the AMP era. Today, the new

Estado Plurinational faces the challenge of achieving a better balance between indigenous demands, the state's need to generate revenue and find new sources of income and investment, and calls for jobs and development from miners and peasants unions in a country that has become more participatory but also more populist than before.

These new laws are probably the most indigenous friendly in the Americas today, and provide a new framework for indigenous rights. For instance, the Autonomy and Decentralization Framework Law provides a very different framework than the AMP had to deal with. The AMP was struggling under a conservative version of mid-twentieth-century liberal legislation with a heavy emphasis on individual property or landownership. Even though current movements like Consejo de Ayllus y Markas del Kollasuyu (CONAMAQ) and Central de Pueblos Indígenas del Oriente de Bolivia (CIDOB) are working in a much more receptive legislative environment, they still face challenges. For instance, there is a group of ayllus in Mallku Quta, northern Potosí, that opposes mining in their territory for religious reasons and because they want to control the mine; they have that right according to the new law, but there are other forces at the local level, such as the peasant unions of the Mallku Quta region and mining unions, that disagree. Despite such challenges, and in the face of enduring racism, many indigenous organizations are working to take advantage of these new laws.

Furthermore, it is not only in the Morales government that we can see the legacy of the AMP's earth politics or decolonization project. Some twenty-first-century acts of decolonization are even being promoted by the Bolivian opposition, which is mostly led by middle-class mestizos. For instance the Movimiento Sin Miedo, which controls La Paz's municipal government, promotes an intercultural fair in El Prado on October 12 that includes worship activities with yatiri (Aymara Indian priests), Catholic priests, and Protestant pastors. In the past interfaith events did not include worshiping Pachamama, and Indian priests were not usually invited.[32]

However, the strongest resonances of earth politics come mainly from the actions of regular people. In the city of La Paz, for example, there are currently ten Aymara sites of worship or wak'as; some of these had been long abandoned but have since been re-activated, and some are even new sites of worship.[33] One of the sites is the wak'a Apacheta, which is where Titiriku used to worship.[34] The active use of wak'as in Bolivia as sites of worship to the Indian gods stands in stark contrast to somewhere like Lima, Peru, where the wak'as Phujllana and Wayllamarka are mostly archeological or touristic sites. The regeneration of many indigenous sites of worship in Bolivia is clear evidence of the significance of indigenous religion to indigenous politics. This adherence to Aymara worship, however, does not always mean that people are setting aside their Catholic or evangelical practices; instead, elements of these religions often enhance Aymara worship.

The cult of ancestors, another way to worship the wak'as, has also widely expanded, so much so that the Catholic Church has taken a stand against this practice and defined them as idolatries. In particular the Catholic Church singled out the cult of ñatitas, which believes that an ancestor or relative's skull, or any other skull of a virtuous person, provides good energy.[35] Indeed, in the Aymara worldview today, skulls are a source of spiritual energy, with the idea that the dead can bring something to the living, especially security and prosperity.[36] These aspects of indigenous religion have nothing to do with the current government, but Bolivia under Evo Morales provides a favorable environment for the reverberation of even sixteenth-century ideas about ancestors and death, which have deep roots in indigenous religion. This also means that indigenous religious rites are still controversial, just as they were in colonial times and in the mid-twentieth century.

In a decolonizing move similar to those of Toribio Miranda, Gregorio Titiriku, and other activists in the AMP, the vice minister of decolonization under the minister of cultures organized wedding rituals according to an Aymara and Andean worldview. On May 7, 2011, 355 couples from different ethnicities were married, and Evo Morales served as the padrino (ceremonial role) of the collective wedding. Other Aymara or originario wedding rituals have not been uncommon in recent times, as evidenced by the indigenous wedding ceremony of the current Bolivian vice president Alvaro Garcia Linera. Indigenous wedding ceremonies are practiced much more widely in today's Bolivia, including by non-indigenous couples who want to marry according to Aymara or originario rituals. These acts resonate with a ceremony performed by Titiriku in August 1944, in which he married a total of 25 couples. Just as when Tiriku and Jach'aqullu performed these wedding rites, for which Jach'aqullu was jailed, the marriages in 2011 were severely criticized by the church.[37] Recalling concerns from the mid-twentieth century, contemporary indigenous people are

FIGURE CONC.2. The festival of Ñatitas in La Paz: Skulls of deceased loved ones, or any other skulls that for historical reasons are believed to provide good energy, are worshipped with blessings and parties that last several days, especially in recent times. Since Catholic priests have been reluctant to take part in this religious activity, yatiris usually perform the blessings. In the photograph two Aymara women worshippers are carrying their Ñatitas for a blessing outside of a church. The festival resembles the worship of the wak'as and panakas previous to the sixteenth century in the Andean world. Courtesy of Petrona Quispe, November 8, 2011, La Paz, Bolivia.

worried about the colonization of basic elements of their culture, such as marriage rituals, and want to decolonize them with these alternative ceremonies. The motivations of the couples who participated in the event in 2011 varied widely; some of them were already married and wanted to have an Aymara ceremony, while others had not been married before. This was probably also the case with the marriages that the AMP organized in the mid-twentieth century.

The continued attempt to decolonize the Spanish names of many places in Bolivia represents another resonance with AMP politics. One recent case revolves around Plaza Murillo, the main plaza of La Paz, where the legislative and executive branches of the Plurinational State of Bolivia are located. The Confederación Nacional de Mujeres Campesinas Indígenas Originarias de Bolivia-Bartolina Sisa has for many years asked to change the name of the plaza to Bartolina Sisa, in honor of an Aymara heroine who was killed in that spot in the 1780s. The only authority that can change the name of the plaza is the municipal government, which is in the hands of

FIGURE CONC. 3. The Aymara wedding celebration of the vice president Álvaro
Garcia Linera in Tiwanaku, Bolivia. *La Razón*, September 8, 2012.

the opposition. Similarly, Gregorio Titiriku insisted on calling the province of Omasuyos by its old name, Qhupaqawayana, and was very persistent in maintaining that it was a way to go back to an older order and reconstruct the Qullasuyu. Evo Morales has asserted that it will still be called Plaza Murillo, but that its "legitimate" name is Bartolina Sisa. Many indigenous peoples have already started calling it Plaza Bartolina Sisa.[38] These older and newer efforts to rename certain sites are just two examples of how Aymaras have attempted to decolonize first names, last names, and place names throughout history. The case of the plaza does show, however, that Gregorio Titiriku and Andrés Jach'aqullu's specific goals resonate in contemporary Bolivia.

Some would argue that the Morales government has not gone far enough in practicing an earth politics. Based on loans from Brazil, the Morales government had planned to build a highway connecting the Pacific and Atlantic oceans via the Departments of Cochabamba and El Beni in Bolivia. However, the planned route passed through the Isiboro-Sécure Indigenous Territory and National Park (TIPNIS), an area the size of Connecticut. In 2011 a new social movement emerged around demands to preserve this land. Voicing their objections to this plan, about two thousand indigenous peoples from TIPNIS and from other indigenous communities in Bolivia marched for sixty-five days on foot from this reserve to La Paz. During the conflict most Bolivians thought that this area should be protected while the government argued that, despite Law 071, it must balance the needs of mother earth with economic development, arguing that Bolivia needed this route in order to progress.[39] Peru, in fact, built a similar highway between Lima and São Paulo (Brazil) that connected the Pacific and Atlantic oceans in 2010. Since its creation in 1825, Bolivia had lacked funds for such a project, and the Morales government was reluctant to put the project on hold. However, the state is currently completing a full consultation with indigenous peoples of the TIPNIS.[40] As I write these words, the electoral office in charge of this process reports that important factions of the TIPNIS are now supporting the highway project. The government, despite the criticism of environmental organizations, seems committed to going forward with the construction of this highway in the future. The government argues that the international highway will be environmentally friendly.[41] Bolivian civil society saw TIPNIS as a clear representation of Pachamama and its intrinsic environmental goals. Radical groups like the CIDOB or CONAMAQ no longer support the current transformations occurring in Bolivia because they do not go far enough in support of an earth politics. Some of these groups seek to restore institutions and Indian ways of life from the sixteenth century, and, in this sense, their goals are closer to the AMP's than Evo Morales's.

Like the AMP, CIDOB and CONAMAQ argue for a more radical relationship between nature, earth politics, land, and territory. These movements include indigenous peoples from the Bolivian Amazon who want to preserve huge regions as natural parks or to control oil and gas exploitation, Bolivia's main source of income. There are also indigenous groups from the highlands that want to maintain control of the exploitation of precious minerals in their territory. Like the AMP, CONAMAQ and CIDOB are fighting to control their own territory. There is now a law of autonomy that can help to make that a reality under the Morales government, although practical politics still makes the application of this law difficult. Bolivia is going through a cultural revolution that includes not only indigenous goals or earth politics but also economic growth and strains of populism and socialism. The reverberations of earth politics today also have limitations that were already clear during the AMP's activism in the mid-twentieth century. Indigenous movements today are still too focused on the "rural world" and lack power in terms of national projects of decolonization. Most Indians now live in the cities, especially the younger generations, but their interests are still underrepresented in contemporary indigenous movements. However, religion, as it relates to the spirit of nature and issues of land and territory, continues to be an emblem of decolonization and where we see the strongest resonance with earth politics today.

This book's articulation of earth politics fits within larger twentieth-century indigenous political projects that combine a modernist desire for democracy and inclusion with a creative articulation of indigenous memory and traditions. The experiences of these four leaders of the AMP illustrate the tensions involved with political consolidation, integration, and the democratization of citizenship. In combining ethnography, biography, and history I have attempted to narrate what it was like to "be an Indian" in mid-twentieth-century Bolivia's colonial, racialized atmosphere. Looking back at the twentieth century from the perspective of the early twenty-first century, and especially within the context of the current globalization of indigenous politics, allows us to examine nation-states through native visions of autonomy and plurality. This book has attempted to provide a better understanding of the dynamics of contemporary Bolivian culture and politics and to uncover the deep roots of its current decolonization agenda.

Appendix 1

Aymara Words and Their Equivalents in Spanish

Alaxsaya	Alajsaya
Ch'aquma	Chacoma
Ch'awarani	Chahuarani
Ch'ikitayox	Chiquitayoj
Chukiawu	Chuquiagu
Chullpa puchu	Chulpapucho
Ch'uqi Ch'uqi	Chuqui Chuqui
Ch'uqutas	Chukutas
Ch'utas	Chutas
Inka	Inca
Inkawasi	Incahuasi
Inqasiwi	Inquisivi
Jach'aqhachi	Achachachi
Jach'aqullu	Jachacollo, Jachakollo, and Achacollo
Jalqas	Jalca
Janqulaimis	Ancoraimes
Jilaqatas	Jilacatas
Kakinqura	Caquingora
Killakas	Quillacas
Killa Killa	Quillaquilla
Llallawa	Llallagua
Luxta	Lojta
Machaqa	Machaca
Machaqmarka	Machacmarca

Mankhasaya	Mankasaya
Marawa	Maragua
Markawi	Marcavi
Misk'i	Misque
Montepuchus	Montepuchos
Moxsa	Mohoza
Muru Muru	Moro Moro
Muxuquya	Mojocoya
Palqa	Palca
Paqajaqi	Pacajes
Paqusillu	Pacosillo
Pasupaya	Pasopaya
Phinas	Peñas
Phuñaqa	Puñaca
Phuxpu	Poopo, Pojpo
Pukarani	Pucarani
Puquata	Pocoata
Purirantes	Poderantes
Qalamarka	Calamarca
Qallapa	Callapa
Qañawa	Cañahua
Qaranqas	Carangas
Qaranqas, Qhara	Carangas, Qharas
Q'araqullu	Caracollo
Q'atawi	Catavi
Q'axiata	Cajiata
Qharaqullu	Caracollo
Qheschwa	Quechua, Kechua
Qhispi	Quispe
Qhuchapuchus	Cochapuchos
Qhupaqawana	Copacabana
Qhupawillki	Copavillque
Qhuphawillki	Copavillque
Qhuyu	Cuyu, Cuyo
Qillaqas	Quillaca
Qiwiñal	Quewiñal, Quehuiñal
Qullasuyu	Collasuyu, Kollasuyu
Qullqichaca	Colquechaca
Qulqi	Colque
Qunquriri	Concoriri
Quntu	Condo
Saqaqa	Sacaca
Sawaya	Sabaya

Saxama	Sajama
Sumala	Somala
Sunimuru	Sunimoro
Sura Suras	Sora Sora
Suruma	Soroma
Taraqu	Taraco
Tarwita	Tarvita
Tikuna	Ticona
Tumina	Tomina, Tominas
Umasuyus	Omasuyos.
Urinuqa	Orinoca
Urqhas	Orca, or Orcas
Waichu	Huaycho
Wak'as	Huacas
Wanqullu	Huancollo
Wanuni	Huanuni
Warachi	Guarachi
Wari	Huari
Wariqallu	Huaricallo
Warisatha	Warizata, Huarisata
Waxt'a	Wajta, Huajta
Waychu	Huaychu (Puerto Acosta)
Wayllamarka	Huayllamarca
Wilaqullu	Vilacollo
Wiraxuchas	Viracochas
Wisk'anchis	Viscanches
Yanapaku	Yanapacu, Yanapaco

Appendix 2

Law of the Rights of Mother Earth
Law 071
December 21, 2010

EVO MORALES AYMA
Constitutional President of the Plurinational State

Whereas, the Plurinational Legislative Assembly has enacted the following Law:
The Plurinational Legislative Assembly,

Resolves:

Law of the Rights of Mother Earth

Chapter I
Purpose and Principles

ARTICLE 1. (SCOPE)
This Act is intended to recognize the rights of Mother Earth and the obligations and duties of the Plurinational State and society to ensure respect for these rights.

ARTICLE 2. (PRINCIPLES)
The binding principles that govern this law are:
1. Harmony: Human activities in the context of plurality and diversity must achieve a dynamic balance with the cycles and processes inherent to the Mother Earth.

2. Collective Good: The interests of society, within the framework of the rights of Mother Earth, must be prevalent in all human activity and above any entitlement.

3. Ensuring the regeneration of Mother Earth: In harmony with the common good, all levels of the state and society must ensure the necessary conditions so that Mother Earth's diverse systems of life can absorb damage, adapt to disturbances, and regenerate without significantly altering their characteristic structure and function, recognizing that living systems are limited in their ability to regenerate and that humans are limited in their ability to reverse their actions.

4. Respect for and defense of the rights of Mother Earth: The State and all individual or collective entities will respect, protect, and guarantee the rights of Mother Earth so that current and future generations can live well.

5. No commercialization: By which the systems of life and the processes that sustain them cannot become commodities nor become part of anyone's private property.

6. Interculturality: The exercise of the rights of Mother Earth requires that the diversity of feelings, values, knowledge, skills, practices, meanings, transformations, sciences, technologies, and standards of all cultures of the world looking to live in harmony with nature be recognized, respected, protected, and discussed.

Chapter II
Mother Earth: Definition and Character

ARTICLE 3. (MOTHER EARTH)

Mother Earth is a living, dynamic system formed by the indivisible community of all life systems and living beings, which are interrelated, interdependent, and complementary, sharing a common destiny.

Mother Earth is considered sacred in the worldviews of peasant indigenous peoples and nations.

ARTICLE 4. (LIFE SYSTEMS)

Life systems are complex and dynamic communities of plants, animals, microorganisms, and other beings in their environment. In life systems, human communities and the rest of nature interact as a functional unit under the influence of climatic, physiographic, and geologic factors, as well as the productive practices and cultural diversity of Bolivians and the worldviews of peasant and indigenous peoples and nations, intercultural communities, and Afro-Bolivian communities.

ARTICLE 5. (LEGAL CHARACTERISTICS OF MOTHER EARTH)

For the purpose of protecting and enforcing its rights, Mother Earth takes on the character of a collective subject of public interest. Mother Earth and all of its components, including human communities, are entitled to all the inherent rights recognized in this Act. The implementation of the rights of Mother Earth will take into account the specificities and peculiarities of its various components defined earlier. The rights in this Act do not limit the existence of other rights of Mother Earth.

ARTICLE 6. (EXERCISING THE RIGHTS OF MOTHER EARTH)

Forming part of the community of beings that make up Mother Earth, all Bolivians exercise the rights established in this Act, in a manner consistent with their individual and collective rights.

The exercise of individual rights are restricted by the exercise of the collective rights of the livelihood of Mother Earth; any conflict between these rights must be resolved so as not to irreversibly affect the functionality of living systems.

Chapter III
Rights of Mother Earth

ARTICLE 7. (RIGHTS OF MOTHER EARTH)

Mother Earth has the following rights:

1. To life: The right to maintain the integrity of life systems and the natural processes that sustain them, as well as the conditions and capacity for their renewal.
2. To the diversity of life: The right to preserve the differentiation and variety of the beings that comprise Mother Earth without being genetically altered or artificially modified in their structure in ways that would threaten their existence, functioning, and future potential.
3. To water: The right to preserve the quality and composition of the water cycle in order to sustain life systems and protect them from pollution for the renewal of the life of Mother Earth and all its components.
4. To clean air: The right to preserve the quality and composition of the air in order to sustain life systems and protect them from pollution for the renewal of the life of Mother Earth and all its components.
5. To equilibrium: The right to maintain or restore the interrelationship, interdependence, complementarity, and functionality of the components of Mother Earth in a balanced manner for the continuation of its cycles and the renewal of its vital processes.
6. To restoration: The right to the timely and effective restoration of life systems affected directly or indirectly by human activities.
7. To live free from contamination: The right to preserve Mother Earth from the contamination of any of its components by toxic and radioactive waste generated by human activities.

ARTICLE 8. (OBLIGATIONS OF THE PLURINATIONAL STATE)

The Plurinational State, at all levels and geographical spheres and across all authorities and institutions, has the following obligations:

1. To develop policies and systematic actions in order to prevent and give early warning of any human activities that lead to the extinction of living populations, that alter the cycles and processes that guarantee life, or that destroy life systems, including the cultural systems that are part of Mother Earth.
2. To develop means of production and consumption patterns that are balanced in such a way that satisfies the needs of the Bolivian people to live well and also safeguards the regenerative capacity and the integrity of the cycles, processes, and vital balances of Mother Earth.
3. To develop policies that defend Mother Earth in the plurinational and international sphere from the exploitation of its components, the commercialization of life systems or the processes that sustain them, and the structural causes of Global Climate Change and its effects.
4. To develop policies that ensure long-term energy sovereignty through reduced use, increased efficiency, and the gradual incorporation into the energy matrix of alternative energy sources that are both clean and renewable.
5. To pursue legal action in the international sphere for the recognition of the debt owed to the environment through the financing of and transition to clean technologies that are effective and consistent with the rights of Mother Earth, as well as through other mechanisms.
6. To promote peace and the elimination of all nuclear, chemical, biological, and other weapons of mass destruction.
7. To promote the recognition and defense of the rights of Mother Earth in the nation's multilateral, regional, and bilateral international relations.

ARTICLE 9. (DUTIES OF PERSONS)

The following are the duties of natural persons and legal entities, public or private:

a) To defend and respect the rights of Mother Earth.
b) To promote the harmony of Mother Earth in all areas of its relationship with other human communities and the rest of nature's living systems.
c) To participate actively, either individually or collectively, in the generation of proposals designed to respect and defend the rights of Mother Earth.
d) To assume production practices and consumption habits that are in harmony with the rights of Mother Earth.
e) To ensure the sustainable use and exploitation of the resources of Mother Earth.
f) To report any action that jeopardizes the rights, life systems, and/or resources of Mother Earth.
g) To respond to the call the competent authorities or civil society organizations to carry out actions aimed at conservation and/or protection of Mother Earth.

ARTICLE 10. (OFFICE OF THE OMBUDSMAN OF MOTHER EARTH)

Creates the office of the Ombudsman of Mother Earth, whose mission it is to ensure the observance, promotion, dissemination, and enforcement of the rights of Mother Earth. A separate law will establish its structure, functions, and powers.

Refer to the Executive Branch for constitutional purposes.

Given in the Hall of Sessions of the Plurinational Legislative Assembly, on the seventh day of December, two thousand and ten.

Signed. Oscar Rene Martinez Callahuanca Zaconeta, Hector Enrique Arce, Andrew A. Villca Daza, Clementina Garnica Cruz, David Cortes, Angel Villegas, Jose Antonio Yucra Paredes.

Therefore, in order to be enacted and obeyed as a law of the State of Bolivia.

Governmental Palace in the city of La Paz, on the twentieth day of December two thousand and ten.

Signed Evo Morales, David Choquehuanca Céspedes, Oscar Coca Antezana, Mary Esther Udaeta Velasquez, Nemesia Achacollo Tola, Carlos Romero Bonifaz, Zulma Yugar Parraga.

Notes

FPDCH	Fondo Prefectura del Departamento de Chuquisaca
FPDLP	Fondo Prefectura del Departamento de La Paz
FPFQ	Fondo Privado de la Familia Quyu
FPFR	Fondo Privado de Francisco Rivera
FPFV	Fondo Privado de Fermín Vallejos
FPGTRR	Fondo Privado de Gregorio Titiriku y Rosa Ramos
FPHC	Fondo Privado de Hilarión Cuellar
FPHE	Fondo Privado de los Hermanos Espirituales
FPLM	Fondo Privado de Lucas Marka
FPMG	Fondo Privado de Melitón Gallardo Saavedra
FPMW	Fondo Privado de Martina Willka
FPTQ	Fondo Privado de Tomás Quevedo
HAM	Honorable Alcaldía Municipal
ILO	International Labour Organization
MITKA	Movimiento Indio Tupac Katari
MNR	Movimiento Nacionalista Revolucionario
SNRA	Servicio Nacional de Reforma Agraria
THOA	Taller de Historia Oral Andina

Chapter 1. Building the Indian Law and a Decolonization Project in Bolivia

1. Titiriku, "Gregorio Titiriku se hablaba así" (memoir), 2–5, APPM.

2. "Testimonio notariado de un legajo de reuniones y posesión de Apoderados" (testimony), Folio 1, 7–13, APAJMC.

3. In my fieldwork in indigenous archives between 1980 and 1985, I found copies of the *garantías* that I refer to as the Indian law in at least nineteen different places in regions such Chuquisaca, Potosí, and La Paz.

4. The Law of the Indies is the entire body of laws issued by the Spanish Crown for its colonial possessions in Latin America and the Philippines. The purpose of the law was to regulate social, political, and economic life, including the inter-actions between the settlers and natives. The most notable collection of these laws is from 1680.

5. "Testimonio notariado de un legajo de reuniones y posesión de Apoderados," Folio 1, 23–25, APAJMC.

6. Ibid., 11.

7. Ibid., 4–5.

8. Ibid., 9–10.

9. Titiriku, "Gregorio Titiriku se hablaba así," 7–9.

10. Choque and Ticona, *Jesús de Machaqa*, 12–45; and Huanca, *Jilirinakasan Amu-yupa Lup'iñataki*, 15–31; Quevedo, "Su historia de Toribio Miranda y Manuela Quevedo" (memoir), 23–44, FPTQ.

11. The five departments are Chuquisaca, Cochabamba, La Paz, Oruro, and Potosí. In the 1980s there were at least two families that collected data about

the membership of each cell in the AMP's network. See APHONS and the Julian Ugarte, "Los antiguos caminantes," APHOMI.

12. Brysk, *From Tribal Village*, 125–245.

13. Gallardo, "Así hemos caminado los antiguos poderantes" (memoir), 7–8, APHONS.

14. Dryzek, *The Politics of the Earth*, 3–15.

15. Larson, *Trials of Nation Making*, 202–45; and Klein, *Bolivia*, 144–78.

16. Langer, *Economic Change*, 188–205.

17. Mamani, *Taraqu*, 13–80.

18. Ashcroft, Griffiths, and Tiffin, *Key Concepts in Post-Colonial Studies*, 71.

19. Said, *Representations of the Intellectual*, 15.

20. Ibid., 40.

21. Addressing the idea of representation in relation to Maya intellectuals, the cultural anthropologist Diane Nelson argues that they are actually "the inappropriate(d) other" because "like computer hackers, who do not control the system they work in but intimately understand the technologies and codes, the Maya are appropriating so-called modern technology and knowledge while refusing to be appropriated into the ladino nation" (*A Finger in The Wound*, 249). Nelson uses the phrase *inappropriate(d) other* to signify that Maya intellectuals, rather than using instruments such as technology in order to integrate successfully into mainstream political discourse in the making of the nation-state, use those resources to empower Maya identity and to reinforce their goals related to the Indian world. In other words, the performance itself constructs the identity, a process she refers to as "performative identity in action."

22. Knight, "Racism, Revolution, and *Indigenismo*," 71–114; Renique, "Race, Region, and Nation," 211–36.

23. Renique, "Race, Region, and Nation," 215.

24. De la Cadena, *Indigenous Mestizos*, 44–130.

25. Sanjinés, *Mestizaje Upside-Down*, 32–65; Salomón, *El espejo indigenista*, 25–70.

26. Mallon, *Decolonizing Native Histories. Collaboration, Knowledge, and Language in the Americas*, 1–19.

27. THOA, *El indio Santos Marka T'ula*, 2–22.

28. Carlos Mamani, another member of the think tank, published the history of a 1930s activist group called the Republic of Qullasuyu that focused on its leader, Eduardo Nina Quispe. See Mamani, *Taraqu*, 10–70. Esteban Ticona published a book on Leandro Nina Quispe, a secretary of caciques and apoderados in the 1920s and 1930s. Both works give examples of the colonial dimensions of the postcolonial Bolivian state. (See Condori Chura and Ticona Alejo, *El escribano de los caciques apoderados*, 50–153).

29. Swartz, *Culture and Power*, 230–95.

30. Rivera Cusicanqui, "La raíz: Colonizadores y colonizados," 27–139.

31. Sanjinés, *Mestizaje Upside-Down*, 32–61; Mignolo, *Local Histories/Global Designs*, 5–19; and Beverley, *Subalternity and Representation*, 3–56.

32. Weistmantel and Eisenman, "Race in the Andes," 121–42.

33. See Gould, *To Die in This Way*, 11–12.

34. Ibid., 10.

35. Nelson, *A Finger in The Wound*, 349.

36. Ibid., 249.

37. Luykx and Foley, *The Citizen Factory*.

38. The word *cholo*, which means hybrid, comes from the Aymara word *ch'ulu*. *Cholo* refers to a hybrid style of dress—different from both whites and Indians—and a hybrid style of speech that mixes native languages with Spanish. See Paredes Candia, *La chola boliviana*, 40.

39. HAM, *Cuarto Centenario*, 3: 480–620.

40. De la Cadena and Starn, *Indigenous Experience Today*, 125–50.

41. "Informe del Instituto de Estadística," *El Diario*, April 2, 1954, 5–6.

42. Larson, *Trials of Nation Making*, 15.

43. Salomón, *El espejo indigenista*, 130–270.

44. Titiriku, "Para recordar a los phawajrunas" (memoir), 3–5, APPM.

45. Lehm and Rivera Cusicanqui, *Los artesanos libertarios*, 170–230.

46. Ibid.

47. Grosby, "Nationality and Religion," 97–119.

48. For more on "oral ethnicities," see Hastings, *The Construction of Nation*, 185–210.

49. Huanca, *El Yatiri en la comunidad aymara*, 11–19; Qulqi, "Inkawawas, la Virgina y su camino de Miranda" (memoir), 17–23, Fondo 1952, APHOA.

50. Rivera, "Las haciendas eran así en su tiempo de Villarroel" (memoir), 33, and Peñaranda, "En su tiempo de Villarroel" (memoir), 21–22, Fondo 11, FPHE.

51. Téllez, "El Gallardo era ch'utita" (memoir), 23, Fondo 2B, FPHE.

52. Nelson, *A Finger in the Wound*, 249; and Warren, *Indigenous Movements and Their Critics*, 177–211.

53. Grandin, *The Blood of Guatemala*, 3–230.

54. Ibid., 13.

55. THOA, *Historia y Memoria*, 1–29. I understand patriarchalism to be a historically specific system of generational as well as gender relations in which children and women are subordinated to the male head of family, who controls the wealth of the family, the sexuality of its women, and the labor power of all its members. See Besse, *Restructuring Patriarchy*, 5–45, 207.

56. Qulqi, "Mi religión es la Pachamama" (memoir), 1–23, APHOA; and THOA, *Historia y Memoria*, 3–21.

57. Antezana and Romero, *Historia de los sindicatos campesinos*, 230–50.

58. De la Cadena, "Women Are More Indian," 89–130.

59. Chura, "Los pachamámicos les decían" (memoir), 3, CDFIA; Apaza, "Andrés Ticona" (oral history), 19, APAJMC; Peralta, "Fausto Reinaga y los alcaldes particulares" (memoir), 19–29, APHOMI; and Villca, "Muruhuta y Mururata Achachila" (oral history), 7–9, FPMG.

60. Portelli, *In the Death of Luigi Trastulli and Other Stories*, 3–341.

61. Williams, *Marxism and Literature*, 35–120.

62. Jach'aqullu, "El indio Uru-Murato, Toribio Miranda y Manuela Quevedo" (memoir), 13, APAJMC; Loayza, "El Congreso de Sucre" (memoir), 9–10, APEO; and Ponce Mamani, "Los poderantes" (memoir), 23, FPHE.

63. Grosby, "Nationality and Religion," 97–120.

64. Rappaport, *The Politics of Memory*, 62–139.

65. Kapsoli, *Los movimientos campesinos en el Perú*, 10–200.

66. Condarco Morales, *Zárate, El "Temible" Willka*, 3–45; and Colque, *El camino de Willkakuti* (memoir), Fondo 4, 11–12, APHOA.

67. Grandin, *The Blood of Guatemala*, 160–220.

68. Klubock, "Ránquil," 121–63; and Becker, "Indigenous Communists and Urban Intellectuals in Cayambe, Ecuador," 41–65.

69. Klubock, "Ránquil," 121, 163; see also Mallon, *Courage Tastes of Blood*, 34–92.

70. Thurner, *From Two Republics to One Divided*, 5–163; Alba Herrera, *Atusparia y la revolución campesina de 1885 en Ancash*, 25–48.

71. Sanders, "'Belonging to the Great Granadian Family,'" 56–86.

72. Díaz Polanco, *Indigenous Peoples in Latin America*, 23–65. See also, Lucero, *Struggles of Voice*, 25–272; Van Cott, *From Movements to Parties in Latin America*, 212–37, and *Indigenous Peoples and Democracy in Latin America*, 23–70.

Chapter 2. Nation Making and the Genealogy of the AMP Indigenous Activists

1. THOA, *El indio Santos Marka T'ula*, 17–43.

2. Démelas, *Nationalisme*, 96; Langer, "El liberalismo," 59–95. See also Irurozqui, *La armonía de las desigualdades*, 30–180.

3. Larson, *Trials of Nation Making*, 59–70.

4. Irurozqui, *La armonía de las desigualdades*, 30–190; Klein, *Bolivia*, 149–88.

5. Klein, *Bolivia*, 149–88.

6. Bonifaz, *Legislación agrario-indígena*, 180–220.

7. Ibid., 225–30.

8. Flores Moncayo, *Legislación boliviana del indio*, 295–96.

9. Choque and Ticona, *Jesús de Machaqa*, 10–210.

10. Dorado, *Impugnación a las ideas federales en Bolivia*, 35–70. See also Langer, "El liberalismo," 59–95.

11. Choque, Soria, Mamani, Ticona, and Conde, *Educación indígena*, 58–89.

12. Platt, *Estado boliviano y ayllu andino*, 50–110.

13. Démelas, *Nationalisme*, 99–100. See also Irurozqui, *La armonía de las desigualdades*, 30–180.

14. Larson, *Trials of Nation Making*, 64.

15. Rivera Cusicanqui, *Oprimidos pero no vencidos*, 23–84.

16. Urquiola, "La población en Bolivia," 193–218.

17. Crespo, *José Manuel Pando*; Gade, "Spatial Displacement of Latin American Seats of Goverment," 43–57; Condarco Morales, *Zárate*, 10–240.

18. Salinas Mariaca, *Vida y muerte*, 35–78; and Condarco Morales, *Zárate*, 35–78.

19. Condarco Morales, *Zárate*, 181–277.

20. Rappaport, *Politics of Memory*, 199–209.

21. Bonifaz, *Legislación agrario-indígena*, 180–220; and Rivera Cusicanqui, *Oprimidos pero no vencidos*, 25–53.

22. Condarco Morales, *Zárate*, 94; "Lista de Apoderados de la provincia Paria, August 9, 1901," 45–53, Folio 2, APAJMC.

23. Condarco Morales, *Zárate*, 248.

24. Ibid., 252–60. See also Platt, "The Andean Experience of Bolivian Liberalism, 1825–1990," 286–327.

25. "De la protocolización de varios documentos de las comunidades Quntu y Qhupawillki," November 11, 1931, FPTQ.

26. Condarco Morales, *Zárate*, 99.

27. Abercrombie, *Pathways of Memory and Power*, 13–230.

28. Condarco Morales, *Zárate*, 81–104.

29. Ibid.

30. Similarly, the great Aymara hero of the eighteenth century Tupak Katari asked a Catholic priest to bless him and say a mass prior to his attack on the whites of La Paz, which demonstrates the long history of hybrid religiosity and indigenous leaders seeking legitimization from the church. See del Valle de Siles, *Historia de la rebelión de Túpac Catari, 1781–1782*, 99–317. See also Thompson, *We Alone Will Rule*.

31. Del Valle de Siles, *Historia de rebelión de Túpac Catari, 1781–1782*, 99–317.

32. Bautista Saavedra, *El Ayllu*, 171–209.

33. Miranda, "Sus luchas de mi padre" (memoir), Folio 3, 3–5, APHOA; and Mamani, *Taraqu*, 15–94.

34. Condarco Morales, *Zárate*, 374.

35. Ibid., 363–403; and Miranda, "Sus luchas de mi padre," 15–21.

36. Anderson, *Imagined Communities*, 23–173.

37. Dress code played a similar role in the eighteenth-century Tupak Amaru and Tupak Katari rebellions in which Indian dress signified being one of them. See Szeminski, *La utopía tupamarista*, 70–210; and Del Valle de Siles, *Historia de la rebelión*, 99–317.

38. Condarco Morales, *Zárate*, 200–53; see also Bonifaz, *Legislación agraria-indígena*, 228.

39. Jach'aqullu, "El indio Uru-Murato, Toribio Miranda y Manuela Quevedo" (memoir), Folio 2, 25, APAJMC.

40. Paredes, *La altiplanicie*, 35–70; Platt, *Estado boliviano y ayllu andino*, 95–180; and Grieshaber, "Survival of Indian Communities in Nineteenth-Century Bolivia," 45–127.

41. Mamani, *Taraqu*, 43–53; and Langer, *Economic Change*, 188–205.

42. "Proceso civil por apropiación de tierras de comunidad entre el Apoderado Mario Ilakita, Turrini y Jorge Monrroy, Diciembre 12, 1921," 4–10, FJA.

43. "Proceso judicial de los comunarios de Ispaya contra Edgar Balderrama, 1921," 12–45, AJA.

44. "Proceso judicial de Juan Fábrica contra Elena vda. de Contreras, 1931–1935," 3–7, AJPD.

45. Ibid., 11–13.

46. Mamani, *Taraqu*, 25–75.

47. Rivera Cusicanqui, *Oprimidos pero no vencidos*, 31, 145; and Grieshaber, "Survival of Indian Communities," 75–165.

48. Mamani, *Taraqu*, 15–94; and Grieshaber, "Survival of Indian Communities," 72–77.

49. Andrade, *José Santos Marka Thola, 1879 a 1939*, 5–7.

50. THOA, *El indio Santos Marka T'ula*, 19–20.

51. Ibid.; and Mamani, *Taraqu*, 13–25.

52. Albó and Mamani, *Achacachi*, 21.

53. Andrade, *José Santos Marka Thola, 1879 a 1939*, 5–7.

54. Lehm and Rivera Cusicanqui, *Los artesanos libertarios*, 21–213; Andrade, *José Santos Marka Thola*, 9–15; "Garantía," 1926, Folio 1, 1–2, APEO.

55. Lora, *Formación de la clase obrera boliviana*, 13–15; Lehm and Rivera Cusicanqui, *Los artesanos libertarios*, 11–16; "Garantía," 1926, Folio 1, 1–2, APEO.

56. "Garantía," 1926, Folio 1, 1–2, APEO.

57. Andrade, *José Santos Marka Thola*, 3–12; THOA, *El indio Santos Marka T'ula*, 15–18.

58. Andrade, *José Santos Marka Thola*, 3–12.

59. THOA, *El indio Santos Marka T'ula*, 15–18.

60. Ibid.

61. THOA, *Historia y memoria*, 19–24.

62. THOA, *El indio Santos Marka T'ula*, 40.

63. Ibid.

64. Titiriku, "Para recordar a los Phawax Runas, 1977," 3–11, APPM.

65. Quevedo, "Tiempos sufridos" (memoir), 3–5, FPTQ.

66. Ibid.

67. THOA, *El indio Santos Marka T'ula*, 49.

68. "Garantía," 1926, Folio 1, 1–2, APEO.

69. "Proceso Judicial de Julio Aruwitu contra Ramón Berdeja, 1930–1932," 23–25, FPAPM.

70. Anderson, *Imagined Communities*, 36–46.

71. THOA, *El indio Santos Marka T'ula*, 11–35; Saavedra, "Lista de AMP," 7–10; Titiriku, "Para recordar a los Phawax Runas, 1977," 9–11. Nabil Saavedra made a list of the AMP membership in 1960, based on Melitón Gallardo's archives and Carlos Torricos Colque's lists.

72. Gotkowitz, *A Revolution for Our Rights*, 233–90.

73. Aymara quotation in Condori Chura and Ticona, *El escribano*, 72.

74. See Thurner, *From Two Republics to One Divided*, 23–87; Stein, *El levantamiento de Atusparia*, 23–78.

75. Condarco Morales, Zárate, 177–94.

76. Rappaport, Politics of Memory, 111–97.

77. Titiriku, "Gregorio Titiriku se hablaba así" (memoir), 10–15, APPM; Quevedo, "Tiempos sufridos," 3–21.

78. "Expediente judicial ex hacienda Wisk'anchis, Fondo Azurduy, 1961," 137–45, SNRA.

79. "Proceso judicial Sunimuru, Apoderado Félix Choque, 1925," 7–19, Inqasiwi, SNRA.

80. "Testamento de Eusebio Quyu y María Kutipa," 23–43, APHOA.

81. "Proceso civil de Apolinar Cuevas contra Isidro Caro, 1923–1932," 19–24, FPFQ; Rivera Cusicanqui with THOA, Ayllus y proyectos de desarrollo en el norte de Potosí, 50–120. For a different categorization of these groups within the ayllus, see Platt, Estado boliviano y ayllu andino, 23–178. Platt defines ethnic categorization through tribute paying in the ayllus of northern Potosí during the nineteenth century. My work adapts this concept by using a categorization based on land tenure for the twentieth century. See also Klein, Haciendas and Ayllus, 12–78.

82. See Gallardo, "Así hemos caminado los antiguos poderantes" (memoir), 33–53, APHONS.

83. Orieta, "Tata Toribio Miranda," 10–13, APHONS.

84. Titiriku, "Gregorio Titiriku se hablaba así," 13–15.

85. Jach'aqullu, "El Kollasuyu y Gregorio Titiriku," 3–15.

86. "Garantía," 1925, 1–2, Folio 1, APEO; Jach'aqullu, "El Kollasuyu y Gregorio Titiriku," 13–19.

87. THOA, El indio Santos Marka T'ula, 49; "Acta notariada de varias reuniones y posesión de Apoderados celebrada por Toribio Miranda, 1924 y 1942," Folio 1, 7–13, APAJMC.

88. Quevedo, "Tiempos sufridos," Folio 1, 33–45.

89. Claure, Las escuelas indigenales, 27–60; Salazar Mostajo, Warisata Mia!, 9–87.

90. Landivar, "Memorias de Vicente Donoso Torrez y la reforma educativa" (oral history), Folio 1, 7–11, APHOA.

91. Claure, Las escuelas indigenales, 27–60; Salazar Mostajo, Warisata Mia!, 9–87.

92. Landivar, "Memorias de Vicente Donoso Torrez y la reforma educativa," Folio 1, 7–11, APHOA.

93. Titiriku, "Gregorio Titiriku se hablaba así," 23–25.

94. Ibid., 5–4.

95. THOA, El indio Santos Marka T'ula, 15–30; Jach'aqullu, "El indio Uru-Murato, Toribio Miranda y Manuela Quevedo," 13–43.

96. Escobari de Querejazu, Caciques, yanaconas y extravagantes, 30–80.

97. For examples of the usage of alcaldes del campo, see Gotkowitz, A Revolution for Our Rights, 233–67.

98. "Garantía," 1936, Folio 4, 7–9, FPFR.

1. Jach'aqullu, "El indio Uru-Murato, Toribio Miranda y Manuela Quevedo"
(memoir), 3–15, and "Acta notariada de la detención de Toribio Miranda, Regi-
miento Policial Camacho. April, 14, 1943," Folio 1, 5, APAJMC.

2. Jach'aqullu, "El indio Uru-Murato, Toribio Miranda y Manuela Quevedo,"
3–15.

3. Ranaboldo, El camino perdido, 3–12; Antezana and Romero, Historia de los sindicatos campesinos, 89–95.

4. "Memorial solicitando el retorno de los cuerpos de Mariano Qhispe y Antonio
García al Ministerio del Interior, por Calixto Peñaranda y otros Alcaldes, Septiembre 4, 1946," Folio 2, 3–6, FPMG.

5. Antezana and Romero, Historia de los sindicatos, 145.

6. Klein, Bolivia, 188–226.

7. Mariátegui, Siete ensayos de interpretación de la realidad peruana, 100–189; Rivera
Cusicanqui with THOA, Ayllus y proyectos de desarrollo en el norte de Potosí, 50–98;
Marof, La tragedia del altiplano, 25–89; Platt, Estado boliviano y ayllu andino, 120–200.

8. Bautista Saavedra had strong connections with the indigenous movement at
the beginning of twentieth century and became president of Bolivia in the 1920s.
See Gómez, Bautista Saavedra, 12–75; Bautista Saavedra, El Ayllu, 20–70; and Q'uyu,
"Su camino de los antiguos caminantes" (memoir), 23–24, FPHE.

9. Ponce Mamani, "Los poderantes" (memoir), 9–10, FPHE.

10. New research has linked the Urus to the Mayas of Central America. For more
on this small Andean ethnic minority, see Wachtel, Gods and Vampires, 10–55; Delgadillo Villegas, La nación de los urus, 1–23; and Olson, Algunas relaciones del chipaya de
Bolivia con las lenguas mayenses, 3–14.

11. Quevedo, "Su historia de Toribio Miranda y Manuela Quevedo," 5–7, FPTQ;
Miranda and Moricio with Barragán, Memorias de un olvido, 21–129.

12. Jach'aqullu, "Su enseñanza del cura Beltrán," Fondo 13, 4–6, APAJMC.

13. Ibid., 7; Beltrán, Colección de opúsculos del cura Carlos Felipe Beltrán, 3–28.

14. Jach'aqullu, "El indio Uru-Murato, Toribio Miranda y Manuela Quevedo,"
2–16.

15. "Carta de Toribio Miranda a Enrique Díaz Mamani, Diciembre 14, 1910,"
Folio 2, 11–15, APAJMC.

16. "Expediente de los ayllus puxpu y poder los jilaqatas a Toribio Miranda,
1909–1927," Fondo 14, 45–49, APAJMC.

17. Ibid., 37–38.

18. In Toribio Miranda's region the Uru economy was a combination of hunting,
fishing, and some agriculture in the 1920s. See Delgadillo Villegas, La nación de los
urus, 1–23.

19. Ibid.

20. "Expediente de las comunidades Phuñaqa y Tinta María contra el Ayllu Uri-
nuqa, Mayo, 1920," Folio 1, 13, APAJMC.

21. Miranda, "Sus luchas de mi padre" (memoir), Fondo 3, 4, APHONS.

22. Jach'aqullu, "El indio Uru-Murato, Toribio Miranda y Manuela Quevedo," 13–17.

23. Ibid., 25.

24. Ibid., 5.

25. "Expediente de las comunidades Phunaqa y Tinta María contra el Ayllu Uri-nuqa, Mayo, 1920," Folio 1, 13, APAJMC.

26. Albó and Mamani, *Desafíos de la solidaridad Aymara*, 5–39.

27. HAM, *Cuarto Centenario*; and Miranda, "Sus luchas de mi padre," 9.

28. Maruja Puquata, "Su thaki de los mallkus," *La Patria*, August 6, 1977, 4.

29. Q'uyu, "Su camino de los antiguos caminantes" (memoir), 7–9, APHOMI; Miranda, "Sus luchas de mi padre," 7.

30. THOA, *El indio Santos Marka T'ula*, 3–15; Condori Chura and Ticona, *El escribano*, 95–102; Jach'aqullu, "El indio Uru-Murato, Toribio Miranda y Manuela Quevedo," 3–55.

31. "Expediente de la demanda interpuesta por los Ayllus de Quntu contra la hacienda de Palqa, 1926–1934," Fondo 2, 7–38, FPTQ.

32. "Garantía," 1926, Fondo 1, 3–5, APEO; THOA, *El indio Santos Marka T'ula*, 15–35.

33. "Carta de Feliciano Marasa a Toribio Miranda, April 13, 1927," Folio 3, 7–9, APAJMC.

34. Ibid.

35. Abercrombie, *Pathways of Memory and Power*, 98–150.

36. Miranda, "Sus luchas de mi padre," 3–4.

37. "Expediente de las comunidades Phuñaqa y Tinta María contra el Ayllu Uri-nuqa, Mayo 1920," Fondo 1, 35, APAJMC.

38. Miranda, "Sus luchas de mi padre," 1–2, 7–8. During colonial times, Indians translated their oral histories using new colonial frames, such as the idea of the flood. The word *qhutusum* may come from an Uru word meaning "the ones who came out of the lake."

39. Jach'aqullu, "El indio Uru-Murato, Toribio Miranda y Manuela Quevedo," 2–16.

40. Miranda, "Sus luchas de mi padre," 1–2.

41. "Garantía," 1926, Fondo 1, 3–5, APEO; THOA, *El indio Santos Marka T'ula*, 15–35.

42. Aguiló, *Uru y Puquina*, 1–3.

43. Barragán, *Indios de arco y flecha*, 1–48.

44. "Expediente de los ayllus puxpu y poder los jilaqatas a Toribio Miranda, 1909–1927," Fondo 14, 45–49, APAJMC.

45. Ibid., 43.

46. Ibid., 10–15.

47. Barragán, *Indios de archo y flecha*, 89–94; "Demanda del Ayllu Condo y comunidad Palqa contra la hacienda Sijcha, 1920–1926," Folio 1920–1928, 35–43, FPTQ;

Langer, "La comercialización de la cebada en los Ayllus y las haciendas de Tarabuco (Chuquisaca) a comienzos del siglo XX," 52–88.

48. Jach'aqullu, "El indio Uru-Murato, Toribio Miranda y Manuela Quevedo," 9–13.

49. Miranda, "Sus luchas de mi padre," 3; Quevedo, "Su historia de Toribio Miranda y Manuela Quevedo," 5–17.

50. "Carta de Manuel Andia a Toribio Miranda, Diciembre 3, 1938," Folio 4, 54–77, APAJMC.

51. Lora, *Formación de la clase obrera boliviana*, 23–50.

52. Ibid.

53. Ponce Mamani, "Los hermanos espirituales" (memoir), 3–5, FPAPM.

54. "Carta de Toribio Miranda a Manuel Andia, Noviembre 21, 1931," Folio 4, APAJMC.

55. THOA, *El indio Santos Marka T'ula*, 13–20; Jach'aqullu, "El indio Uru-Murato, Toribio Miranda y Manuela Quevedo," 13–15.

56. "Carta de Toribio Miranda a Luciano Negrete, Abril 11, 1936," Folio 1, 2–4, AJPM.

57. "Memorial del jilanku del ayllu Bombo, Miguel Hurtado, solicitando que la subprefectura de la provincia Dalence le ayude a recuperar tierras de vallada en la provincia Misk'i, Enero 14, 1931," Fondo 35, 3–4, AJPD; Dandler, "El Congreso Nacional Indígena," 98–240; Gordillo, *Arando en la historia*, 55–99; and *La Razón*, June 14, 1948, 4–5.

58. Jorge Cordoba, "Así nos castigaban" (testimony), Fondo 5, 23–27, APHONS; and Langer, *Economic Change*, 77–87.

59. "Carta de Toribio Miranda a Pascual Ichu, comunicándole su matrimonio con Berna Andia, Mayo 10, 1938," Folio 2, 7, FPHC.

60. Ibid., 9.

61. Vallejos, "Mi camino de Jampiri y la provincia Mizque" (memoir), FPMG.

62. "Testamento de Petrona Andia," August 17, 1957, Folio 1, FPFV.

63. Letter with a seal with the names of Toribio Miranda and Berna Andia, Chinguri, November 4, 1940, to Hermelindo Vargas, folio 2, FPFV.

64. Consejo Episcopal Americano, *Método Cala*, 10–51.

65. Gotkowitz, *A Revolution for Our Rights*, 101–31.

66. Ibid.

67. The word *gamonal* means "large landowner" and refers to the exploitation of the Indian population, mainly by landowners of European descent.

68. Klein, *Bolivia*, 148–88; Céspedes, *El dictador suicida*, 177–83.

69. Rivera Cusicanqui, *Oprimidos pero no vencidos*, 66–76; Córdoba, "La hacienda el Novillero" (testimony), 23–27, APJC; Dandler, "El Congreso Nacional Indígena," 133–200.

70. Antezana and Romero, *La historia de los sindicatos campesinos*, 119–202.

71. "Declaración ante la Policía Rural de Francisco Mamani, Noviembre 14, 1948," Fondo 1, 3, APJC.

72. Jach'aqullu, "El indio Uru-Murato, Toribio Miranda y Manuela Quevedo," 13–15.

73. Gallardo, "Así hemos caminado" (memoir), Fondo 3, 25–31, APHONS.

74. Quevedo, "Tiempos sufridos" (memoir), Fondo 1, 33–35, FPTQ.

75. Ibid.

76. Arias, Historia de una esperanza, 41–57.

77. Oral history records say that he was participating in the ritual of kintu, in which people invite each other with a few select coca leaves and then chew them. So Miranda held coca leaves and talked about Pachamama because coca leaves are considered one of the representations of her in the indigenous tradition. See Felipa Cardozo, "Memorias de Toribio Miranda," Folio 2, 5, FPFV.

78. Jacha'qullu, "El indio Uru-Murato, Toribio Miranda y Manuela Quevedo," 2.

79. Gotkowitz, A Revolution for Our Rights, 157; Vallejos, "Los purirantes" (testimony), Folio 1, 7, FPFV.

80. "Expediente de los ayllus puxpu y poder los jilaqatas a Toribio Miranda, 1909–1927," Fondo 14, 7, APAJMC.

81. Rivera, "Chunca Cancha, 1948" (memoir), Fondo 4, FPHE.

82. Teodoro Tellez, "El Gallardo era ch'utita" (memoir), 3–4, FPHE; Q'uyu, "Su camino de los antiguos caminantes," 17–19; and Peñaranda, "En su tiempo de Villarroel" (memoir), 13–14, FPHE.

83. Peñaranda, "En su tiempo de Villarroel," 13–14, FPHE.

84. Dandler, "El Congreso Nacional Indígena," 135–200.

85. "Expediente de los ayllus puxpu y poder los jilaqatas a Toribio Miranda, 1909–1927," Fondo 14, 7, APAJMC; Gotkowitz, A Revolution for Our Rights, 233–67.

86. Guibernau and Hutchinson, Understanding Nationalism, 15.

87. Orieta, "Tata Toribio Miranda" (testimony), APHONS; Ticona Alejo, Rojas Ortuste, and Albó, Votos y Wiplhalas, 83.

88. Said, Representations of the Intellectual, 15–33.

89. Lora, Formación de la clase obrera boliviana, 43–68.

90. "Carta de Gregorio Titiriku a Ezequiel Orieta, Diciembre 14, 1948," Fondo 2, 2, APEO.

Chapter 4. Against Cholification: Gregorio Titiriku's Urban Experience and the Development of Earth Politics in Segregated Times

1. "Acta de detención de Mariano Qhispi, Estación de la Policía, La Paz, August 1925," Folio 1, 3, FPMG.

2. Ibid.

3. Ari-Chachaki, "Dos repúblicas," 7.

4. Gómez, Bautista Saavedra, 240.

5. Arguedas, Pueblo enfermo, 55.

6. Ramos, "Así le he ayudado" (memoir), 11–12, APHOA.

7. For similar cases in Mexico in the early twentieth century, see Beezley, Judas

at the Jockey Club and Other Episodes of Porfirian Mexico, 57–102; Beezley, Martin, and French, Rituals of Rule, Rituals of Resistance, 23–70.

8. Rivera Cusicanqui, Oprimidos pero no vencidos, 3–20; and THOA, El indio Santos Marka T'ula, 13–25.

9. Titiriku, "Gregorio Titiriku se hablaba así" (memoir), 15–16.

10. Choque, "La sociedad," 13–16; Mamani, Taraqu, 55–169.

11. Nelson, A Finger in the Wound, 249.

12. "Carta de Gregorio Titiriku a Eusebio Canqui, Marzo 14, 1945," Fondo 1, 45, APAJMC; see also Anderson, Imagined Communities, 23–178.

13. Jach'aqullu, "El Kollasuyu y Gregorio Titiriku" (memoir), Folio 2, 7–8, APAJMC; Gotkowitz, A Revolution for Our Rights, 69–100.

14. Gregorio Titiriku's petition to the Minister of Education, February 27, 1937, Folio 1, 3, FPGTRR.

15. Huanacuni, Filosofía, políticas, estrategias y experiencias regionales, 37–95.

16. Torero, "Lingüística e historia de la sociedad andina," 2–50; and Bouysee-Cassagne, La identidad Aymara, aproximación histórica (siglo XV, siglo XVI), 15–78.

17. Titiriku "Gregorio Titiriku se hablaba así," 9–12.

18. Choque, Sociedad y economía colonial en el sur andino, 150–238; Choque and Albó, Cinco siglos de historia, 130–270.

19. Titiriku, "Gregorio Titiriku se hablaba así," 9–12.

20. Titiriku, "Para recordar a los phawajrunas" (memoir), 3–5, APPM.

21. "Memorial de Gregorio Titiriku en defensa del despojo que sufren las comunidades de Zamora y Turrine, Noviembre 12,1914," Fondo 1, 4, APPM.

22. Titiriku, "Para recordar a los phawajrunas," Fondo 2, 4.

23. "Carta de Gregorio Titiriku a Andres Titiriku, Marzo, 1923," Fondo 7, APPM.

24. Titiriku, "Gregorio Titiriku se hablaba así," 9–12.

25. Jach'aqullu, "El Kollasuyu y Gregorio Titiriku," Folio 2, 7–9. Also see HAM, Cuarto Centenario, 480–620.

26. Carmona, "El tiempo de Peñaranda" (memoir), Fondo 3, 3–5, APHONS.

27. "Expediente de demanda del Ayllu Condo y comunidad Palqa contra la hacienda Luwichutu, 1926–1934," Fondo 1920–1945, 3–17, FPAPM; Barragán, Indios de arco y flecha, 21–76.

28. Ramos, "Así le he ayudado," 11–12.

29. Titiriku, "Gregorio Titiriku se hablaba así," 9–12.

30. Jach'aqullu, "Sobre Gregorio Titiriku," Fondo 2, 3–6, APAJMC.

31. Lehm and Rivera Cusicanqui, Los artesanos libertarios, 48–59; El hombre libre, February 23, 1926, 3–4; Ramos, "Así le he ayudado," 12.

32. Lehm and Rivera Cusicanqui, Los artesanos libertarios, 51–63; and El hombre libre, February 23, 1926, 3–4.

33. Jach'aqullu, "El Kollasuyu y Gregorio Titiriku," Fondo 2, 7, 80–120.

34. Arias, "Memorias de Florencia Burgoa Chachaki," Fondo 5, 6–8, APHOA.

35. Thompson, "La cuestión India en Bolivia a comienzos del siglos," 83–116.

36. Arguedas, Pueblo enfermo, 69.

37. "Los lugares céntricos y la vestimenta de los autóctonos," *La República*, Abril 21, 1925, 6.

38. Ibid.

39. Gómez, *Bautista Saavedra*, 240.

40. El *Diario*, February, 11, 1924, 5; and El *Diario*, September, 23, 1925, 7. See also Lehm and Rivera Cusicanqui, *Los artesanos libertarios*, 72–173.

41. Lehm and Rivera Cusicanqui, *Los artesanos libertarios*, 153–98.

42. Ramos, "Así le he ayudado," 9,

43. Arguedas, *Pueblo enfermo*, 55–65.

44. Gill, *Precarious Dependencies*, 37–77, 141–52. This book contains a good description of cholas as plebeian woman in the late twentieth century. See also, Barragán, "Entre polleras, lliqllas y ñañacas," 85–127.

45. Fernando Olmos, "Oruro y el progreso," *La Trinchera*, February 18, 1938, 5–6, Folio 3, APAJMQ.

46. Arguedas, *Pueblo enfermo*, 55.

47. "Demanda por violación y calumnias de José Mamani contra Carlos Reinaga, 1927–1935," Folio 3, 37–41, AJPD.

48. "Declaración de Antonio García en la Estación de Policía Camacho," Folio 3, 2, FPHE.

49. "Demanda por violación y calumnias de José Mamani contra Carlos Reinaga, 1927–1935," Folio 3, 37–41, AJPD.

50. For example, Bolivian public jails had a three-tiered provisioning system in 1925. Continuing a colonial policy, the jailer provided high-quality food to whites (gente decente), a medium quality to mestizos, and the worst food of all to Indians. See "Interesante petición de Indígenas," *La República*, October 25, 1925, 3.

51. Memorial de Pablo Condo, "Los indios después de Daza," Folio 1, 10, FPFQ.

52. Arze, *Guerras y conflictos sociales*, 15–45. See also Hylton, "Tierra común: Caciques, artesanos e intelectuales radicales y la rebelión de Chayanta," in *Ya es otro tiempo el presente: Cuatro momentos de insurgencia indígena*, edited by Forrest Hylton, Felix Patzi, Sergio Serulnkov, and Sinclair Thompson (La Paz: Muela del Diablo, 2003), 134–98; and "El Federalismo Insurgente," 99–118.

53. Klein, *Bolivia*, 88–227.

54. Medinaceli, *La Chaskañawi*, 15–98; Romero Pittari, *Las Claudinas*, 15–30. Romero Pittari expresses the perspective of white men who see cholas as objects of love and sex. Although Medinaceli sees love and sex between whites and cholas as leading to the degeneration of whites, his is the best sample of Bolivian literature addressing this topic.

55. Lehm and Rivera Cusicanqui, *Los artesanos libertarios*, 5–75; Condori Chura and Ticona, *El escribano*, 22–55; Mamani, *Taraqu*, 43–45, 127–34.

56. Gallardo, "Chutas y Cholos, 1972" (memoir), 20–23, APHONS; Ari-Chachaki, "Apuntes para una perspectiva comparativa de los ch'utas en La Paz y Sucre," 3–8.

57. Lora, *Formación de la clase obrera boliviana*, 25–75; Arze, *Guerras y conflictos sociales*, 15–55; and Lazarte Rojas, *Movimiento obrero y procesos políticos en Bolivia*, 50–189.

58. Lehm and Rivera Cusicanqui, *Los artesanos libertarios*, 21–113.

59. Aronna, "*Pueblos enfermos*," 15–108.

60. Arguedas, *Pueblo enfermo*, 58; Salomón, *El espejo indigenista en Bolivia*, 63–73.

61. Tamayo, *Obras escogidas*, 3–105.

62. "Acta de buena conducta entre Gregorio Titiriku y Jacinto Díaz Quispe y Pedro Conde Iturri, 1934," Fondo 1, 3–5, FPGTRR.

63. Ibid.

64. Titiriku, "Gregorio Titiriku se hablaba así," 5–7.

65. Díaz Machicao, *Historia de Bolivia*, 56–80.

66. Ibid., 45–190.

67. "Carta de Gregorio Titiriku a Honorato Rocha, Enero 14, 1928," Fondo 2, APEO.

68. Titiriku, "Gregorio Titiriku se hablaba así," 5–7.

69. Jach'aqullu, "El Kollasuyu y Gregorio Titiriku," 4–8; Choque and Ticona, *Jesús de Machaqa*, 21–35; and Langer, *Economic Change*, 52–87.

70. Ugarte, "Los antiguos caminantes" (memoir), Folio 2, 5, APHOMI.

71. Iquiapaza, "Titiriku y su camino" (testimony), Folio 3, 5, APHOA.

72. Ibid., 3.

73. "Acta de posesión del Alcalde Particular Carlos Condori, Septiembre 12, 1936," Fondo 1, 1, FPHE.

74. Sallez, "El sufrimiento de los Alcaldes Particulares" (testimony), 3–6, FPFR.

75. "Carta de Gregorio Titiriku a Felix Choque, Mayo 22, 1937," Fondo 2, APPM.

76. "Carta de Gregorio Titiriku a Andrés Jachakollo, Marzo 21, 1941," Fondo 1, 2, FPTQ.

77. "Acta de detención de Mariano Qhispi, Estación de la Policía, La Paz, August 1925," Folio 1, 3, FPMG.

78. Iquiapaza, "Titiriku y su camino," Folio 3, 5. See also Ugarte, "Los antiguos caminantes," Folio 2, 5.

79. Ramos, "Así le he ayudado," 13.

80. Ibid.

81. "Denuncia de la propietaria de la hacienda Churumatas, Diciembre 15, 1939," Folio 3, FPFR.

82. "Informe del Corregidor Don Pedro Molle, Noviembre 1947," Folio 1, 3, FPLM.

83. Ibid., 2.

84. Ugarte, "Los antiguos caminantes," Folio 2.

85. "Informe del Corregidor, Febrero 15, 1944," Folio 7, 13, AJA.

86. Titiriku, "Gregorio Titiriku se hablaba así," 8–9.

87. "Sumario informativo contra Carlos Rivera y Timoteo Sotomayor por abusos denunciados," Folio 3, 2–3, FPHC.

88. Ibid., 4.

89. Ibid., 1–2.

90. Ibid., 5.

91. Ibid.

92. Ibid., 6.

93. "Declaración de Antonio García en la Estación de Policía Camacho," Folio 3, 2, FPHE.

94. Ibid., 2–3.

95. Titiriku, *Historia de la llegada de la Iglesia Evangélica Metodista en Bolivia*, 3–9; Titiriku, "Gregorio Titiriku se hablaba así," 5–13.

96. "Carta de Gregorio Titiriku a Lorenzo Titiriku, Julio 1, 1935," Fondo 1, 3, FPTQ.

97. Pérez, *Warisata*, 50–120; Salazar Mostajo, *La Taika*, 60–90. See also Larson, "'La invención del indio iletrado,'" 117–47.

98. "Carta de Gregorio Titiriku a Mateo Apaza, Febrero 25, 1938," Fondo 4, 33, FPTQ; Velasco, *La escuela indígenal de Warisata*, 1–69.

99. Velasco, *La escuela indígenal de Warisata*, 10–45.

100. Pérez, *Warisata*, 334–401.

101. "Carta de Gregorio Titiriku a Isidro Mullisaca, Abril 14, 1939," Fondo 1, 1, APEO.

102. "Carta y listas de Alcaldes, de Gregorio Titiriku a Manuel Iquiapaza, Junio 6, 1944," Fondo 1, 7, APEO.

103. "Carta de Gregorio Titiriku a Andrés Jachaqullu, Enero, 3, 1941," Fondo 1, 2, APEO.

104. "Carta de Gregorio Titiriku a Toribio Miranda, Septiembre 1, 1936," Fondo 2, 12, FPTQ.

105. Velasco, *La escuela indígenal de Warisata*, 25–67; Pérez, *Warisata*, 21–220.

106. Choque, Soria, Mamani, Ticona, and Conde, *Educación indígena*, 23–75.

107. "Carta de Toribio Miranda a Lucas Marka, Marzo 6, 1937," Fondo 2, 13–15, APAJMC.

108. Ibid., 3.

109. Ibid., 1.

110. Saavedra, "Lista de Alcaldes Mayores Particulares," 10–35, APHONS.

111. "Acta de posesión del Alcalde Particular Carlos Condori, Abril 15, 1937," Folio 1, 15, FPHE.

112. "Carta de Gregorio Titiriku a Melitón Gallardo, Diciembre 12, 1945," Fondo 3, 33, FPMG.

113. "Carta de Gregorio Titiriku a Fermín Vallejos, Mayo 14, 1944," Fondo 3, 7, APJC.

114. Ramos, "Así le he ayudado," 9.

115. Titiriku, "Gregorio Titiriku se hablaba así," 20–21.

116. Titiriku, "Para recordar a los phawajrunas," 25–28.

117. Titiriku, "Gregorio Titiriku se hablaba así," 3–6.

118. Titiriku, "Para recordar a los phawajrunas," Fondo 3, 15–17; Orieta, "Tata Toribio Miranda" (testimony), Fondo 2B, 11–13, APHONS.

119. Q'uyu, "Su camino de los antiguos caminantes" (testimony), 9–19, FPFQ.

120. Titiriku, "Gregorio Titiriku se hablaba así," 19–21.

121. Ibid.

122. Grandin, The Blood of Guatemala, 130–220.

123. Ibid., 1–52, 230–35.

124. Ibid., 130–220.

125. Eskildsen, "Of Civilization and Savages," 388–418.

126. For the conflictual relationship between Aymaras migrants and the city of La Paz after the national revolution of 1952, see Albó and Sandoval, Chukiawu, 10–180; Albó and Mamani, Khitipxtansa.

127. In the 1920s there were two important wak'as (funerary towers) of Aymara ancestors that Titiriku worshiped. One was Qunchupata and the other was Killi-Killi (Titiriku, "Para recordar a los phawajrunas," Folio 4, 3).

128. Titiriku, "Para recordar a los phawajrunas," 6–10.

129. Ramos, "Sutalaya y una experiencia en La Paz" (memoir), 3, APHOA.

Chapter 5. Between Internal Colonialism and War:
Melitón Gallardo in the Southern Andean Estates

1. "Sumario de proceso penal contra Melitón Gallardo por instigaciones y ca-lumnias, Febrero, 1947," Fondo Judicial, 1945–47, 3–5, CDHSFX. In this court case Melitón narrated the events of November 13, 1946, that resulted in his severe injury.

2. Klein, Bolivia, 188–227.

3. José Dandler, "El Congreso Nacional Indígena de 1945 y la rebelión de Ayo-paya (1947)," 224–95; "Sumario informativo sobre la muerte de Carlos Condori y ciertos rumores, Diciembre, 1947," Fondo 2, 6–7, FPFR.

4. "Sumario de proceso penal contra Melitón Gallardo por instigaciones y ca-lumnias, Febrero 1947," Fondo Judicial, 1945–47, 8–11, CDHSFX; "Denuncia de Mario Pari por el asesinato del esposo de su hija, Carlos Condori Puquaqa," Fondo 2, 2, FPHE.

5. Carlos Inturias, "En el tiempo de Fermín Vallejos y las haciendas," FPFV; Arias, Historia de una Esperanza, 39–107; Arias, El tata Fermín, 12–53; "Sumario de proceso penal de Melitón Gallardo contra Anselmo Cosolich, 1946–1947," Fondo 4, 3–5, FPMG. See also similarities with the Chayanta Rebellion in Langer, "Andean Rituals of Revolt," 227–53.

6. "Sumario de proceso penal de Melitón Gallardo contra Anselmo Cosolich, 1946–1947," 11–13.

7. Ibid., 9–10.

8. "Denuncia de Mario Pari por el asesinato del esposo de su hija, Carlos Condori Poquaqa, 1947," Fondo 2, 4, FPHE; "Así fue asesinado Carlos Condori," La Calle, February 7, 1948, 5–6.

9. "La Muerte de Marcelino Mamani," Nueva Vanguardia, April 21, 1947, Fondo 2, 7–8, FPMG.

10. Saavedra, "La vida y obra y Melitón Gallardo" (memoir), Fondo 1, 2–3, FPMG.

11. Gallardo, "Así hemos caminado los antiguos poderantes" (testimony), 9–11; Torrico, "Memorias de la Guerra del Chaco del Melitón Gallardo" (memoir), Fondo 1H, 3–7, FPTQ.

12. Inturias, "En el tiempo de Fermín Vallejos y las haciendas" (testimony), 13–15, 5–9.

13. Gallardo, "Así hemos caminado los antiguos poderantes," Fondo 1, 5–7.

14. Ibid., Fondo 2, 8–11; "Expediente agrario de Tapalillas, 1961," 60–61, Tapalillas, Puxpu, Fondo Oropeza, SNRA.

15. Gallardo, "Así hemos caminado los antiguos poderantes," Fondo 1A, 17–21.

16. Ibid., 23.

17. Torrico, "Memorias de la Guerra del Chaco del Melitón Gallardo," Fondo 2, 14–15.

18. Ibid., 5–7.

19. "Carta de Melitón Gallardo al presidente Villarroel pidiendo una audiencia mientras estaba en La Paz, May 3, 1945," Fondo 4, 3–4, FPMG.

20. Gallardo, "Así hemos caminado los antiguos poderantes," Fondo 1A, 18–21.

21. Saavedra, "La vida y obra de Melitón Gallardo" (memoir), Fondo 1, 19–25, FPMG.

22. Gallardo, "Así hemos caminado los antiguos poderantes," Fondo 2, 13–15.

23. Ibid., 10.

24. Ibid., 35. See also Arze, Guerras y conflictos sociales, 35–78.

25. Torrico, "Memorias de la guerra del Chaco del Melitón Gallardo," 4.

26. Saavedra, "La vida y obra de Melitón Gallardo," Fondo 1, 18–21.

27. "Nota del jefe de personal de la prefectura de Chuquisaca, Febrero 21, 1937," Fondo Prefectural, 1937, CDHSFX.

28. La Calle, April 6, 1942, 14.

29. Gallardo, "Así hemos caminado los antiguos poderantes," 12–13.

30. Siles, "El anarquismo en la capital de la república, 1953," Fondo 2A, 3–5, FPMG.

31. Gallardo, "Así hemos caminado los antiguos poderantes," 10; Saavedra, "La vida y obra de Melitón Gallardo," 5–8.

32. Orieta, "Tata Toribio Miranda" (testimony), 3, APHONS.

33. Gallardo, "Así hemos caminado los antiguos poderantes," 10.

34. Saavedra, "La vida y obra de Melitón Gallardo," 7–10.

35. Ibid., 17, and Gallardo, "Así hemos caminado los antiguos poderantes," 11.

36. Quevedo, "Tiempos sufridos," (memoir, 1979), 3–23.

37. Titiriku, "Para recordar a los phawajrunas," (memoir, 1977), 3–7.

38. Orieta, "Tata Toribio Miranda," 11.

39. García Quintanilla, "Monografía de la Provincia Zudáñez," 400–421.

40. "Expediente agrario Uyuni," 78–83; Fondo Zudañes, SNRA; and Barragán, *Indios de arco y flecha*, 1–48.

41. Quevedo, "Su historia" (memoir, 1979), 13–15.

42. García Quintanilla, "Monografía de la Provincia Zudáñez," 400–421. See also Arias, *Historia de una Esperanza*, 39–108.

43. "Expedientes agrarios de hacienda Sumala," 135–57; "Churumatas," 115–25; "Suruma," 23–25, Fondo Zudáñez SNRA; and García Quintanilla, "Monografía de la Provincia Zudáñez," 400–421.

44. "Expedientes agrarios de hacienda Sumala," 135–57; "Churumatas," 115–25, "Suruma," 23–25, Fondo Zudáñez SNRA; and García Quintanilla, "Monografía de la Provincia Zudáñez," 400–421; Orieta, "Tata Toribio Miranda," Fondo Kolla-suyus, 7; Rivera, "Las haciendas eran así en su tiempo de Villarroel" (memoir), Fondo 3, 23, FPHE; Rivera, "Chunca Cancha, 1948," Fondo 3D, 3, FPFR. For Chuquisaca in general, see Langer, *Economic Change*, 10–198.

45. Orieta, "Tata Toribio Miranda," 14.

46. "Sumario de proceso penal contra Melitón Gallardo por instigaciones y calumnias," Fondo Judicial, 1945–47, 3–5, CDHSFX.

47. "Nota de Melitón Gallardo dirigida a Francisco Rivera," November 23, 1947, 48; "Sumario de proceso penal contra Melitón Gallardo por instigaciones y calumnias, 1946–47," Fondo Judicial 1945–47, 3–5, CDHSFX.

48. "Carta de Meliton Gallardo a Juan Wallpa, Abril 23, 1044," Folio 3E, 6, APHOA. Muruhuta Mountain is located in La Paz, the heart of the Aymara world.

49. "Nota de Melitón Gallardo dirigida a Francisco Rivera," November 23, 1947, 48; "Sumario de proceso penal contra Melitón Gallardo por instigaciones y calumnias. 1946–47," Fondo Judicial, 1945–47, 3–5, CDHSFX. See also Barragán, *Indios de arco y flecha*, 9–98.

50. Saavedra, "La vida y obra de Melitón Gallardo," Fondo 1, 23–25.

51. Ibid.; see also Barragán, *Indios de arco y flecha*, 9–95.

52. "Carta de Melitón Gallardo dirigida a Andrés T'ika, Abril 21, 1944," Fondo 2, 47, FPHE.

53. Gallardo, "Así hemos caminado los antiguos poderantes," 21–25; Loayza, "El Congreso de Sucre" (memoir), Fondo 3H, 2–3, APEO; Sallez, "El sufrimiento de los Alcaldes Particulares" (testimony), Fondo 13, 17–18, FPFR; Rivera, "Las haciendas eran así en su tiempo de Villarroel," 3–5; Cari, "Sumala" (memoir), Fondo 3B, 6–7, FPFR.

54. Barragán, *Indios de arco y flecha*, 1–48; García Quintanilla, "Monografía de la Provincia Zudáñez," 400–421.

55. Grosby, "Nationality and Religion," 97–119. See also Grosby, "The Chosen People of Ancient Israel and the Occident," 357–80.

56. Guha, *A Subaltern Studies Reader*, 10–390.

57. Thompson, "Was There Race in Colonial Latin America?," 72–91.

58. Gallardo, "Así hemos caminado los antiguos poderantes," 21–25.

59. La Calle, November 6, 1940, 3–5.

60. Andean communities used to complete their diet with food produced in different ecological zones, highlands and subtropical. See Murra, "An Aymara Kingdom in 1567," 115–51.

61. "Informe sobre sumario contra llameros agitadores, Icla," Fondo Prefectural 1940, 14–16, CDHSFX.

62. Semanario La Plata, April 11, 1929, 4, APEO.

63. Escobar, Testimonio de un militante obrero, 12–56.

64. Aisakayu, "Andrés Jach'aqullu" (memoir), 9–11, APAJMC.

65. Escobar, Testimonio de un militante obrero, 12–56; Zavaleta Mercado, Bolivia Hoy, 150–240.

66. See "Carta de Feliciano Inka Marasa and Pablo Espinoza Marasa," Fondo 3, 1–3, FPHE.

67. "Carta de Feliciano Inka Marasa al Prof. Estanislao Ari," January 7, 1943, Fondo 1, FPHE.

68. "Primer Congreso Kechua," Boletín informativo Congreso Kechua, May 1942, 1–2, Fondo 3, APEO.

69. Condarco Morales, Zárate, 10–240.

70. Siles, "El anarquismo en la capital de república," Fondo 3, 3–5.

71. Ibid., 7.

72. Ibid., 3–4.

73. "Palabras de los Delegados," Boletín Informativo Congreso Kechua, June 1942, Fondo 4, FPMG.

74. Rivera, "Las haciendas eran así en su tiempo de Villarroel," 21–25; García, "En su tiempo de Peñaranda" (memoir), Fondo 1E, 3–5, FPHC; and Gallardo, "Así hemos caminado los antiguos poderantes," 21–25.

75. La Razón, November 17, 1944, 5.

76. Antezana and Romero, Historia de los sindicatos campesinos, 28–45.

77. "Nota de Ezequiel Orieta a Eleuterio Díaz," April 27, 1944, Fondo 1, FPHE; La Razón, November 3, 1944, 5–6.

78. "Expediente Agrario Sumala," 37, and "Expediente agrario Soruma," 40, Fondo Zudáñez SNRA.

79. Antezana and Romero, Historia de los sindicatos campesinos, 38.

80. See "Sumario de proceso penal contra Melitón Gallardo por instigaciones y calumnias, 1946–1947," 3–5.

81. Ibid., 9; Gallardo, "Así hemos caminado los antiguos poderantes," 23–25.

82. "Expediente Agrario Sumala," 23–43, Fonda Zudáñez SNRA.

83. Arias, Historia de una Esperanza, 23–64; and Ponce Mamani, "Los poderantes" (testimony), 3–5, FPHE.

84. "Proceso sumarial por instigar a la toma de tierras de la hacienda Sipiqani," November 1947, Fondo Judicial, 3–4, CDHSFX; La Razón, April 1, 1947.

85. "Proceso sumarial por instigar a la toma de tierras de la hacienda Sipiqani," 7–8.

86. Rivera Cusicanqui with THOA, *Ayllus y proyectos*, 40–65. Also see Langer, "Andean Rituals of Revolt," 227–53.

87. "Sumario por instigar falsos cultos, Septiembre, 1947," Fondo 1, 2–3, FPFR.

88. Ibid., 5–7.

89. Ponce Mamani, "Los poderantes," 33–35; and Peñaranda, "En su tiempo de Villarroel" (memoir), Fondo Kollasuyus, 3–4, FPHE.

90. Rivera, "Las haciendas eran así en su tiempo de Villarroel," 33; and Peñaranda, "En su tiempo de Villarroel," Fondo 11, 21–22.

91. Téllez, "El Gallardo era ch'utita" (memoir), Fondo 2B, 23, FPHE.

92. Gallardo, "Así hemos caminado los antiguos poderantes," Fondo 2B, 21–25.

93. Luis Velas's letter to Ignacio Aduviri, November, 23, 1948, Fondo 2, FPMG.

94. Antezana and Romero, *Historia de los sindicatos campesinos*, 23–45.

95. "Carta de Anastasia Reina dirigida a Fidelia Lora, Diciembre 3, 1947," Fondo Judicial, 1947–1950, Fondo 7, 33, CDHSFX.

96. Rivera, "Las haciendas eran así en su tiempo de Villarroel" (memoir), 11; Saavedra, "La vida y obra de Melitón Gallardo," 5; "Carta de Melitón Gallardo dirigida a Ezequiel Orieta," Fondo 1, 38, Enero 13, 1947, FPHE.

97. "Sumario de los líos de Febrero de 1948 en Chunca Cancha," Fondo 3, 7–8, FPMG.

98. Joseph and Nugent, *Everyday Forms of State Formation*, 69–326.

Chapter 6. Against Whitening: Andrés Jach'aqullu's Movement between Worlds in the Era of the Bolivian National Revolution of 1952

1. "Proceso judicial Vela contra Reina, 1953–1956," 7–11, CDHSFX.

2. Rivera Cusicanqui, *Oprimidos*, 120–70.

3. "Decreto Supremo 3937," *La Gaceta de Bolivia*, July 3, 1956.

4. Antezana and Bedregal Gutiérrez, *Origen, fundación y futuro del M.N.R.*, 1–35.

5. Calderón, and Dandler, *Bolivia, la fuerza histórica del campesinadoa*, 135–200.

6. Rivera Cusicanqui, *Oprimidos*, 15; Arias, *Historia de una Esperanza*, 50–120.

7. Rivera Cusicanqui, *Oprimidos*, 9–11.

8. Healy, *Caciques y patrones*, 50–320.

9. "Demanda judicial de Felix Cutrina," April 11, 1958, 2–3, APJC.

10. Ibid., 5–6.

11. "Carta de Pedro Añawaya dirigida al Corregidor de Janqulaime," September 15, 1957, 3–5, APHOMI; "Demanda de Filberto Quispe contra Reynaldo Ramires, Enero 3, 1958," 6–7, APEO.

12. "Demanda judicial de Felix Cutrina," April 11, 1958, 3–10.

13. Aisakayu, "Andrés Jach'aqullu" (memoir), 4–6, APAJMC.

14. Klein, *Bolivia*, 149–88.

15. Ibid.

16. Aisakayu, "Andrés Jach'aqullu," 13–16.

17. Harris and Albó, *Monteras y guardatojos*, 4–6.

18. "Proceso judicial Vela contra Reina, 1953–1956," 3–10, CDHSFX; Rivera Cusicanqui, *Oprimidos*, 19–21.

19. Jach'aqullu, "Bayetas camisas sabían decirnos" (memoir), Fondo 17A, 33–45, APAJMC; and Lora, *Formación de la clase obrera boliviana*, 19–83.

20. Jach'aqullu, "Phichuwawas sabían decirnos" (memoir), Fondo 3, 11–17, APHOA.

21. Aisakayu, "Andrés Jach'aqullu," Fondo 1, 13–16.

22. Villca, "Muruhuta y Mururata Achachila" (memoir), Fondo 1, 5, FPAPM.

23. Ibid., 5–9.

24. Jach'aqullu, "Phichuwawas sabían decirnos," 21–27.

25. Ibid., 11–15.

26. Aisakayu, "Andrés Jach'aqullu," 13–16.

27. "Hojas de servicios de Andrés Cerrogrande, 1944," Comando Departamental de la Policía Boliviana, Oruro, Fondo 4, 2–4, APAJMC.

28. Qulqi, "Inkawawas, la Virgina y su camino de Miranda" (memoir) Fondo 2, 13–15, APHOA, and Aisakayu, "Andrés Jach'aqullu," 13–16.

29. Jach'aqullu, "Pichuwawas sabían decirnos," 21–25; Aisakayu, "Andrés Jach'aqullu," 15–19.

30. "Los hijos del Sol," *Revista del Trabajo* 9 (1956): 22–23, Fondo 7, APAJMC.

31. "Carta de Toribio Miranda a Andrés Jach'aqullu nombrándolo su apoderado," April 11, 1951, Fondo 8, APAJMC.

32. Albó and Mamani, *Achacachi*, 16–38.

33. Rivera Cusicanqui, et al., *Ser mujer, indígena*, 17–85, 163–285.

34. Julio Sallez, "El sufrimiento de los Alcaldes Particulares" (testimony), Folio 2, 14, 16, FPFR.

35. "Expediente Paredes vs. Iturri, 1928–1932," 7–23, FPGTRR.

36. Ibid., 17.

37. Rivera Cusicanqui, et al., *Ser mujer, indígena*, 163–285; Stephenson, *Gender and Modernity in Andean Bolivia*, 1–34.

38. Gómez, *Bautista Saavedra*, 229.

39. Jach'aqullu, "Phichuwawas sabían decirnos," Folio 3, 11.

40. Lehm and Rivera Cusicanqui, *Los artesanos libertarios*, 129.

41. "Manifiesto de la Federación Agraria Departamental La Paz, Octubre 1939," Fondo Prefectural, 1940, 3–5, AHLP.

42. Andrade, *José Santos Marka Thola*, 14–17.

43. Antezana and Romero, *Historia de los sindicatos campesinos*, 101–11.

44. "Algo que Pudo Parecer Insólito," *La Calle*, May 11, 1945, 4.

45. Getulio Vargas, the president and dictator of Brazil, was admired by Villarroel and other socialist military officers in Bolivia. Villarroel admired Vargas for fostering "updated" or "modernized" labor relations in Brazil in the 1930s. See "Memorias of Raul Riveros, Villarroel, Vargas y Brazil," La Paz, APHOA, 1972.

46. Jach'aqullu, "Phichuwawas sabían decirnos," 11–15.

47. Céspedes, Sangre de mestizos, 35–70.

48. Zavaleta Mercado, Bolivia, 129–49.

49. Malloy, Bolivia, 3–75.

50. Klein, Bolivia, 227–45.

51. Antezana and Romero, Historia de los sindicatos campesinos, 203–64.

52. Huizer, The Revolutionary Potential of the Peasant in Latin America, 94.

53. Larson, Trials of Nation Making, 246–54.

54. El Diario, April 2, 1954, 5–6.

55. Guillén Pinto, La educación del indio, 23–89.

56. Joseph and Nugent, Everyday Forms of State Formation, 1–24.

57. Antezana and Romero, Historia de los sindicatos campesinos, 228.

58. Albó and Mamani, Achacachi, 37–86.

59. Paredes, El indio Machaca y la República Aymara, 3–12.

60. Gordillo, Arando en la historia, 19–38; Los hombres de la revolución, 10–35.

61. Rivera Cusicanqui, Oprimidos, 85–114. See also Joseph and Nugent, Everyday Forms of State Formation, 1–24, 355–67.

62. Rivera Cusicanqui, Oprimidos, 101–8; Arias, Historia de una Esperanza, 109–60.

63. "Informe del Corregidor De Icla al Prefecto del Departamento de Chuquisaca, Agosto de 1958," Folio 14, 34; "Correspondencia de la Prefectura 1958–1964," CDHSFX; "Memorial de la Central Agraria de Sumala, Enero 3, 1956," Folio 16, 34–37; "Expediente de Sumala," Fondo Zudañéz, SNRA.

64. "Expediente agrario de las ex haciendas Sumala," 101–12; and "Expediente Churumatas," 98–99, Fondo Zudanéz, SNRA.

65. El Diario, October 20, 1956, 13.

66. "Carta de Francisco Rivera sobre la escuela de Chunca Cancha y quejas sobre la profesora Irma Malpartida, April 8, 1958," Folio 3, 2, FPFR.

67. Juan Apaza, "Andrés Ticona" (oral history), Folio 5, 23–24, APAJMC.

68. Guzmán Aspiazu, Hombres sin tierra, 33–55.

69. Gómez, "Campesinos," 30–35.

70. "Carta de Sebastián Aruwitu al Corregidor de Janqulaime, April 12, 1956," Folio 3, 34, FJA.

71. "Nota de Nataniel Vera, Corregidor de Ambaná a la Central Agraria de Ambaná, Marzo, 14, 54," Folio 1, 35, APPM.

72. "Demanda civil de Teodora Cari contra Sebastián Illaquita, Noviembre, 1964," Folio 1, 13–18, AJA.

73. Aisakayu, "Andrés Jach'aqullu," Folio 7, 19.

74. Villca, "Mururata y Mururata Achachila," (memoir, 1981), 11–13; Jach'aqullu, "Phichuwawas sabían decirnos," 25–30; Aisakayu, "Andrés Jach'aqullu," 19–21.

75. Ramos, "Sutalaya y una experiencia de La Paz" (memoir), Folio 3, 11–12, APHOA.

76. "El Kollasuyu," La Patria, September 2, 1953, 3.

77. "Declaración del diacono Edgar Silva sobre los Kollasuyus de la loma de Huanuni," September 22, 1953, Fondo 4, 5–9, APAJMC.

78. "Sumario judicial que inicia el diacono de Bombo contra falsos sacerdotes," Fondo 1945–1958, 9–11, AJPD.

79. "Certificado de matrimonio bajo la Ley de Indios de Julio Cutrina y Berna Ledesma, September, 21, 1950," 45, Fondo 7, APAJMC.

80. Aisakayu, "Andrés Jach'aqullu," 13–16, 9–11.

81. "Acta de libertad del reo Andrés Jach'aqullu," February 28, 1952, Fondo 1, APAJMC.

82. Ibid., 14–15.

83. Jach'aqullu, "El Kollasuyu y Gregorio Titiriku" (memoir), 33–35, APAJMC; Qulqi, "Inkawawas, la Virgina y su camino de Miranda" (memoir), 12–14; "Sumario judicial que inicia el diacono de Bombo contra falsos sacerdotes," 9–11, Fondo 1950–1960, Judicatura de la Prov. Dalence, Wanuni, Oruro.

84. "Nota de Luciano Negrete dirigida a Gregorio Titirico," May 10, 1954, 1; "Nota de Venancia Inturias dirigida a Toribio Miranda," June 14, 1955, 45–46; Jach'aqullu, "El Kollasuyu y Gregorio Titiriku," 23–25.

85. Quevedo, "Su historia de Toribio Miranda y Manuela Quevedo" (memoir), 23–25, FPTQ; Titiriku, "Para recordar a los phawajrunas" (memoir), 13–15, APPM.

86. Jach'aqullu, "El indio Uru-Murato, Toribio Miranda y Manuela Quevedo" (memoir), Fondo 3, 33–35, APAJMC; and Orieta, "Tata Toribio Miranda" (memoir), 3, APHONS.

87. "Proceso agrario de la hacienda Churumatas, 1954–1962," 124, Fondo Zudáñez, SNRA.

88. "Informe del jefe del Comando del MNR, Enero 1954," 23–25, Fondo Prefectural, 1950–1955, CDHSFX.

89. Ibid.; Antezana and Romero, *Historia de los sindicatos campesinos*, 145–53.

90. 'Expediente agrario de Qullachiwanway, 1953," 23–45, Fondo Zudáñez, SNRA.

91. "Demanda contra Zenón Ibáñez por compra fraudulenta de un lote, Enero 1956," Fondo 6, 5–7, APAJMC. Piqueros owned land, either on or off a hacienda. After the agrarian reform piqueros tended to have larger plots of land than excolonos; this gave them more influence on the structures of local power.

92. "Felipe Lima, Mallku Mayor del Ayllu Qillu Qullana quejándose contra Qarita por apropiarse tierras del ayllu, 1957," Fondo 2, 35, APPM.

93. "Carta Pastoral del Cardenal Maurer, Julio 6, 1956," Fondo 2, FPTQ.

94. "Carta de Andrés Jach'aqullu a Matilde Qulqi, Mayo 4, 1958," Fondo 7, APAJMC.

95. "Carta de Andrés Jach'aqullu a Fermín Vallejos, Enero 3, 1958," Fondo 3, FPFV.

96. "Expedientes agrarios Sumala," 87; "Soroma, 1959," 53; "Viscanches, 1958," 21; "Jatun Mayo 13, 1961," Fondo Zudañes, SNRA.

97. "Sumario informativo contra Andrés Jachaqullu, Francisco Rivera y otros conocidos como hombres voladores, Diciembre, 1957," Fondo 1, 7–8, FPTQ.

98. Ibid.

99. "Solicitud de reactivación de proceso contra hombres voladores del Corregidor de Icla, Angel Estrada, al Juez de Tarabuco, Enero 1959," Fondo Prefectural, 1950–1959, 5–8, CDHSFX.

100. "Carta de Francisco Rivera, a Fermín Vallejos, Marzo 3, 1959," Fondo 3, 1, FPHE; Orieta, "Tata Toribio Miranda," Fondo Kollasuyus, 14.

101. "Informe del Subprefecto de Azurduy, Julio Maturana, Febrero 1960," Fondo Prefectural, 1960–1973, 2–3, CDHSFX.

102. "La Plata, Abril 1960," 1, Fondo 3, FPHE.

103. "Expediente agrario Qullachiwanway, 1959–1966," 67, Fondo Zudáñez, SNRA.

104. Aisakayu, "Andrés Jach'aqullu," 13–16.

105. Ponce Mamani, "Los poderantes" (memoir), 4–71, FPHE.

106. "Expediente agrario Marapampa, 1956–1967," 98–103, Fondo Azurduy, SNRA.

107. "Expediente agrarios de Quinua Chacra, 1954–1969," 33–35, Fondo Azurduy; "Redención Pampa, 1956–1964," 51–53, Fondo Zudáñez, SNRA; Rivera Cusicanqui, Oprimidos, 17–78.

108. Salamanca Trujillo, Los campesinos, 10–210.

109. Antezana and Romero, Historia de los sindicatos campesinos, 35–45; Salamanca Trujillo, Los campesinos, 99–108; and Gordillo, Campesinos revolucionarios en Bolivia, 50–125.

110. Rivera Cusicanqui, Oprimidos, 70–125.

111. Jach'aqullu, "El indio Uru-Murato, Toribio Miranda y Manuela Quevedo" Fondo 3, 33; Orieta, "Tata Toribio Miranda," 34; Titiriku, "Para recordar a los phawajrunas," 35.

112. "Denuncia ante el juzgado penal de Misk'i del Subprefecto de la provincia, Febrero 14, 1964," Fondo 1, 3–4, FPMG.

113. Paredes, El indio Machaca y la República Aymara, 10–43.

114. Ramos, "Sutalaya y una experiencia en La Paz" (memoir), Folio 1, 13–15, APHOA.

115. Monje, "El Kollasuyu," Revista Andina 9 (1956): 22–33, Fondo 7, APAJMC.

116. Aisakayu, "Andrés Jach'aqullu," 38–41.

117. Feierman, Peasant Intellectuals, 23–50.

118. Aisakayu, "Andrés Jach'aqullu," 12–34.

119. Qulqi, "Inkawawas, la Virgina y su camino de Miranda," 23–28.

120. Jach'aqullu, "El Kollasuyu y Gregorio Titiriku," 35–39.

121. Ibid., 13–18.

122. Ponce Mamani, "Los poderantes" 23.

123. Ibid.

124. Orieta, "Tata Toribio Miranda," 23–28; and Quevedo, "Su historia de Toribio Miranda y Manuela Quevedo," 17–21.

125. Peralta, "Fausto Reinaga y los alcaldes particulares" (memoir), 14–17, APHOMI; Ponce Mamani, "Los poderantes," 23, 29.

126. Rivera, "Las haciendas eran así en su tiempo de Villarroel" (memoir), 14, 18, FPHE; and Ponce Mamani, "Los poderantes," 5–7.

127. Loayza, "El Congreso de Sucre" (memoir), 5–8, APEO; and Orieta, "Tata Toribio Miranda," 21–23.

128. Arias, *Historia de una Esperanza*, 177–8.

129. Ibid., 33; and Hurtado, *El katarismo*, 240–60.

130. Apaza, "Andrés Ticona," Fondo 5, 11–15; Qulqi, "Inkawawas, la Virgina y su camino de Miranda," Fondo 2, 18–22.

131. Villca, "Muruhuta y Mururata Achachila," 15–18.

132. "Primeros pobladores," *Presencia*, December 14, 1978, 11–15.

133. Ugarte, "Los antiguos caminantes," (memoir), 23–28, APHOMI; Orieta, "Tata Toribio Miranda," 15.

134. Ponce Mamani, "Los poderantes," 23.

135. Ugarte, "Los antiguos caminantes," 27.

136. Peralta, "Fausto Reinaga y los alcaldes particulares," 11.

137. Qulqi, "Mi religión es la Pachamama y soy hija de los phichuwawa" (memoir), Fondo 2, 28–32, APHOA; Titiriku, "Para recordar a los phawajrunas," 35–39.

138. Arias, "Felipe Quispe y los Ayllus Rojos en Chuquisaca," 3, APHOA.

139. Rivera Cusicanqui, *Oprimidos*, 115–73.

140. Huizer, *The Revolutionary Potential of the Peasant in Latin America*, 94.

141. Antezana and Romero, *Historia de los sindicatos campesinos*, 203–64.

142. Aisakayu, "Andrés Jach'aqullu," 23–33.

Conclusion: The AMP's Innovations and Its Legacy in Bolivia under Evo Morales

1. Regarding the role of oral history and memory in Bolivia's Aymara and Quechua movements, see Ticona and THOA, "El papel de la memoria historica," *Temas Sociales*, 30–84. On the transmission of memory and its interpretation through documents among the indigenous peoples of Colombia, see Rappaport, *The Politics of Memory*, 1–27. See also Mallon, *Courage Tastes of Blood*, 228–48.

2. Javier Hurtado and Diego Pacheco have documented Aymara and Quechua activism both during the years of military dictatorship and once democracy was reinstated in Bolivia. See Hurtado, *El katarismo*, 30–180; Pacheco, *El Indianismo y los indios contemporáneos en Bolivia*, 20–190.

3. Rivera Cusicanqui, *Oprimidos*, 178–84.

4. Baud and Rutten, *Popular Intellectuals and Social Movements*, 197.

5. Orta, *Catechizing Culture*, 1–25, 147–327.

6. Ibid., 206.

7. Ibid., 207.

8. Ibid.

9. Ibid., 209.

10. Rivera Cusicanqui, "La raíz," 27–139.

11. Baud and Rutten, *Popular Intellectuals and Social Movements*, 41–65.

12. Albó and Mamani, *Achacachi*, 25–45.

13. Lecocq, "Unemployed Intellectuals in the Sahara," 87–110.

14. Saavedra, "Lista de de Alcaldes Mayores Particulares," 1–23; Titiriku, "Gregorio Titiriku se hablaba así," 23–66.

15. Ibid.

16. "Carta de Andrés Jach'aqullu a Fernando Diez de Medina, Enero 31, 1951," Fondo 8B, 37–38, APAJMC.

17. Baud and Rutten, *Popular Intellectuals and Social Movements*, 217.

18. Hastings, *The Construction of Nationhood*, 185–210. Hastings especially focuses on ethnic social movements.

19. "Expediente de demanda del ayllu Condo y comunidad Palca contra la hacienda Phuxpu, 1926–1936," 3–17, FPAPM.

20. Jach'aqullu, "El Kollasuyu y Gregorio Titiriku," 14–18.

21. Paz Arauco, *Los Cambios detrás del cambio*, 30–109.

22. "El candidato: Evo Morales," *Opinion*, February 18, 2002, 17–19.

23. "Decreto Supremo, October 12, 2011: Día de la descolonización," *Gaceta Oficial de Bolivia*, 2011.

24. "Ley Marco de Agrupaciones Ciudadanas y Pueblos Indígenas," *Gaceta Oficial de Bolivia*, 2004. For more on gender in contemporary Bolivia and with a comparative perspective, see Swanson, "A Messy Success"; and Gamez, "United in Sisterhood."

25. "Mujeres en el Poder," *La Razón*, September 30, 2012, 5; http://www.un.org/womenwatch/daw/beijing15/general_discussion/Bolivia.pdf.

26. "Los Guaraníes: Esclavos del siglo xxi," *Los Tiempos*, 2008, 10. See also Gustafson, *New Languages of the State*, 30–150; and Postero, *Now We Are Citizens*, 10–120.

27. Paz Arauco, *Los Cambios detrás del cambio*, 30–109.

28. "Ley 737/2010-Contra el Racismo y toda forma de discriminación," *Gaceta Oficial de Bolivia*.

29. "Ley 071, December 21, 2010," *Gaceta Oficial de Bolivia*.

30. "Ley 300, Ley Marco de la madre tierra y del desarrollo integral para vivir bien," *Gaceta Oficial de Bolivia*.

31. Gotkowitz, *Histories of Race and Racism*, 15–330. This volume has a significant number of articles regarding the history of racism in Bolivia, including several that treat the contemporary era.

32. "Feria de las culturas," *Página Siete*, October 12, 2011, 1.

33. "La Paz tiene 10 wakas para pedir salud, trabajo y justicia," *La Razón*, October 9, 2011, 1.

34. Ramos, "Así le he ayudado," Folio 1, 3, APHOA.

35. "Extirpación de idolatrías, siglo XXI," *La Razón*, August 8, 2011, 3.

36. "Ñatitas: En el Alto las ñatitas fueron agasajadas con rezos y música," *Página Siete*, November 9, 2011, 1; "Atribuyen a las ñatitas divinos favores de salud," *La Razón*, November 9, 2011, 1.

37. "Cardenal: La iglesia no puede ser acallada," *Los Tiempos*, May 9, 2011, 1.

38. "Evo: Seguirá llamándose Plaza Murillo, pero 'legítimamente' será Bartolina Sisa," *La Razón*, September 5, 2011, 1.

39. "No somos fundamentalistas medioambientalistas," *La Razón*, September 4, 2011, 1.

40. "Ministro de Gobierno afirma que se respetara la decisión de comunidades del TIPNIS a no ser consultadas," *La Razón*, November 24, 2012, 3.

41. Ramos, "Así le he ayudado," Folio 1, 3; "El TIPNIS destapa interés y abre debate," *Los Tiempos*, October 1, 2011.

Glossary

Achachila (Aymara): Good spirit, grandfathers, grandparents, ancestors.

Agregado: An indigenous peasant born in an indigenous community, whose ancestors had received a portion of land from the original inhabitants of the ayllu.

Alaxsaya/Manqhasaya (Aymara): Upper side, one half of an ayllu/lower side, the other half of the ayllu; see also Aransaya/Urinsaya.

Alcalde Escolar: Indigenous educational officer charged with the ayllu's schooling activities. An Alcalde Escolar usually lived in the community.

Alcaldes mayores: High-level leaders among Indians from late colonial times to 1953. They replaced the mallkus (Aymara) or kuraqas (Quechua) from pre-Spanish times and colonial times.

Alcaldes Mayores Particulares (AMP): A large network of indigenous activists who promoted the Indian law, literally means major autonomous mayors.

Ama sua, ama llulla, ama khella (Quechua): The trilogy or Inka moral code: Don't steal, don't lie, and don't be lazy.

Apacheta (Aymara): A sacred place, dedicated to the spirit of the mountains, a favorite place of worship among Aymara.

Apoderado: A person with the power of attorney for the ayllu or Indian community. Since 1874 the term has referred to the legal Indian representative of an Indian community.

Aransaya/Urinsaya (Quechua): A section of the ayllu, meaning one half, for instance a lower part and a higher part. See also Alaxsaya/Manqhasaya.

Arrendero: Peon that rents land.

Arriendo: The land that peons work; peons do not directly own land, so they pay rent to the landlord or hacendado.

Arriero: Mule driver.

Arrimante: Peons that work for an arrendero and therefore neither own lands nor work directly for the landlord.

Ayllu (pukina): Economic and political organization of a large number of communities in the Aymara and Andean world; a social segment within a network of ayllus is called a marka.

Bartolina Sisa: Eighteenth-century Aymara heroine; today she is a national heroine in Bolivia and an emblem of indigenous women's organizations.

Bayeta de la tierra: A handmade textile made with sheep wool or llama and alpaca fibers. This fabric was primarily used to make Indian clothing before 1952.

Birlocha: A racialized term used by the white elite to refer to female children of cholas. Birlochas do not wear the traditional ethnic dress of cholas.

Bofedales: Wetlands in the Andean highlands that have good grass for llamas and alpacas.

Cabecillas: A derogatory term that the white elite in the mid-twentieth century used for indigenous activists. The term in Spanish literally means "little heads."

Cabildos: Groups of indigenous people organized for the purpose of discussing political, social, and educational activism based on ancestral practices.

Caciques de sangre: Descendants of mallkus, the main indigenous chiefs in the eighteenth century.

Caudillos: Charismatic figures that sometimes used authoritarianism to maintain power.

Certificos: Paperwork issued by the AMP that emphasized that Indians should be protected by the state, based in some colonial ideas; AMP adherents sometimes used certificos instead of ID cards, birth certificates, and marriage certificates.

Chachawarmi (Aymara): Worldview of gender that emphasizes reciprocity, harmony, and collaboration between sexes. In practice, any office of Aymara governance must have a female counterpart because of this ideology. For instance the mallku or jilaqata's office has the corresponding office of the mama t'alla.

Challxasiris (Aymara): Exchange of agricultural products without the use of currency.

Charque or ch'arki (Aymara): Dehydrated meat; jerky, especially when made of dried llama meat.

Cholo: A person who might be of Indian or mestizo origin but wears Western clothes and develops a unique ethnic style. They frequently define their identity as being distinct from Indian.

Chu'kuta or chucuta (Aymara): The modern name for the urban Aymaras of La Paz. It dates to the time of the 1920s Bolivian Cultural Revolution.

Chullpa (pukina): Ancestors to be worshiped, Andean mummies.

Chullpapuchus (pukina/Aymara): The term that Urus used to refer to Aymaras in the 1920s.

Chuño: Dehydrated potatoes.

Ch'uta or chuta: A person who is changing his or her identity from Indian to cholo and starts to wear a mixture of cholo and Indian clothing, retaining some indigenous fabrics as a part of his or her dress.

Chuxlla (Quechua): A seasonal indigenous housing structure in the agricultural fields.

Corregidores: Highest government official at the cantonal level. Term originated in a colonial-era position that had responsibility for overseeing judicial proceedings and tax collection.

Emisario: An emissary of the AMP.

Escribano: Someone who copies manuscripts and acts as secretary for the AMP or other indigenous activists before 1952.

Escuelas particulares: Autonomous indigenous schools, literally means "autonomous school."

Ethnic economy: Andean communities used to complement their diet with food production from different ecological levels, such as the highlands, the coast, and subtropical and tropical regions. Aymara macro ayllus of the highlands had their economic enclaves in tropical, or coastal regions.

Forastero: A relatively new member of the ayllu, who was not part of the original group but whose ancestors joined the ayllu later. They have different rights than originarios or agregados.

Gamonales: Large landowners and/or local political bosses, bossism.

Garantías: Indigenous activists' documents compiled from fragments of the Law of the Indies and correspondence with government officials that affirmed their rights. The AMP popularized the use of garantías in the 1930s and 1940s.

Illa (Aymara): Representation of a deity, talisman.

Indianista: In Bolivia an Indianista is an Aymara or originario who argues in favor of indigenous rights or seeks an Indian revolution.

Indian law: An idea that combined the colonial-era Law of the Indies with Aymara religious and political ideas from the first half of the twentieth century. Rather than a single document, the Indian law is a reinterpretation and re-elaboration of fragments of the Law of the Indies that advocated for two separate republics: one Indian, the other white (or Spanish).

Indigenista: An elite person or mestizo who argues in favor of retaining traditional indigenous cultural practices and opposes modernization or change for indigenous peoples.

Jallp'a sangres: Term that mixes Quechua and Spanish; used by Melitón Gallardo to inspire among supporters of the AMP racial pride and religious devotion to Indian deities; means "the blood of our lands."

Jalqa (Aymara): An ethnic group of Chuquisaca that emerged in the second half of the nineteenth century as a result of the combination of Aymara and Uru communities.

Jaqi (Aymara): Literally "people" in Aymara; from the colonial period to the first half of the twentieth century it was used to denominate Aymara or Qulla peoples (including Quechua speaking).

Jilaqatas (Aymara): An Aymara word that means older brother; the term is used to refer to an intermediate level of indigenous leadership within the ayllu or hacienda structure.

Katarista: Late twentieth-century ethnic movement inspired by Túpac Katari, an eighteenth-century Aymara hero.

Kollasuyus: Name given to the adherents of the AMP in the mid-twentieth century.

Latifundio: A large landed estate.

Ley de exvinculación (Disentailment Law): Bolivian law passed in 1874 that mandated the sale of community land at public auction unless communities obtained new property titles from the government within three months.

Llameros: Shepherds of llama caravans.

Luxt'a: A libation made of a sweet substance and alcohol to offer to the indigenous deities, including the mother earth.

Mallku: An Aymara Indian chief who has authority over an ayllu or marka.

Mama T'alla: A mallku's wife, who has responsibilities within the Aymara political system and holds an official office.

Mank'asaya (Aymara): Lower side, one half of an ayllu.

Marka: A large conglomerate of ayllus within the Aymara world.

Mesa: Offering to the Aymara deities that consists of sweet cookies and aromatic herbs put together in a colorful preparation. There are many types of mesas depending on one's religious motives.

Mestizaje: A twentieth-century racial discourse of nation making through homogenization that usually implied elimination of indigenous cultural markers.

Mistis: Literally means "elite" in Aymara, usually refers to white and mestizo elites.

Mita: A method of dispersing the population to different ecological regions in pre-Inka times; a system of public service under Inka rule and a system of forced labor mostly for indigenous people under Spanish rule.

Montepuchus: Term that Urus used to refer to Quechuas in the 1920s.

Ñatitas: Skulls believed to be carriers of good wishes, skulls of ancestors or any other who can carry good luck to Aymara people.

Originarios: The ancestral people of Latin America, refers to indigenous peoples. The term also has a more specific meaning from the colonial and postcolonial history of the ayllus: the original member of an ayllu, who consequently enjoyed more rights in relation to agregados and forasteros.

Pachakuti: In the Aymara philosophy, this means time of change; the same notion is used today in all Andean languages and cultures.

Pachamama: Mother Earth, the main Aymara goddess, who also became a pan-Andean divinity.

Pachamamar waxtañ (Aymara): The act of giving libations to Pachamama.

Pachamámicos: People who emphasize devotion to Pachamama.

Palqas or calzones partidos: Ethnic pants that La Paz's Aymaras wore before the cultural revolution of 1925.

Phanaqa or panaca: Inka remains that were worshiped as deities in the late inka empire.

Phawajrunas: A mocking term for members of the AMP in the region of Chuquisaca that literally means "the men that fly"; originated from myths that emerged in the 1960s based on the fact that the AMP prayed on the mountaintops.

Piquera: A women who owns land, either on or off a hacienda.

Poncho: Ethnic piece of clothing made with the wool of llamas and alpacas, often in bright colors.

Pongueaje: Indentured servitude.

Pucara falda: Pre-Inka site of worship.

Puchu (Aymara): Vestige.

Puna: Arid plateau.

Purirantes: Term that mixes Spanish and Aymara, derived from apoderados; means power of attorney for the community or Aymara ayllu.

Qañawa: A young quinoa plant.

Q'aras: Literally, "bare skinned." In Aymara the term is used to refer to the descendents of the Spaniards.

Qhuchapuchus: The term that Urus used in the 1920s to refer to themselves and differentiate themselves from Aymaras and Quechuas.

Qixu qixu: The deity of lightning.

Quinoa: A nutritious grain grown in the Andes.

Qulla: Refers to Aymaras and, in modern days, also to Quechuas.

Qullasuyu: Aymara territory in pre-Inka times. In modern usage, this term came to signify an imagined community promoted by the AMP.

Ramas: Donations of cash or goods that indigenous activists collected to promote the Indian cause before 1952.

Republic of Indians or Republic of Qullasuyu: A term referring to an imagined community of people of pre-Inka heritage, including notions of ethnicity and religion as promoted by the AMP.

Rosca: A term used by the Bolivian working class for the white elite. It refers to the fact that Bolivian elites are powerful despite being tiny in number.

Segunda mayor: In the system of Indian authorities, the position of segunda mayor is superior to the jilaqata and inferior to the alcalde mayor; in pre-Inka times the position was called mallku or kuraka.

Sumaqamaña (Aymara): Philosophical approach to life, it translates as "to live well" and is in opposition to market-oriented and consumerist lifestyles.

Surco: Besides being the cut that the plow makes in the earth, it serves to measure land.

Tambos: Shelter, lodging, hostel. A big house where agricultural producers bring their products for sale. Also a meeting place for indigenous peasants from diverse regions.

Tata (Aymara/Quechua): Literally means "father"; term of respect for men equivalent to "Mr."

Tatala (Aymara/Quechua): Elders, specifically Aymara elders involved in petty trade in inter-ethnic zones.

Tituleros: Nickname that the AMP used to vilify the caciques apoderados' political strategy of seeking land title; implies an "addiction" to titles.

Tupac Katari: An eighteenth-century Aymara hero; today a national hero in Bolivia and an emblem of the Aymara transnational movement.

Uma jalsus (Aymara): Place of the water deity; literally means "place where water sprouts."

Uma kankaña (Aymara): Refers to the existence of water.

Umasuyus: The region of Lake Titikaka on the Bolivian side.

Urus: An ancient nation of the Bolivian altiplano. Urus are a pre-Aymara people in the highlands.

Utawawa: Literally, "children of the house." Refers to an Indian who worked for both white and mestizo bosses, as well as for priests and powerful Indians, usually as a domestic servant or general helper.

Vecinos de pueblo: Rural elite, usually racialized as white or mestizo.

Wak'a: Masculine or feminine deity that takes care of an ayllu, region, or nation; ancestors' remains in the Aymara religion prior to sixteenth century. Wak'as are sometimes represented by stones with anthropomorphous shapes.

Waxt'a (Aymara): A sacrifice and offering that is given to Pachamama in a ceremonial act. Also means gift, talent, and endowment.

Wiraxuchas: The name of an Andean god; however, after the arrival of the Spaniards, it changed to mean "sir."

Yanapaku: Laborer who works in agriculture.

Yatiri: Aymara priest.

Selected Bibliography

Primary Sources

ARCHIVES

Chuquisaca
Archivo Privado de Ezequiel Orieta, Churumumu (APEO)
Archivo Privado de Historia Oral de Manuel Ilaquita, El Alto (APHOMI)
Archivo Privado de Historia Oral de Nabil Saavedra, Mesa Verde (APHONS)
Biblioteca Nacional de Bolivia (BNB)
Centro Documental é Histórico de San Francisco Xavier (CDHSFX)
Centro Documental Privado Fundación Indígena Amauta (CDFIA)
Fondo Corte Superior del Distrito de Chuquisaca, 1920–1950 (FCSDCH)
Fondo Judicial Provincias Yamparáez y Zudáñez, 1930–1970 (FJPY and FJPZ)
Fondo Prefectura del Departamento de Chuquisaca, 1930–1970 (FPDCH)
Fondo Privado de Agapito Ponce Mamani, Marapampa (FPAPM)
Fondo Privado de Francisco Rivera, Sumala (FPFR)
Fondo Privado de los Hermanos Espirituales, Roditoyoj (FPHE)
Fondo Privado de Melitón Gallardo Saavedra (FPMG)
Fondo Privado de Tomás Quevedo, Guerra Loma (FPTQ)
Servicio Nacional de Reforma Agraria (SNRA)

Cochabamba
Archivo Judicial de la Provincia Campero, Aiquile (AJPC)
Archivo Judicial de la Provincia Mizque, Mizque (AJPM)
Fondo Privado de Fermín Vallejos, Raqaypampa (FPFV)

La Paz

Archivo Histórico de La Paz (AHLP)
Archivo Judicial de Ambaná (AJA)
Archivo Judicial (Mínima Cuantía) de Ancoraimes (AJMA)
Archivo Privado de Historia Oral Amuykisipxasiñasataki (APHOA)
Archivo Privado de Pedro Mamani (APPM)
Biblioteca del Congreso Nacional de Bolivia (BCNB)
Centro Documental Privado Fundación Kechuaymara (FDLP)
Centro Documental Taller de Historia Oral Andina (THOA)
Correspondencia en Asuntos Indígenas y Educación, 1940–1950
Fondo Prefectura del Departamento de La Paz, 1940 (FPDLP)
Fondo Privado de Gregorio Titiriku y Rosa Ramos (FPGTRR)
Fondo Privado de Lucas Marka, Huayllamarca (FPLM)
Fondo Privado de Martina Willka (FPMW)

Oruro

Archivo Judicial de la Provincia Dalence, Huanuni (AJPD)
Archivo Privado de Andrés Jachakollo y Matilde Colque (APAJMC)

Potosí

Archivo Judicial de la Provincia Bustillos, Uncía (AJPB)
Fondo Privado de Hilarión Cuellar, Cala Cala (FPHC)
Fondo Privado de la Familia Quyu, Cala Cala (FPFQ)

NEWSPAPERS AND JOURNALS

Cochabamba

La Nación, 1940–1949
Los tiempos, 2010–2011
Opinión, 1953 and 2002

La Paz

El Diario, 1940–1970
El Fígaro, 1915–1919
El Hombre Libre, 1923–1925
El Norte, 1912–1917
El Trabajo, 1957–1959
La Calle, 1946–1948
La Gaceta de Bolivia, 1940–1960 and 2010–2012
La Razón, 1940–1948 and 2010–2011
La República, 1925
Pagina Siete, 2011
Presencia, 1978

Oruro

La Patria, 1953–1978

Sucre

La Plata, 1929
La Trinchera, 1938
Nueva Vanguardia, 1947

Secondary Sources

UNPUBLISHED MANUSCRIPTS

Aisakayu, Marcos. "Andrés Jach'aqllu." Oruro: APAJMC, 1984.

Apaza, Juan. "Andrés Ticona." La Paz: APAJMC, 1984.

Arias, Juan. "Entrevistas a Emma Gutiérrez de Bedregal." La Paz: APHOA, 1975.

———. "Felipe Quispe y los Ayllus Rojos en Chuquisaca." La Paz: APHOA, 1994.

———. "Memorias de Florencia Burgoa Chachaki." La Paz: APHOA, 1979.

Ari-Chachaki, Waskar. "Apuntes para una perspectiva comparativa de los ch'utas en La Paz y Sucre." La Paz: APHOA, 1997.

———. "Dos repúblicas: Las plazas de Ambaná y Achacachi." La Paz: APHOA, 1992.

Cari, Pedro. "Sumala." Ruditayoj (Chuquisaca): FPFR, 1981.

Carmona, Ezequiel. "El tiempo de Peñaranda." Sucre: APHONS, 1975.

Chura, Pedro. "Así nos castigaban." Laguna Grande (Cochabamba): APJC, 1985.

———. "Los pachamámicos les decían." CDFIA, April 1979.

Córdoba, Jorge. "La hacienda el Novillero." Laguna Grande (Cochabamba): APJC, 1957.

Gallardo, Melitón. "Así hemos caminado los antiguos poderantes." Sucre: APHONS, 1968.

———. "Chutas y Cholos, 1972." APHONS, 1982.

García, Carlos Antonio. "Ch'utas y cholos en su tiempo de Peñaranda." Tarabuco: FPHC, 1979.

———. "En su tiempo de Peñaranda." Llallawa: FPHC, 1974.

Grieshaber, Erwin. "Survival of Indian Communities in Nineteenth-Century Bolivia." PhD dissertation, University of North Carolina, 1977.

Huariqallu, Angelino. "El mallku Machaca." La Paz: APHOMI, 1991.

Inturias, Carlos. "En el tiempo de Fermín Vallejos y las haciendas." Chinguri (Cochabamba): FPFV, 1969.

Iquiapaza, Juan. "Titiriku y su camino." Uncía (Potosí): FPFQ, 1969.

Jach'aqllu, Andrés. "Bayetas camisas sabían decirnos." Oruro: APAJMC, 1977.

———. "El indio Uru-Murato, Toribio Miranda y Manuela Quevedo." Oruro: APAJMC, 1977.

———. "El Kollasuyu y Gregorio Titiriku." Oruro: APAJMC, circa 1984.

————. "Phichuwawas sabían decirnos." La Paz: APHOA, 1977.

————. "Sobre Gregorio Titiriku." Oruro: APAJMC, 1972.

————. "Su enseñanza del cura Beltrán." Oruro: APAJMC, 1977.

Landivar, Molly. "Memorias de Vicente Donoso Torrez y la reforma educativa." La Paz: APHOA, 1984.

Loayza, Juan de Dios. "El Congreso de Sucre." Churumumu (Chuquisaca): APEO, 1973.

Miranda, Benjamín. "Sus luchas de mi padre." Sucre: APHONS, 1977.

Orieta, Ezequiel. "Tata Toribio Miranda." Sucre: APHONS, 1957.

Peñaranda, Calixto. "En su tiempo de Villarroel." Ruditayoj (Chuquisaca): FPHE, 1977.

Peralta, Celestino. "Fausto Reinaga y los alcaldes particulares." QalaQala (Potosí): APHOMI, 1979.

Ponce Mamani, Agapito. "Los hermanos espirituales" (memoir), FPAPM.

————. "Los poderantes." Ruditayoj (Chuquisaca): FPHE, 1982.

Quevedo, Tomás. "Su historia de Toribio Miranda y Manuela Quevedo." La Paz: FPTQ, 1979.

————. "Tiempos sufridos." Sucre: FPTQ, 1979.

Qulqi, Matilde. "Inkawawas, la Virgina y su camino de Miranda." La Paz: APHOA, 1981.

————. "Mi religión es la Pachamama y soy hija de los phichuwawa." La Paz: APHOA, 1979.

Q'uyu, Eusebio. "Su camino de los antiguos caminantes." QalaQala (Potosí): FPFQ, 1969.

Ramos, Anacleto. "Sutalaya y una experiencia en La Paz." La Paz: APHOA, 1973.

Ramos, Rosa. "Así le he ayudado." La Paz: APHOA, 1977.

Rivera, Francisco. "Chunca Cancha, 1948." FPLM, 1981.

————. "Las haciendas eran así en su tiempo de Villarroel." FPHE, 1978.

Riveros, Raul. "Villarroel, Vargas y Brasil." La Paz: APHOA, 1972.

Saavedra, Abraham. "La vida y obra de Melitón Gallardo." Sucre: FPMG, 1982.

————. "Lista de Alcaldes Mayores Particulares." Sucre: APHONS, 1982.

Saavedra, Juan Carlos. "La vida y obra y Melitón Gallardo." Sucre: FPMG, 1982.

Sallez, Julio. "El sufrimiento de los Alcaldes Particulares." Ruditayoj: FPFR, 1964.

Siles, Agar. "El anarquismo en la capital de la república." Sucre: FPMG, 1953.

Téllez, Teodoro. "El Gallardo era ch'utita." Ruditayoj (Chuquisaca): FPHE, 1987.

Titiriku, Manuel. "Para recordar a los phawax Runas, 1977." Ancoraimes: APPM, 1977.

Titiriku, María. "Gregorio Titiriku se hablaba así." Ancoraimes: APPM, 1979.

Torero, Alfredo. "Le Puqina, la troisième langue générale du Pérou." Tesis de doctorado lingüística, Universidad de Paris, 1965.

Torrico, Benito. "Memorias de la guerra del Chaco del Melitón Gallardo." Sucre: FPTQ, 1985.

Ugarte, Julián. "Los antiguos caminantes." Sucre: APHOMI, 1979.

Vallejos, Dorotea. "Los purirantes." FPFV, 1954.

Vallejos, Fermín. "Mi camino de Jampiri y la provincia Mizque." Sucre: FPMG, 1978.

Villca, José. "Muruhuta y Mururata Achachila." Wanuni (Oruro): FPMG, 1981.

BOOKS AND ARTICLES

Abercrombie, Thomas. *Pathways of Memory and Power: Ethnography and History among an Andean People.* Madison: University of Wisconsin Press, 1998.

———. "Q'aqchas and la Plebe in 'Rebellion': Carnival vs. Lent in Eighteenth-Century Potosí." *Journal of Latin American Anthropology* 2, no. 1 (1996): 62–111.

Aguiló, Federico. *Uru y Puquina.* Cochabamba: UMSS-CP, 1987.

Alba Herrera, Augusto. *Atusparia y la revolución campesina de 1885 en Ancash.* Austin: University of Texas Press, 2000.

Albarracín, Juan. *El poder minero.* La Paz: Urquizo, 1972.

Albó, Xavier, and Joseph Barnadas. *La cara campesina de nuestra historia.* La Paz: CIPCA, 1985.

Albó, Xavier, and Mauricio Mamani. *Achacachi: Medio siglo de lucha campesina.* La Paz: CIPCA, 1979.

———. "Andean People in the Twentieth Century." In *The Cambridge History of the Native People of the America,* edited by Stuart Schwartz and Frank Salomon, 765–871. Cambridge: Cambridge University Press, 1999.

———. *Desafíos de la solidaridad Aymara.* La Paz: CIPCA, 1985.

———. *Esposos, suegros y padrinos entre los Aymaras.* La Paz: CIPCA, 1972.

———. *Khitipxtansa: Identidad localista, étnica y clasista.* La Paz: CIPCA, 1976.

Albó, Xavier, and Godofredo Sandoval. *Chukiawu: La cara Aymara de La Paz.* La Paz: CIPCA, 1983.

Anderson, Benedict. *Imagined Communities.* London: Verso, 1991.

Andrade, Claudio. *José Santos Marka Thola, 1879 a 1939: Cronología del primer "sindicalista" campesino.* Sucre: TIFAP, 1989.

Antezana Ergueta, Luis, and Guillermo Bedregal Gutiérrez. *Origen, fundación y futuro del M.N.R.* La Paz: Ediciones Abril, 1992.

Antezana Ergueta, Luis, and Hugo Romero. *Historia de los sindicatos campesinos: Un proceso de integración nacional en Bolivia.* La Paz: MACA/CNRA, Investigaciones Sociales, 1979.

Appelbaum, Nancy P., Anne S. Macpherson, and Karin Alejandra Rosemblatt, eds. *Race and Nation in Modern Latin America.* Chapel Hill: University of North Carolina Press, 2003.

Arce, José Roberto. *Bosquejo sociodialéctico de la historia de Bolivia.* La Paz: Camarlinghi, 1978.

Arguedas, Alcides. *Pueblo enfermo.* Santiago de Chile: Ercilla, 1937.

Arias, Juan Félix. *El tata Fermín.* Cochabamba: Cenda, 1996.

———. *Historia de una Esperanza.* La Paz: Aruwiyiri-THOA, 1994.

Ari-Chachaki, Waskar, ed. *Aruskipasipxañasataki: El siglo XXI y el futuro del pueblo Aymara.* La Paz: Amtasiñataki, 2001.

Arnold, Denise Y. *Hacia un orden andino de las cosas: Tres pistas de los Andes Meridionales.* La Paz: Hisbol/ILCA, 1992.

———. *Más allá del Silencio: Las fronteras del género en los Andes.* La Paz: CIASE/ILCA, 1997.

Aronna, Michael. *"Pueblos enfermos": The Discourse of Illness in the Turn of the Century Spanish and Latin American Essay.* Chapel Hill: University of North Carolina, Department of Romance Languages, 1999.

Arze, José Antonio. *Bolivia neofascista.* Lima: Editorial Peruana, 1945.

———. *Bosquejo socio-dialéctico de la historia de Bolivia.* La Paz: Camarlinghi, 1978.

———. *El Imperio Incaico.* La Paz: Nuevo Amanecer, 1930.

Arze, René Danilo. *Guerras y conflictos sociales: El caso rural boliviano durante la campaña del Chaco.* La Paz: CERES, 1987.

Arze, Silvia, ed. *Etnicidad economía y simbolismo en los Andes.* La Paz: Hisbol-IFEA, 1992.

Ashcroft, Bill, and Pal Ahluwalia. *Edward Said: The Paradox of Identity.* London: Routledge, 2000.

Ashcroft, Bill, and Gareth Griffiths, with Helen Tiffin. *Key Concepts in Post-Colonial Studies.* London: Routledge, 1998.

Barragán, Rossana. "Entre polleras, lliqllas y ñañacas: Los mestizos y la emergencia de la tercera república." In *Etnicidad economía y simbolismo en los Andes,* edited by Silvia Arze et al., 85–117. La Paz: Hisbol-IFEA, 1992.

———. *Indios de arco y flecha: Entre la historia y la arqueología de las poblaciones del norte de Chuquisaca.* Sucre: ASUR, 1994.

Barrios, Raúl, and Xavier Albó, eds. *Violencias encubiertas en Bolivia: Cultura y política.* La Paz: CIPCA, 1993.

Baud, Michiel, and Rosanne Rutten, eds. *Popular Intellectuals and Social Movements: Framing Protest in Asia, Africa, and Latin America.* Cambridge: Cambridge University Press, 2004.

Becker, Marc. "Indigenous Communists and Urban Intellectuals in Cayambe, Ecuador." In *Popular Intellectuals and Social Movements: Framing Protest in Asia, Africa, and Latin America,* edited by Michiel Baud and Rosanne Rutten, 41–63. Cambridge: Cambridge University Press, 2004.

Bedregal Gutiérrez, Guillermo. *Origen, fundación y futuro del M.N.R.* La Paz: Ediciones "Abril," 1992.

Beezley, William. *Judas at the Jockey Club and Other Episodes of Porfirian Mexico.* Lincoln: University of Nebraska Press, 1987.

Beezley, William, Cheryl English Martin, and William French. *Rituals of Rule, Rituals of Resistance: Public Celebration and Popular Culture in Mexico.* Wilmington: SR Books, 1994.

Beltrán, Carlos Felipe. *Colección de opúsculos del cura Carlos Felipe Beltrán dedicados al General Agustín Morales.* Oruro: El Progreso, 1872.

Bertonio, Ludovico. *Vocabulario de la Lengua Aymara.* La Paz: CERES, 1984 [1612].

Besse, Susan. *Restructuring Patriarchy: The Modernization of Gender Inequality in Brazil 1914–1940.* Chapel Hill: University of North Carolina Press, 1996.

Beverley, John. *Subalternity and Representation.* Durham: Duke University Press, 1999.

Bonifaz, Miguel. *Legislación agrario-indígena.* Cochabamba: UMSS, 1953.

Bouysee-Cassagne, Thérèse. *La identidad Aymara, aproximación histórica (siglo XV, siglo XVI).* La Paz: Hisbol-IFEA, 1997.

Brysk, Alison. *From Tribal Village to Global Village: Indian Rights and International Relations in Latin America.* Stanford: Stanford University Press, 2000.

Butler, Judith. *Gender Trouble: Feminism and the Subversion of Identity.* New York: Routledge, 1999.

Calderón, Fernando, and Jorge Dandler. *Bolivia, la fuerza histórica del campesinado.* La Paz: CERES, UNRISD, 1984.

Caulfield, Sue Ann. *In Defense of Honor: Sexual Morality, Modernity, and Nation in Early Twentieth-Century Brazil.* Durham: Duke University Press, 2000.

Céspedes, Augusto. *El dictador suicida.* La Paz: "Juventud," Séptima edición, 2002.

———. *Sangre de mestizos.* Santiago: Claridad, 1956.

Chakrabarty, Dipesh. *Provincializing Europe: Postcolonial Thought and Historical Difference.* Princeton: Princeton University Press, 2000.

Chaturvedi, Vinayak. *Mapping Subaltern Studies and the Postcolonial.* London: Verso, 2000.

Choque, Roberto. "La sociedad república del Kollasuyu, 1930." *Chitakolla* (1989): 9–12.

———. *Sociedad y economía colonial en el sur andino.* La Paz: Hisbol, 2003.

Choque, Roberto, and Xavier Albó. *Cinco siglos de historia.* La Paz: Plural y CIPCA, 2003.

Choque, Roberto, Vitaliano Soria, Humberto Mamani, Esteban Ticona, and Ramón Conde. *Educación indígena: Ciudadanía ó colonización.* La Paz: Hisbol, 1992.

Choque, Roberto, and Esteban Ticona. *Jesús de Machaqa: Sublevación y Masacre de 1921.* La Paz: CIPCA, CEDOIN, 1996.

Chow, Rey. *Primitive Passions: Visuality, Sexuality, Ethnography, and Contemporary Chinese Cinema.* New York: Columbia University Press, 1995.

Clark, Kim. "Race 'Culture' and Mestizaje: The Statistical Construction of the Ecuadorian Nation 1930–1950." *Journal of Historical Sociology* 16, no. 1 (1998): 352–423.

Claure, Karen. *Las escuelas indigenales: Otra forma de resistencia comunitaria.* La Paz: Hisbol, 1989.

Condarco Morales, Ramiro. *Zárate, el "Temible" Willka: Historia de la rebelión indígena de 1899.* La Paz: Renovacion, 1983.

Condori Chura, Leandro, and Esteban Ticona Alejo. *El escribano de los caciques apoderados-kasikinakan purirarunakan qillqiripa.* La Paz: Hisbol/THOA, 1992.

Consejo Episcopal Americano. *Método Cala.* Cochabamba: Cala, 1961.

Crespo, Luis S. *José Manuel Pando.* La Paz: Alenkar, 1982.

Dandler, Jorge. "El Congreso Nacional Indígena de 1945 y la rebelión de Ayopaya (1947)." In *Bolivia: La fuerza histórica del campesinado*, edited by Fernando Calderón and Jorge Dandler, eds., 133–200. La Paz: CERES/UNSRSID, 1984.

De la Cadena, Marisol. *Indigenous Mestizos: The Politics of Race and Culture in Cuzco, Peru, 1919–1991*. Durham: Duke University Press, 2000.

———. "Women Are More Indian." In *Ethnicity, Markets, and Migration in the Andes: At the Crossroads of History and Anthropology*, edited by Brooke Larson, Olivia Harris, and Enrique Tandeter, 328–48. Durham: Duke University Press, 1991.

De la Cadena, Marisol, and Orin Starn. *Indigenous Experience Today*. New York: Berg Editorial, 2007.

Delgadillo Villegas, Julio. *La nación de los urus: Chipaya*. Centro Diocesano de Pastoral Social, 1998.

Delgado, Richard. *Critical Race Theory: The Cutting Edge*. Philadelphia: Temple University Press, 1995.

Del Valle de Siles, María Eugenia. *Historia de la rebelión de Túpac Catari, 1781–1782*. La Paz: Don Bosco, 1990.

Démelas, Daniéle. *Nationalisme sans nation? La Bolivie aux XIXe-XXe siécles*. Toulouse: CNRS, 1980.

Díaz Machicao, Porfirio. *Historia de Bolivia: Saavedra, 1920–1925*. La Paz: Don Bosco, 1954.

Díaz Polanco, Hector. *Indigenous Peoples in Latin America: The Quest for Self-Determination*. Boulder: Westview Press, 1997.

Díaz Villamil, Antonio. *La niña de sus ojos*. La Paz: La Juventud, 1956.

Dorado, José Vicente. *Impugnación a las ideas federales en Bolivia*. Sucre: Imprenta de Pedro España, 1877.

Dryzek, John. *The Politics of the Earth: Environmental Discourses*. New York: Oxford University Press, 1997.

Escobar, Filemón. *Testimonio de un militante obrero*. La Paz: CIPCA, 1980.

Escobari de Querejazu, Laura. *Caciques, yanaconas y extravagantes: la sociedad colonial en Charcas s. XVI–XVIII*. La Paz: Plural Editores, 2005.

Eskildsen, Robert. "Of Civilization and Savages: The Mimetic Imperialism of Japan's 1874 Expedition to Taiwan." *American Historical Review* 102, no. 2 (2002): 388–418.

Esposito, John, and John Voll. *Makers of Contemporary Islam*. Oxford: Oxford University Press, 2001.

Facultad de Derecho, Universidad Mayor de San Andrés. *Anales de Legislación*. La Paz: Facultad de Derecho, 1955.

Feierman, Steven. *Peasant Intellectuals: Anthropology and History in Tanzania*. Madison: University of Wisconsin Press, 1990.

Ferreira da Silva, Denise. "'Facts of Blackness,' Brazil Is Not (Quite) the United States and Racial Politics in Brazil." *Social Identities* 4, no. 2 (1998): 10–90.

Fisher, Edward, and R. McKenna Brown. *Maya Cultural Activism in Guatemala*. Austin: University of Texas Press, 1996.

Flores Apaza, Policarpio, with Fernando Montes, Elizabeth Andia, and Fernando Huanacuni. *El hombre que volvió a nacer: Vida, saberes y reflexiones de un Amawt'a de Tiwanaku.* La Paz: Plural, 1999.

Flores Moncayo, José. *Legislación boliviana del indio: Recopilación 1825–1953.* La Paz: IIB, 1953.

Freyre, Gilberto. *The Masters and the Slaves: A Study in the Development of Brazilian Civilization.* New York: Knopf, 1956.

Foucault, Michel. *The Foucault Reader.* New York: Pantheon, 1984.

Gade, Daniel. "Spatial Displacement of Latin American Seats of Government: From Sucre to La Paz as National Capital of Bolivia." *Revista Geográfica* 73 (1970): 43–57.

Gamez, Elizabeth. "United in Sisterhood." *Bolivia Reborn* (2011): 75–77.

García Quintanilla, Julio. "Monografía de la Provincia Zudáñez." *Boletín de la Sociedad Geográfica de Sucre* 49 (1979), 264–321.

Gerstle, Gary. *American Crucible: Race and Nation in the Twentieth Century.* Princeton: Princeton University Press, 2001.

Gill, Leslie. *Precarious Dependencies: Gender, Class, and Domestic Service in Bolivia.* New York: Columbia University Press, 1994.

Gilroy, Paul. *The Black Atlantic: Modernity and Double Consciousness.* Cambridge: Harvard University Press, 1993.

Gómez, Eugenio. *Bautista Saavedra.* La Paz: Biblioteca del Sesquicentenario, 1975.

Gómez, Oscar. "Campesinos." *Cordillera* 6, no. 114 (1954): 30–45.

Gordillo, José M. *Arando en la historia. La experiencia política campesina en Cochabamba.* La Paz: Plural/CERES/UMSS, 1998.

———. *Campesinos revolucionarios en Bolivia. Identidad, territorio y sexualidad en el valle Alto de Cochabamba, 1952–1964.* La Paz: Plural, 2002.

———. *Los hombres de la revolución: Memorias de un líder campesino, Sinforoso Rivas Antezana.* La Paz: Plural, 2000.

Gotkowitz, Laura, ed. *Histories of Race and Racism: The Andes and Mesoamerica from Colonial Times to the Present.* Durham: Duke University Press, 2011.

———. *A Revolution for Our Rights: Indigenous Struggles for Land and Justice in Bolivia, 1880–1952.* Durham: Duke University Press, 2007.

Gould, Jeffrey L. *To Die in This Way: Nicaraguan Indians and the Myth of Mestizaje, 1880–1965.* Durham: Duke University Press, 1998.

Graham, Richard, ed. *The Idea of Race in Latin America, 1870–1940.* Austin: University of Texas Press, 1990.

Gramsci, Antonio. *Selections from the Prison Notebooks.* New York: International Publisher, 1971 [1947].

Grandin, Greg. *The Blood of Guatemala: A History of Race and Nation.* Durham: Duke University Press, 2000.

Grandin, Greg, and Gilbert Joseph, eds. *A Century of Revolution: Insurgent and Counterinsurgent Violence during Latin America's Long Cold War.* Durham: Duke University Press, 2010.

Grosby, Steve. "The Chosen People of Ancient Israel and the Occident: Why Does Nationality Exist and Survive?" *Nations and Nationalism* 5, no. 3 (1999): 357–80.

———. "Nationality and Religion." In *Understanding Nationalism*, edited by Montserrat Guiberneau and John Hutchinson, 97–119. Cambridge: Blackwell Publishers, 2001.

Guha, Ranajit. *Dominance without Hegemony: History and Power in Colonial India*. Cambridge: Harvard University Press, 1997.

———. *Elementary Aspects of Peasant Insurgency in Colonial India*. Durham: Duke University Press, 1992.

———, ed. *A Subaltern Studies Reader, 1986–1995*. Minneapolis: University of Minnesota Press. 1997.

Guibernau, Montserrat, and John Hutchinson, eds. *Understanding Nationalism*. Cambridge: Blackwell Publishers, 2001.

Guillén Pinto, Alfredo. *La educación del indio*. La Paz: Gonzáles Medina, 1919.

Gustafson, Bret. *New Languages of the State: Indigenous Resurgence and the Politics of Knowledge in Bolivia*. Durham: Duke University Press, 2007.

Gutman, Matthew, ed. *Changing Men and Masculinities in Latin America*. Durham: Duke University Press, 2003.

Guzmán Aspiazu, Mario. *Hombres sin tierra*. La Paz: Burillo, 1956.

Guzmán de Rojas, Iván. *Logical and Linguistic Problems of Social Communication with the Aymara People*. Ottawa: IDRC, 1985.

Harris, Olivia, and Xavier Albó. *Monteras y guardatojos: Campesinos y mineros en el Norte de Potosí*. La Paz: CIPCA, 1989.

Hastings, Adrian. *The Construction of Nationhood: Ethnicity, Religion and Nationalism*. Cambridge: Cambridge University Press, 2001.

Healy, Kevin. *Caciques y patrones*. Cochabamba: El Buitre, 1987.

Hedrick, Tace. *Mestizo Modernism: Race, Nation and Identity in Latin American Culture, 1900–1940*. New Brunswick: Rutgers University Press, 2003.

Hobsbawm, Eric. *Captain Swing*. London: Lawrence and Wishart, 1969.

———. *Primitive Rebels: Studies in Archaic Forms of Social Movement in the Nineteenth and Twentieth Centuries*. Manchester: Manchester University Press, 1971.

Howard-Malverde, Rosaleen. *The Speaking of History: "Willapaakushayki" or Quechua Ways of Telling the Past*. London: University of London, 1990.

Huanacuni, Fernando. *Filosofía, políticas, estrategias y experiencias regionales*. La Paz: CAB, 2010.

Huanca, Tomás Laura. *El Yatiri en la comunidad aymara*. La Paz: CADA, 1992.

———. *Jilirinaksan Amuyupa Lup'iñataki: El saber de nuestros mayores para la reflexión*. La Paz: THOA, 1991.

Huizer, Gerrit. *The Revolutionary Potential of the Peasant in Latin America*. Lexington: Lexington Books, 1972.

Hurtado, Javier. *El katarismo*. La Paz: Hisbol, 1986.

Hutchinson, John, and Anthony D. Smith, eds. *Nationalism*. Oxford: Oxford University Press, 1994.

Hylton, Forrest. "El Federalismo Insurgente: Una aproximación a Juan Lero, los comunarios y la guerra federal." *T'inkasos* 7, no. 16 (2004): 99–118.

Hylton, Forrest, Felix Patzi, Sergio Serulnkov, and Sinclair Thompson. *Ya es otro tiempo el presente: Cuatro momentos de insurgencia indígena.* La Paz: Muela del Diablo, 2003.

Irurozqui, Marta. *A bala, piedra y palo: La construcción de la ciudadanía política en Bolivia, 1826–1952.* Sevilla: DS, 2000.

———. *La armonía de las desigualdades: Elites y conflictos de poder en Bolivia, 1880–1920.* Madrid: CIC/CERABC, 1994.

Irurozqui, Marta, and Víctor Peralta. *Por la concordia, la fusión y el unitarismo: Estado y caudillismo en Bolivia, 1825–1880.* Madrid: CSIC, 2000.

Jones, Kristine. "Warfare, Reorganization, and Readaptation at the Margins of Spanish Rule: The Southern Margin, (1573–1882)." In *The Cambridge History of the Native Peoples of the Americas,* edited by Frank Salomon and Stuart B. Schwartz, 138–87. Vol. 2. Cambridge: Cambridge University Press, 1999.

Joseph, Gilbert, and Daniel Nugent. *Everyday Forms of State Formation.* Durham: Duke University Press, 1994.

Kapsoli, Wilfredo. *Los movimientos campesinos en el Perú.* Lima: El Sol, 1987.

Kearney, Michel. *Reconceptualizing the Peasantry: Anthropology in Global Perspective.* Boulder: Westview Press, 1996.

Klein, Herbert. *Bolivia: The Evolution of a Multiethnic Society.* New York: Oxford University Press, 1992.

———. *Haciendas and Ayllus: Rural Society in the Bolivian Andes in the Eighteenth and Nineteenth Centuries.* Stanford: Stanford University Press, 1993.

Klubock, Thomas. *Contested Communities: Class, Gender, and Politics in Chile's El Teniente Copper Mine, 1904–1951.* Durham: Duke University Press, 1998.

———. "Ránquil: Violence and Peasant Politics on Chile's Southern Frontier." In *A Century of Revolution: Insurgent and Counterinsurgent Violence during Latin America's Long Cold War,* edited by Greg Grandin and Gilbert Joseph, 121–62. Durham: Duke University Press, 2010.

Knight, Alan. "Racism, Revolution and Indigenismo." In *The Idea of Race in Latin America, 1870–1945,* edited by Richard Graham, 71–114. Austin: University of Texas Press, 1990.

Lame Chantre, Manuel Quintin, with Juan Friede. *Los pensamientos del indio que se educó dentro de las selvas colombianas.* Bogotá: MLCS, 1983.

Langer, Erick. "Andean Rituals of Revolt: The Chayanta Rebellion of 1927." *Ethnohistory* 37, no. 3 (1990): 227–53.

———. *Economic Change and Rural Resistance in Southern Bolivia, 1880–1930.* Stanford: Stanford University Press, 1989.

———. "El Liberalismo y la abolición de la comunidad indígena en el siglo XIX." *Historia y Cultura* 14 (1988): 59–95.

———. "La comercialización de la cebada en los Ayllus y las haciendas de Tarabuco (Chuquisaca) a comienzos del siglo XX." In *La participación indígena en los mercados surandinos*, edited by Brooke Larson and Olivia Harris, 583–601. La Paz: CERES, 1988.

Larson, Brooke. *Cochabamba, 1550–1900: Colonialism and Agrarian Transformation in Bolivia*. Durham: Duke University Press, 1998.

———. "'La invención del indio iletrado': La pedagogía de la raza en los Andes bolivianos." In *Formaciones de Indianidad: Articulations raciales, mestizajes y nación en América Latina*, edited by Marisol de la Cadena, 117–48. Lima-Bogotá: EnVision, 2008.

———. *Trials of Nation Making: Liberalism: Race and Ethnicity in the Andes, 1810–1910*. Cambridge: Cambridge University Press, 2004.

Larson, Brooke, Olivia Harris, and Enrique Tandeter, eds. *Ethnicity, Markets, and Migration in the Andes: At the Crossroads of History and Anthropology*. Durham: Duke University Press, 1991.

Lazarte Rojas, Jorge. *Movimiento obrero y procesos políticos en Bolivia: Historia de la COB, 1952–1987*. La Paz: Editorial Al Frente Bolivia, 1989.

Lecocq, Baz. "Unemployed Intellectuals in the Sahara: The Teshumara Nationalist Movement and the Revolutions in Tuareg Society." In *Popular Intellectuals and Social Movements: Framing Protest in Asia, Africa, and Latin America*, edited by Michiel Baud and Rosanne Rutten, 87–110. Cambridge: Cambridge University Press, 2004.

Lehm, Zulema, and Silvia Rivera Cusicanqui. *Los artesanos libertarios y la ética del trabajo*. La Paz: THOA, 1988.

Lewis, Earl. *In Their Own Interests: Race, Class and Power in Twentieth-Century Norfolk, Virginia*. Berkeley: University of California Press, 1991.

Lewis, Stephen. *The Ambivalent Revolution: Forging State and Nation in Chiapas, 1910–1945*. Albuquerque: University of New Mexico Press, 2005.

Lomnitz-Adler, Claudio. *Exits from the Labyrinth: Culture and Ideology in the Mexican National Space*. Berkeley: University of California Press, 1992.

Lora, Guillermo. *Bolivia: Diccionario político histórico cultural*. La Paz: Masas, 1983.

———. *Formación de la clase obrera boliviana*. La Paz: Masas, 1980.

Lucero, José Antonio. *Struggles of Voice. Politics of Indigenous Representation in the Andes*. Pittsburgh: University of Pittsburgh Press, 2008.

Luykx, Aurolyn, and Douglas Foley. *The Citizen Factory: Schooling and Cultural Production in Bolivia*. New York: SUNY Press, 1999.

Mallon, Florencia. *Courage Tastes of Blood: The Mapuche Community of Nicolás Ailio and the Chilean State, 1906–2001*. Durham: Duke University Press, 2010.

———. *Peasant and Nation: The Making of Postcolonial Mexico and Peru*. Berkeley: University of California Press, 1995.

———, ed. *Decolonizing Native Histories. Collaboration, Knowledge, and Language in the Americas*. Durham: Duke University Press, 2012.

Malloy, James. *Bolivia: The Uncompleted Revolution*. Pittsburgh: Pittsburgh University Press, 1970.

Mamani, Carlos. *Historia y prehistoria: ¿Dónde nos encontramos los indios?* La Paz: Editorial Aruwiri, 1992.

———. *Taraqu: Masacre, guerra, y "renovación" en la biografía de Eduardo Nina Qhispi.* La Paz: Editorial Aruwiri, 1991.

Mannheim, Bruce. *The Language of the Inkas since the European Invasion.* Austin: University of Texas Press, 1991.

Mariátegui, José Carlos. *Siete ensayos de interpretación de la realidad peruana.* Lima: Biblioteca Amauta, 1928.

Marof, Tristán. *Experimento nacionalista.* Mexico City, 1945.

———. *La tragedia del altiplano: La justicia del Inka.* Buenos Aires: Claridad, 1934.

Martin, Tony. *Race First: The Ideological and Organizational Struggles of Marcus Garvey and the Universal Negro Improvement Association.* Dover, Mass: The Majority Press, 1976.

Medinaceli, Carlos. *La Chaskañawi.* La Paz: Fundación Patiño, 1947.

Mendoza, Jaime. *El macizo boliviano.* La Paz: Ministerio de Educación, 1957.

Mignolo, Walter D. *Local Histories/Global Designs: Coloniality, Subaltern Knowledges, and Border Thinking.* Princeton: Princeton University Press, 2000.

Miranda, Lucas, and Daniel Moricio, with Rossana Barragán. *Memorias de un olvido: Testimonios de vida Uru-Muratos.* La Paz: ASUR/Hisbol, 1992.

Montenegro, Carlos. *Nacionalismo y Coloniaje.* La Paz: La Juventud, 1979.

Montoya, Rodrigo y Luis Enrique López. *¿Quiénes somos? El tema de la identidad en el Altiplano.* Lima: Mosca Azul Editores y Universidad Nacional del Altiplano, 1982.

Morley, David, and Kuan-Hsing Chen. *Stuart Hall: Critical Dialogues in Cultural Studies.* London: Routledge, 1996.

Municipalidad de La Paz. *La Paz en su Cuarto Centenario.* 4 vols. La Paz: HAM, 1948.

Murra, John. "An Aymara Kingdom in 1567." *Ethnohistory* 15, no. 2 (1968): 115–51.

Nelson, Diane M. *A Finger in the Wound: Body Politics in Quincentennial Guatemala.* Durham: Duke University Press, 1999.

Olson, Ronald D. *Algunas relaciones del chipaya de Bolivia con las lenguas mayenses.* Riberalta: Instituto Lingüístico del Verano en colaboración con el Ministerio de Educación y Cultura, 1980.

Orta, Andrew. *Catechizing Culture: Missionaries, Aymara, and the "New Evangelization."* New York: Columbia University Press, 2004.

Pachecho, Diego. *El Indianismo y los indios contemporáneos en Bolivia.* La Paz: Hisbol/MUSEF, 1992.

Paredes, Alfonsina. *El indio Machaca y la República Aymara.* La Paz: Producciones Isla, 1980.

Paredes, Manuel Rigoberto. *La altiplanicie.* La Paz, Argote, 1914.

Paredes Candia, Antonio. *La chola boliviana.* La Paz: Isla, 1992.

Paz Arauco, Verónica, ed. *Los Cambios detrás del cambio: Desigualdades y movilidad social en Bolivia.* 2nd ed. La Paz: PNUD, 2011.

Pérez, Elizardo. *Warisata, la escuela Ayllu.* Buenos Aires: Burillo, 1962.

Pérez Torrico, Alexis. *El estado oligárquico y los empresarios de Atacama (1871–1878).* La Paz: Ediciones Gráficas, 1994.

Platt, Tristan. "The Andean Experience of Bolivian Liberalism, 1825–1990: Roots of Rebellion in Nineteenth-Century Chayanta (Potosí)." In *Resistance, Rebellion and Consciousness in the Andean Peasant World: Eighteenth to Twentieth Century,* edited by Steve Stern, 280–326. Madison: University of Wisconsin Press, 1987.

———. *Estado boliviano y ayllu andino: Tierra y tributo en el norte de Potosí.* Lima: IEP, 1982.

Ponce Sanginés, Carlos, and Ana María Montaño Duran. *La Revolución Federal 1898–1899.* La Paz: La Juventud, 1999.

Poole, Deborah. *Vision, Race and Modernity: A Visual Economy of the Andean Image World.* Princeton: Princeton University Press, 1997.

Portelli, Alessandro. *In the Death of Luigi Trastulli and Other Stories: Forms and Meaning in Oral History.* Albany: SUNY Press, 1991.

Postero, Nancy. *Now We Are Citizens: Indigenous Politics in Postmulticultural Bolivia.* Stanford: Stanford University Press, 2007.

Pratt, Mary Louis. *Imperial Eyes: Travel Writing and Transculturation.* London: Routledge, 1997.

Quispe, Felipe. *El indio en escena.* La Paz: Pachacuti, 1999.

Rafael, Vicente. *Contracting Colonialism: Translation and Christian Conversion in Tagalog Society under Early Spanish Rule.* Durham: Duke University Press, 1993.

Ramos, Alcida Rita. *Indigenism: Ethnic Politics in Brazil.* Madison: University of Wisconsin Press, 1998.

Ranaboldo, Claudia. *El camino perdido: Biografía del líder campesino kallawaya. Antonio Álvarez Mamani.* La Paz: Sempta, 1987.

Rappaport, Joanne. *Cumbe Reborn: An Andean Ethnography of History.* Chicago: University of Chicago Press, 1994.

———. *The Politics of Memory: Native History and Interpretation in the Colombian Andes.* Durham: Duke University Press, 1998.

Renique, Gerardo. "Race, Region, and Nation: Sonora's Anti-Chinese Racism and Mexico's Postrevolutionary Nationalism, 1920s –1930s." In *Race and Nation in Modern Latin America,* edited by Nancy P. Appelbaum, Anne S. Macpherson, and Karin Alejandra Rosemblatt, 211–36. Chapel Hill: University of North Carolina Press, 2003.

Retamoso, Abel. *Civilización y cultura indígena.* La Paz: La Prensa, 1927.

Rivera Cusicanqui, Silvia. "La raíz: Colonizadores y colonizados." In *Violencias encubiertas en Bolivia: Cultura y política,* edited by Raúl Barrios and Xavier Albó, 25–139. La Paz: CIPCA, 1993.

———. *Oprimidos pero no vencidos, luchas del campesinado Aymara y Qhechwa de Bolivia 1900–1980.* La Paz: Hisbol, 1984.

Rivera Cusicanqui, Silvia, Denise Arnold, Zulema Lehm, Susan Paulson, and Juan de Dios Yapita. *Ser mujer, indígena: Chola o birlocha en la Bolivia postcolonial de los años 90.* La Paz: Subsecretaría de Asuntos de Género, 1996.

Rivera Cusicanqui, Silvia, with THOA. *Ayllus y proyectos de desarrollo en el norte de Potosí*. La Paz, Aruwiyiri, 1992.

Robertson, Roland. "Glocalization: Time-space and Homogeneity-Heterogeneity." In *Global Modernities*, edited by Mike Featherstone, Scott Lash, and Roland Robertson, 45–68. London: Sage, 1995.

Romero Pittari, Salvador. *Las Claudinas: Libros y sensibilidades a principios del siglo en Bolivia*. La Paz: Garza Azul, 1998.

Saavedra, Bautista. *El Ayllu*. La Paz: El Porvenir, 1993.

Said, Edward. *Representations of the Intellectual*. New York: Random House, 1994.

Salamanca Trujillo, Daniel. *Los campesinos en el proceso político boliviano*. Oruro: Quelco, 1978.

Salazar Mostajo, Carlos. *La Taika: Teoría y práctica de la Escuela Ayllu*. La Paz: UMSA, 1986.

———. *¡Warisata Mía!* La Paz: Editorial Amerindia, 1989.

Salinas Mariaca, Ramón. *Vida y muerte de Pando*. La Paz: Ultima Hora, 1978.

Salomón, Josefa. *El espejo indigenista en Bolivia: 1900–1956*. La Paz: Plural, 1997.

Sanders, James. "'Belonging to the Great Granadian Family': Partisan Struggle in the Construction of Indigenous Identity and Politics in Southwestern Colombia, 1849–1890." In *Race and Nation in Modern Latin America*, edited by Nancy P. Appelbaum, Anne S. Macpherson, and Karin Alejandra Rosemblatt, 56–86. Chapel Hill: University of North Carolina Press, 2003.

Sanjines, Javier. *Mestizaje Upside-Down: Aesthetic Politics in Modern Bolivia*. Pittsburgh: University of Pittsburgh Press, 2004.

Shanklin, Eugenia. 2000. "Representations of Race and Racism in American Anthropology." *Current Anthropology* 41, no. 1 (2000): 99–102.

Smith, Carol, and Marilyn Moors, eds. *Guatemalan Indians and the State: 1540 to 1988*. Austin: University of Texas Press, 1990.

Sommer, Doris. *Proceed with Caution: When Engaged by Minority Writing in the Americas*. Cambridge: Harvard University Press, 1999.

Spalding, Karen. *Huarochiri: An Andean Society under Inca Spanish Rule*. Stanford: Stanford University Press, 1984.

Spivak, Gayatri Chakravorty. "Can the Subaltern Speak?" In *Marxism and the Interpretation of Culture*, edited by Cary Nelson and Lawrence Grossberg, 271–313. Urbana: University of Illinois Press, 1988.

Stein, William. *El levantamiento de Atusparia: El movimiento popular ancashino de 1885, un estudio de documentos*. San Isidro: Mosca Azul, 1988.

Stepan, Nancy. *The Hour of Eugenics: Race, Gender, and Nation in Latin America*. Ithaca: Cornell University Press, 1991.

Stephenson, Marcia. *Gender and Modernity in Andean Bolivia*. Austin: University of Texas Press, 1999.

Stern, Steve, ed. *Peru's Indian Peoples and the Challenge of Spanish Conquest: Huamanga to 1640*. 2nd ed. Madison: University of Wisconsin Press, 1993 [1982].

————. *Resistance, Rebellion, and Consciousness in the Andean Peasant World: Eighteenth to Twentieth Centuries*. Madison: University of Wisconsin Press, 1987.

Swanson, Justin. "A Messy Success." *Bolivia Reborn* (2011): 40–56.

Swartz, David. *Culture and Power: The Sociology of Pierre Bourdieu*. Chicago: University of Chicago Press, 1980.

Szeminski, Jan. *La utopía tupamarista*. Lima: Pontificia Universidad Católica del Perú, 1984.

Tamayo, Franz. *Obras escogidas*. Caracas: Biblioteca Ayacucho, 1979.

Tapia, Luciano (Lusiku Qhispi Mamani). *Ukhamawa Jakawisaxa/Así es nuestra vida: Autobiografía de un Aymara*. La Paz: Hisbol, 1995.

THOA. *El indio Santos Marka T'ula: Cacique principal de los Ayllus de Qallapa y Apoderado General de las comunidades originarias de la República*. La Paz: Aruwiri, 1984.

————. *Historia y memoria: Mujer y resistencia comunitaria*. La Paz: Hisbol, 1986.

Thompson, Sinclair. "La cuestión India en Bolivia a comienzos del siglos: El caso de Manuel Rigoberto Paredes." In *Autodeterminación*, 42–48. La Paz: Plural, 1986.

————. "Was There Race in Colonial Latin America?: Identifying Selves and Others in the Insurgent Andes." In *Histories of Race and Racism: The Andes and Meso-america from Colonial Times to the Present*, edited by Laura Gotkowitz, 72–94. Durham: Duke University Press, 2011.

————. *We Alone Will Rule: Native Andean Politics in the Age of Insurgency*. Madison: University of Wisconsin Press, 2002.

Thurner, Mark. *From Two Republics to One Divided: Contradictions of Postcolonial Nation-making in Andean Peru*. Durham: Duke University Press, 1997.

Ticona Alejo, Esteban, Gonzalo Rojas Ortuste, and Xavier Albó. *Votos y Wiplhalas: Campesinos y pueblos originarios en democracia*. La Paz: CIPCA, 1995.

Titiriku, Lorenzo. *Historia de la llegada de la Iglesia Evangélica Metodista en Bolivia: El caso del Altiplano (Ancoraimes, La Paz)*. La Paz: IEMB, 1984.

Toranzo, Carlos, ed. *Bolivia en el siglo XX*. La Paz: Harvard Club de Bolivia, 1999.

Torero, Alfredo. "Lingüística e historia de la sociedad andina." In *El reto del multilingüismo en el Perú*, edited by Alberto Escobar, 2–50. Lima: IEP, 1972.

Trinh T. Minh-ha. *When the Moon Waxes Red: Representing Gender and Cultural Politics*. New York: Routledge, 1991.

Urban, Greg, and Joel Sherzer. *Nation-States and Indians in Latin America*. Austin: University of Texas Press, 1991.

Urquiola, José. "La población en Bolivia." In *Bolivia en el siglo XX*, edited by Carlos Toranzo, 193–218. La Paz: Harvard Club de Bolivia, 1999.

Van Cott, Donna Lee. *From Movements to Parties in Latin America*. Cambridge: Cambridge University Press, 2005.

————. *Indigenous Peoples and Democracy in Latin America*. New York: Palgrave Macmillan, 1995.

Velasco, Adolfo. *La escuela indígenal de Warisata*. Mexico City: Departamento de Asuntos indígenas, 1940.

Wachtel, Nathan. *Gods and Vampires: Return to Chipaya*. Chicago: University of Chicago Press, 1994.

Warren, Kay. *Indigenous Movements and Their Critics: Pan Maya Activism in Guatemala*. Princeton: Princeton University Press, 1998.

Weismantel, Mary. *Cholas and Phistacos: Stories of Race and Sex in the Andes*. Chicago: University of Chicago Press, 2001.

Weismantel, Mary, and Stephen F. Eisenman. "Race in the Andes: Global Movements and Popular Ontologies." *Bulletin of Latin American Research* 17, no. 2 (1998): 121–42.

Williams, Raymond. *Marxism and Literature*. London: Oxford University Press, 1977.

Zavaleta Mercado, René. *Bolivia: El desarrollo de la conciencia nacional*. La Paz: Crítica, 1973.

———, ed. *Bolivia Hoy*. México, D.F.: Siglo Veintiuno Editores, 1983.

———. *El Poder dual en América Latina*. México, D.F.: Siglo Veintiuno Editores, 1979.

———. *Lo nacional-popular en Bolivia*. México, D.F.: Siglo Veintiuno Editores, 1986.

Zilveti Arce, Pedro. *Bajo el signo de la barbarie: Matanzas de noviembre*. Santiago: El Orbe, 1946.

Zulawski, Ann. *They Eat from Their Labor: Work and Social Change in Colonial Bolivia*. Pittsburgh: University of Pittsburgh Press, 1990.

Index

Made in the USA
San Bernardino, CA
23 August 2018